ALSO BY P. W. SINGER

Corporate Warriors:
The Rise of the Privatized Military Industry

Children at War

P. W. SINGER

Pantheon Books, New York

Library of Congress Cataloging-in-Publication Data

Singer, P. W. (Peter Warren)
Children at war / P. W. Singer.
p. cm.
Includes index.
ISBN 0-375-42349-4
1. Child soldiers—History—20th century.   2. Child soldiers—
History—21st century.   I. Title.

UB416.S56 2005
355'.0083—dc22   2004053448

www.pantheonbooks.com

Printed in the United States of America

First Edition

2 4 6 8 9 7 5 3 1

Children at War

When one has no one left on the earth, neither father nor mother, neither brother nor sister, and when one is small, a little boy in a damned and barbaric country where everyone slashes each other's throats, what does one do? Of course, one becomes a child soldier, a small soldier, to get one's fair share of eating and butchering as well. Only that remains.

—AHMADOU KOUROUMA, *Allah n'est pas obligé*

CONTENTS

Contents

Over the course of researching and writing this book, I have been asked many times why I would ever want to write about a topic so shocking and disheartening as child soldiers.

The vast changes in warfare that we are witnessing in the twenty-first century, most particularly the rise of new conflict groups, have long interested me. While we commonly think of war as men in uniform, fighting for the political causes of their states, it is not the case. The wars of our times are actually fought by men, women, and now children. Their causes are often political, but they also fight for economic, social, religious, or even criminal motives. The groups that they fight within can be anything from a state army or a terrorist cell to a warlord's gang or a drug cartel's paramilitaries.

I first became interested in child soldiers through my prior study, *Corporate Warriors,* which looks at another new participant in war—private businesses—that now carry out the jobs that soldiers used to perform. As these new soldiers of the private market discussed their experiences, I was amazed to learn that their adversaries in combat repeatedly included young children. I quickly discovered that this was a growing and global phenomenon, but one that few analysts, policymakers, or even soldiers in Western militaries were aware of.

Little was understood of the issue, not only where, why, and how the practice of using children in war came about, but also what it means and, most importantly, what to do about it. An international alliance of nongovernmental organizations, the Coalition to Stop the Use of Child Soldiers, has emerged to bring attention to the issue, and passing media coverage has been paid to isolated cases of child soldiers (which tend to find their way into the press mainly because of heartrending photos, such as the broadly carried image of the cigar-smoking Htoo brothers, two child soldiers from Myanmar). But the overall issue of child soldiers was and still is a largely invisible one to both researchers and policymakers. For example, among those political scientists who study modern-day world politics and warfare, the treatment of the phenomenon is at best peripheral. It has either focused on the specific conflicts in which child soldiers were present or on issues that are indirectly linked, such as the small arms trade. The existing scholarship of psychologists, historians, and sociologists who study behavior in war all generally ignores the issue.

This is not just a problem for academia, but is a problem that has clear policy implications that should concern us all. Until we understand the nature of the problem and what to do about it, we can, at best, only express how terrible and tragic it is. At worst, we will develop responses that are either lacking or even counterproductive. Many of the noble-minded political and advocacy efforts designed to end the use of child soldiers are often not connected to the real underlying causes and, for all their energy and good intent, have been largely ineffective. In the military and intelligence realm, little awareness and no counter to the phenomenon has been developed despite children's general presence in contemporary warfare. Our soldiers must deal with the complex dilemmas of facing children on the battlefield without proper intelligence warnings or training to help prepare or guide them. In the humanitarian realm, the repeated failure to appreciate the unique risks and problems of child soldiers has repeatedly crippled demobilization and rehabilitation efforts once the wars are over. We cannot even begin to think that we have a handle on what to do about the dynamics of present-day armed conflict until we have a better understanding of the role children play in it.

The topic of children at war is admittedly not an easy one, neither to research nor to read about. These new soldiers are not simply children; they can also be callous killers capable of the most terrible acts of cruelty and brutality. Many are adrift, having lost their entire families, including some by their own hands; they may know nothing except a world of violence. At the same time, they are still children whom society has an obligation to protect. Their understanding of the power and consequences of their acts is often limited. Indeed, children's immaturity and inexperience is often the very reason they are exploited. It is this innocence of youth placed within the context of war that is perhaps the most difficult to deal with.

To accomplish the research for this book, I relied on an extensive body of primary and secondary literature from a number of disparate fields, including psychiatry, pediatric medicine, anthropology, military history, sociology, and political science. The biggest challenge was not the creation of new knowledge, but rather discerning and integrating what was already known across many different areas into a more focused and useful understanding. As such, the work reflects the hard work of many before me, including the reporting of countless aid and rehabilitation workers who collected this data and gained this experience. They are to be applauded for their dedication and, most of all, their humanity.

Most importantly, though, this book would not have been possible without the assistance of those who consented to speak with me about their experiences. They ranged from former child soldiers who fought in a number of conflicts (including in Colombia, Lebanon, Liberia, Kashmir, Kosovo, Sierra Leone, Sri Lanka, and Sudan), to aid and humanitarian workers around the globe, to many of the individual soldiers, both public and private, who have been put in the terrible position of having to fight children. Where quotes are used, they are most often from sources already in the public domain or who use pseudonyms. This reflects my rather unique starting point in the secretive private military industry, but also addresses a broader concern I had throughout the process of writing this book. I preserve the anonymity of interviewees both as a means to maintaining future access and a way of encouraging a greater frankness of discussions. It also stays within what I believe are my proper bounds as a political science analyst trained neither as a counselor nor health practitioner. The cooperation and willingness of all to speak with me is deeply appreciated.

This book could not have been completed without the support of family, friends, and colleagues, to whom I owe heartfelt thanks. Susan Morrison-Singer provided my strength in the times when this topic brought me down. Jo Becker, Charlie Borchini, Dan Byman, Laura Donohue, Anne Edgerton, Martha Kaplan, Sasha Kishinch, Megan Kraushaar, Hadia Mubarak, Ben Runkle, and Vicky Wilson all provided great aid and guidance during the research, writing, and editing. James Steinberg and my other colleagues at the Foreign Policy Studies program at the Brookings Institution assisted in the project throughout.

I would like to thank the Brookings Institution, the John M. Olin Foundation, and the Belfer Center for Science and International Affairs at Harvard University for their organizational support. The smart policies that change the world often find origin in their backing of research.

The views expressed here are my own and should not be ascribed to those acknowledged or to the trustees, officers, or other staff members of the Brookings Institution.

PART I

Children at War

CHAPTER I

Children and War

The rebels told me to join them, but I said no. Then they killed my smaller brother. I changed my mind. —L., age seven[1]

One of the original sins of humanity has been its inability to live at peace. From the very beginning of history, conflicts over food, territory, riches, power, and prestige have been an almost constant recurrence. Indeed, much of what is written in human history is simply a history of warfare. The world that we know today, from the states that we live in to the technology that we use daily, has been greatly shaped by violent struggle.[2]

Yet even in this most terrible realm of societal violence, rules of behavior developed. Among the very first was the differentiation between warriors and civilians. In even the most primitive societies, a distinction was made between those who chose to bear the risks involved in the profession of fighting and those who lay outside the field of battle. In a sense, a bargain was struck. Honor and power were accorded to the warriors. In exchange, civilians were granted a sort of guarantee of protection from their depredations. While it applied to all those who were unarmed, special immunity was usually given to certain groups: the old, the infirm, women, and, most particularly, children.[3]

While certainly not always complied with, this "law of the innocents" had been one of the most enduring rules of war, arguably the most important of what legal theorists term *jus in bello* (laws in war). The deliberate targeting of civilians, in particular children, has been the single greatest taboo of all, extending from ancient Chinese philosophy and traditional African tribal societies to the state signatories of the modern-day Geneva Conventions.

Unfortunately, in the chaos and callousness of modern-day warfare, this law has seemingly broken down. Where rules and limits once governed the practice of war, these standards no longer hold in much of warfare at the turn of the twenty-first century. Michael Ignatieff, an ethicist at Harvard University, sums up the changes as simply being a massive breakdown in what he terms the "Warrior's Honor."[4] The participants in battle are often no longer honored warriors, guided by an ethical code, but rather new predators, who target the weakest of society. The result of this breakdown has been a disturbing change in the morbidity of contemporary conflicts.

> *If you join the paramilitaries [the AUC in Colombia], your first duty is to kill. They tell you, "Here you are going to kill." From the very beginning, they teach you how to kill. I mean when you arrive at the camp, the first thing they do is kill a guy, and if you are a recruit they call you over to prick at him, to chop off his hands and arms.* —A., age twelve[5]

The ancient distinction between combatants and civilians as targets of violence has arguably disappeared, or, even worse, swung the other way, creating a new pattern of warfare. Civilians have always suffered in war, but the difference is that in many present-day conflicts they are the primary target. Tactics of ethnic cleansing and genocide have replaced the strict codes of conduct and chivalry that guided such military social orders as medieval European feudalism and ancient Japanese Bushido. Whereas wars were once fought almost exclusively between soldiers, in recent decades the worldwide percentage of victims from wars has become predominantly civilian. In World War I, the percentage of casualties that were civilian was under 10 percent of the total; in World War II, the percentage had risen to nearly 50 percent. The evolution continued through the next fifty years, to the point that now the overwhelming majority of those killed in conflicts are civilians instead of soldiers. For example, of all the persons killed in African conflicts in the late twentieth century, the overwhelming preponderance (92 percent) were civilians. Similar figures hold true for the wars in the Balkans.[6] Civilians once had no place on the battlefield; now the battlefield is almost incomplete without them.

Michael Klare, a professor at Hampshire College who studies modern warfare, describes this change:

> The widespread slaughter of civilians in recent conflicts forces us to rethink what we mean by the concept of war. In the past, "war" meant a series of armed encounters between the armed forces of established states, usually for the purpose of territorial conquest or some other clearly defined strategic objective. But the conflicts of the current era bear little resemblance to this model: most take place within the borders of a single state and entail attacks by paramilitary and irregular forces on unarmed civilians for the purpose of pillage, rape, or ethnic slaughter— or some combination of all three.[7]

Because the most basic laws of war have increasingly been abandoned, conflicts have been characterized by horrific levels of violence. In particular, the once unimaginable targeting of children has become a widespread tactic of war. Examples run from the Serb snipers during the Sarajevo siege who deliberately shot at children walking between their parents, to Rwandan radio broadcasts before the 1994 genocide that reminded genocidal Hutu killers to be sure not to forget "the little ones." The resulting tolls from this shift in attitudes are staggering. In the last decade of warfare, more than two million children have been killed, a rate of more than five hundred a day, or one every three minutes, for a full ten years.

For those children who are touched by war but still survive, the experiences are nonetheless devastating. Six million more children have been disabled or seriously injured in wars over the last decade, and one million children have been orphaned. Almost twenty-five million more children have been driven from their homes by conflict, roughly 50 percent of the current total number of refugees in the world. Another ten million children have been psychologically traumatized by war.[8] As you read this book, these numbers are growing only larger.

The New Warriors

As the most basic laws of war have been increasingly violated, there is a new, perhaps even more disturbing element. Not only have children become the new targets of violence and atrocities in war, but many now have also become the perpetrators.

As the twenty-first century opens, a new practice in warfare has emerged. Indeed, it is becoming so common that it can be thought of as an entirely new doctrine of warfare ("doctrines" are what militaries think of as a set of guidelines about the use of force). While not formalized in a drill manual, it represents a new body of fundamental principles, deliberate instrumental choices, and transferred teachings about how to fight.[9] This new doctrine, though, is the dark underbelly of the display of high technology and clean, distant precision used by U.S. forces in Afghanistan and Iraq, commonly referred to as the Revolution in Military Affairs, or RMA. Instead, it encapsulates modern warfare in its rawest and most troubling form. This new doctrine prescribes the methods and circumstances of children's employment in battle.

The use of child soldiers is far more widespread than the scant attention it typically receives. In over three fourths of the armed conflicts around the world, there are now significant numbers of children participating as active combatants. These are not just youths who are on the cusp of adulthood, but also include minors as young as six years old.

We were frightened because we were young children and we didn't know anything about the army. Even on the shooting range, when they tell you to fire, you're always very scared. For me to overcome that fear, I had to kill someone at the training camp. They brought someone to me one night when I was on duty guarding an entrance. It was a child, whose face they'd covered, and they told

me he was a rebel, an enemy, and I had to kill him. That's exactly
what I did. On the spot. With my knife. That night, after doing
that, I couldn't sleep. —G., age ten[10]

A "child soldier" is generally defined (under both international law
and common practice) as any person under eighteen years of age who is
engaged in deadly combat or combat support as part of an armed force
or group.[11] That this definition is even necessary is a horrifying proof of
how the nature of the warrior has changed. The presence of children
has become a fact of modern combat, violating the once universal rule
that they simply have no part in warfare, either as target or participant.

While this definition seems simple enough, the choice of eighteen
as the onset of adulthood has sometimes been a source of contention.
Obviously, childhood is a not a fixed state, simply bounded by eighteen
years as its upper limit. What determines an individual's capacities is
shaped by social, political, and economic contexts, as well as by genetic
heritage.

However, every culture withholds powers and responsibilities from
youngsters and places them under the care and control of guardians.
These are usually the parents, but also include the broader community
as well, which exercises its guidance through differing laws and practices that seek to regulate the treatment of children. Once they are
judged able to conduct themselves in a mature and fully rational manner, they are granted equal standing as adults. Pre-literate societies were
not able to keep age records, so certain physical events (generally
puberty) or social rites of passage marked the transition to adulthood.
In our modern societies, adulthood is granted at the onset of a prede-
termined age.[12]

Around the world, eighteen years has become the generally
accepted transition point to adulthood. Not only do the overwhelming
majority of UN states not grant political rights, such as the right to
vote, until a citizen is that age, but they also generally apply their laws
and distribute their public services differently to those below this
threshold. For example, criminal sanctions are lighter for those under
the age of eighteen, including special dispensations with regard to the
death penalty in the United States, while those below eighteen qualify

for different social benefits, such as education and health care. Simply put, the age itself has emerged as the international norm for adulthood. As explored in the following chapters, this age point also had carried over into the military realm, generally determining who was allowed to serve as a warrior and who was ineligible to be targeted.[13]

CHAPTER 2

It's a Small World After All: Child Soldiers Around the Globe

The use of child soldiers is probably the world's most unrecognized form of child abuse. —*New York Times*[1]

From its very beginning, human warfare has been an almost exclusively adult male domain. The battlefield was an arena generally closed to all others for nearly four millennia.[2] Indeed, only within the last few decades have able-bodied adult women even been considered capable of participating in war, and this change is far from widespread.

Children and War: The View from History

The exclusion of children from warfare has held true in almost every traditional culture. For example, in pre-colonial African armies the general practice was that the warriors typically joined three to four years after puberty. In the Zulu tribe, for instance, it was not until the ages of eighteen to twenty that members were eligible for *ukubuthwa* (the drafting or enrollment into the tribal regiments).[3] In the Kano region of West Africa, only married men were conscripted, as those unmarried were considered too immature for such an important job as war.[4] When children of lesser ages served in ancient armies, such as the

9

enrollment of Spartan boys into military training, at ages seven to nine, they typically did not serve in combat. Instead, they carried out more menial chores, such as herding cattle or bearing shields and mats for the more senior warriors. In absolutely no cases were traditional tribes or ancient civilizations reliant on fighting forces made up of young boys or girls.

The exclusion of children from war was not simply a matter of principle but was pragmatic too, as adult strength and training were needed to use pre-modern weapons. It also reflected the general importance of age in tribal organization. Most traditional cultures relied on a system of age grades for their ruling structures. These were social groupings determined by age cohorts that cut across ties created by kinship and common residence. Such a system enabled senior rulers and tribal elders to maintain command over young—and potentially unruly—subjects. For instance, in the Achioli tribe, in what is now northern Uganda, the system was known as "Lapir." Not only were children and women not to be targeted by the tribe's warriors, but clan elders were the only ones who could decide whether to go to war. This acted as an inherent force of stability.[5] Today, within this same tribe, the Lapir system has been turned on its head. Over the last decade, the area has become engulfed in conflict, with most of the fighting carried out by abducted child soldiers targeting civilians.

> *I grew up in a society where the concept of lapir was very strong. Lapir denotes the cleanliness and weight of one's claim, which then attracts the blessing of the ancestors in recognition and support of that claim.*
>
> *Before declaring war, the elders would carefully examine their lapir—to be sure that their community had a deep and well-founded grievance against the other side. If this was established to be the case, war might be declared, but never lightly. And in order to preserve one's lapir, strict injunctions would be issued to regulate the actual conduct of the war. You did not attack children, women or the elderly; you did not destroy crops, granary stores or livestock. For to commit such taboos would be to soil your lapir, with the*

consequence that you would forfeit the blessing of the ancestors, and thereby risk losing the war itself. . . .

But today, to paraphrase the poet W. B. Yeats, things have fallen apart, the moral centre is no longer holding. In so many conflicts today, anything goes. Children, women, the elderly, granary stores, crops, livestock—all have become fair game in the single-minded struggle for power, in an attempt not just to prevail but to humiliate, not simply to subdue but to annihilate the "enemy community" altogether. This is the phenomenon of total war.

—OLARA OTUNNU, UN special representative
for children and armed conflict[6]

Similarly in European history, the exclusion of children was a general rule. However, some male children did play military roles, though not as active soldiers. Boy pages helped arm and maintain the knights of medieval Europe, while drummer boys and "powder monkeys" (small boys who ran ammunition to cannon crews) were a requisite part of any army and navy in the seventeenth and eighteenth centuries. The key is that these boys fulfilled minor or ancillary support roles and were not considered true combatants. They neither dealt out death nor were considered legitimate targets. Indeed, Henry V was so angered at the breaking of this rule at the battle of Agincourt (1415), where some of his army's boy pages were killed, that he in turn slaughtered all his French prisoners, as famously described by Shakespeare.

FLUELLEN: *Kill the boys and the luggage! 'Tis expressly against the law of arms: 'tis as arrant a piece of knavery, mark you now, as can be offer't: in your conscience now, is it not?*

GOWER: *'Tis certain there's not a boy left alive; and the cowardly rascals that ran from the battle ha' done this slaughter: besides, they have burned and carried away all that was in the King's tent; wherefore the King, most worthily, hath caused every soldier to cut his prisoner's throat. Oh, 'tis a gallant King!*

—WILLIAM SHAKESPEARE, *Henry the Fifth*[7]

Even the new mass armies and general mobilization of society that the French Revolution brought about in 1798 did not lead to children serving as soldiers. Rather, children who joined worked exclusively behind the lines, helping women and elderly tend to the wounded.

Perhaps the most well-known use of supposed child soldiers in history is the famous Children's Crusade in the Middle Ages. Interestingly, the reality is that the crusade was not an actual case of children at war. Instead, it was a march of thousands of mostly unarmed boys from northern France and western Germany who sought to take back the Holy Land by the sheer power of their faith. Crowds of disenfranchised boys, who had been excluded from the prevailing feudal social structure, were inspired by a French peasant boy named Stephen from a village near Vendôme and a German boy named Nicholas from Cologne. The two claimed to have met Jesus Christ, whom they said had given them a plan to succeed at taking back Jerusalem where the adult crusaders had failed. The boys would march to the Mediterranean Sea, which would part for them, and they would continue on to the Holy Land, whereupon the infidels would bow down before their innocence. What actually happened is that while Stephen and Nicholas succeeded in gathering roughly thirty thousand boys, the crowd was robbed and attacked along its way to the Mediterranean. Once there, the sea did not part. Eventually, a small number of the children were able to embark on seven boats provided by local merchants in Marseilles. Two of the boats sank with all lives lost. The other five did not make it to the Holy Land but landed instead in Algiers, whereupon the boat captains sold the children into slavery to the local ruler.[8]

Another historic myth of child soldiers was the Janissary of the Ottoman Empire. This was a corps made up of Christian captives, often youths rounded up by the civil authorities as a form of tax on non-Muslim families. Separated from their families, they were crafted into an elite group that was answerable only to the sultan. The youths, though, were not deployed until they had gone through a strict program of education, religious instruction, and then military training, thus only until they had become adults. The Janissary evolved into one of the first standing professional armies and thus gave the Ottomans an edge over the Western feudal armies of the period. Because of its gain in power and influence, the Janissary corps soon became a hereditary organization and lost any youth or Christian aspect. In time, it became a primary palace guard rather than a feared army. It was folded by Sultan Mahmud II in 1826 because he feared its threat to his power.

Stories of children's involvement in warfare are also found in American history, all the way back to the fictional Johnny Tremain, who grows from apprentice to patriot during the Revolution.[9] While the earliest regulations of the U.S. Army (1802) stated that no person under the age of twenty-one could enlist without his parents' permission, there was no minimum age if the child had his parents' consent.[10] This meant that a small number of young boys served as musicians, powder monkeys, and midshipmen (teenage gentlemen officers in training) in the nascent American military. In 1813 new rules lowered the age of admission without parental permission to eighteen, but also standardized the roles of those younger with parental permission. The regulations stated that "healthy, active" boys between fourteen and eighteen could enlist as musicians with parental consent. These boys' musician positions existed until 1916.

The musicians, though, were different from regular soldiers or sailors. The boys were clearly differentiated from active combatants, often by different uniforms. Additionally, U.S. forces were far from reliant on their presence. Their roles still did entail great risk, though, and many conducted themselves with bravery, sometimes going outside their established areas. Perhaps the most notable boy to serve in the U.S. Army was fifteen-year-old bugler John Cook, the only child to ever win the Medal of Honor. At the Civil War battle of Antietam (September 17, 1862), the bloodiest day in U.S. history, Cook was serving as a courier for a Union artillery battery. While running messages to other units, he discovered two unmanned cannons. He then took it upon himself to serve them. Just five feet tall, he single-handedly carried out the job of a four-man gun crew. While he was firing the guns, Union brigadier general John Gibbon spotted him. While it certainly wasn't the best role for either the boy or the general, Gibbon jumped off his horse and joined Cook in firing the guns until the end of the battle. By the end of the war, Cook had served in more than twenty battles.[11]

*I was fifteen years of age, and was bugler of Battery B, which suf-
fered fearful losses in the field at Antietam where I won my Medal
of Honor. . . . At this battle we lost forty-four men, killed and
wounded, and about forty horses, which shows what a hard fight
it was.* —JOHN COOK[12]

Thus, while the rule held that children were not to be soldiers,
there were some exceptions in the grand span of history. Small numbers of underage children certainly lied about their ages to join armies,
while others like Cook found ways to go outside their designated roles.
In addition, a few states sent children to fight in their last gasps of
defeat. Perhaps the most notable instances were the Virginia Military
Institute cadets who fought at the battle of New Market in May 1864
and the arming of the Hitler Jugend (Hitler Youth) when Allied armies
entered Nazi Germany in the spring of 1945. At New Market, Union
forces marched down the Shenandoah Valley, hoping to cut the Virgin-
ian Central Railroad, a key supply line. Southern general John Breck-
inridge found himself with the only Confederate force in the area,
commanding just fifteen hundred men, so he ordered the corps of
cadets from the nearby VMI military academy to join him. Two hundred forty-seven strong (roughly twenty-five were sixteen years old or
younger), they waited out most of the battle until its final stages. Then,
in a fairly dramatic charge, they overran a key Union artillery battery.
Ten cadets were killed and forty-five were wounded. Ultimately,
though, their role was for naught. Within the year, the Union would
capture the Shenandoah and with it the rest of the Confederacy.[13]

The Hitler Jugend were young boys who had received quasi-
military training as part of a political program to maintain Nazi rule
through indoctrination. During most of World War II, the youths only
joined German military forces (including the SS, for which they were a
feeder organization) once they reached the age of maturity. However,
when Allied forces invaded German territory in the final months of the
war, Hitler's regime ordered these boys to fight as well. It was a desperate gambit to hold off the invasion until new "miracle" weapons (like
the V-2 rocket and Me-262 jet fighter) could turn the tide. Lightly
armed and mostly sent out in small ambush squads, scores of Hitler

Jugend were killed in futile skirmishes, all occurring after the war had essentially been decided.[14]

> *I swear by God this Holy Oath: I will render unconditional Obedience to the Führer of the German Reich and the people, Adolf Hitler, the supreme commander of the Armed Forces and will be ready as a brave soldier, to stake my life at any time for this oath.*
> —Oath taken by Hitler Jugend[15]

In sum, while there were isolated instances in which children did serve in armies or other groups at war, a general norm held against child soldiers across the last four millennia of warfare. The small number of cases were qualitatively different from a general practice, being isolated in time, geographic space, and scope. Moreover, the children were never an integral or essential part of any of the limited number of forces they served in. New Market, for example, was the first and only major battle in all U.S. history to see their use. It involved only 247 boys total, and no other countries in that period rushed to copy the example. All told, the incidents are the exceptions to what the rule used to be.

The New Child Soldiers

The nature of armed conflict has changed greatly since these times. The case of Sierra Leone, a small country in West Africa, captures just how much. Sierra Leone is often at the center of the child soldier discussion, not simply because the country has suffered through a terrible civil war that lasted from 1991 to 2001, but because of the prominent role of children in fighting it. In the rebel Revolutionary United Front (RUF) organization that initiated the violence, as much as 80 percent of all fighters were aged seven to fourteen, many of them abducted.[16] Moreover, children were brought into the fighting at the very start, not at a later point when adult soldiers ran short, as had been the case in some earlier instances. However, the RUF was not the only group in Sierra Leone to use child soldiers; both the government and its tribal militia allies recruited them as well. The overall total of child soldiers for all the sides is close to ten thousand, putting them in the majority of total fighters in the conflict.

Sierra Leone is no exception, though. By the turn of the twenty-first century, child soldiers had served in significant numbers on every continent of the globe but Antarctica. They have become integral parts of both organized military units and nonmilitary but still violent political organizations, including rebel and terrorist groups. They serve as combatants in a variety of roles: infantry shock troops, raiders, sentries, spies, sappers, and porters. In short, the participation of children in armed conflict is now global in scope and massive in number.

A quick tour around the world reveals the extent and activity of this new practice of war over the last decade.

The Western Hemisphere

In the Americas since 1990, child soldiers have fought in Colombia, Ecuador, El Salvador, Guatemala, Mexico (in the Chiapas conflict), Nicaragua, Paraguay, and Peru. The most substantial numbers are in Colombia. There, more than eleven thousand children are being used as soldiers, meaning that one out of every four irregular combatants is underage. They serve on both the rebel side, in the Revolutionary Armed Forces of Colombia (FARC) and National Liberation Army (ELN) organizations, and with the Colombian government's military and rightist paramilitary groups such as the United Self-Defense Forces (AUC). As many as two thirds of these children fighters are under fifteen years of age, with the youngest recruited being seven years old.[17]

Child soldiers in Colombia are nicknamed "little bells" by the military that use them as expendable sentries and "little bees" by the FARC guerrillas, because they "sting" their enemies before they know they are under attack. In urban militias, they are called "little carts," as they can sneak weapons through checkpoints without suspicion. Up to 30 percent of some guerrilla units are made up of children. Child guerrillas are used to collect intelligence, make and deploy mines, and serve as advance troops in ambush attacks against paramilitaries, soldiers, and police officers. For example, when the FARC attacked the Guatape hydroelectric facility in 1998, the employees of the power plant reported that some of the attackers were as young as eight years old. In

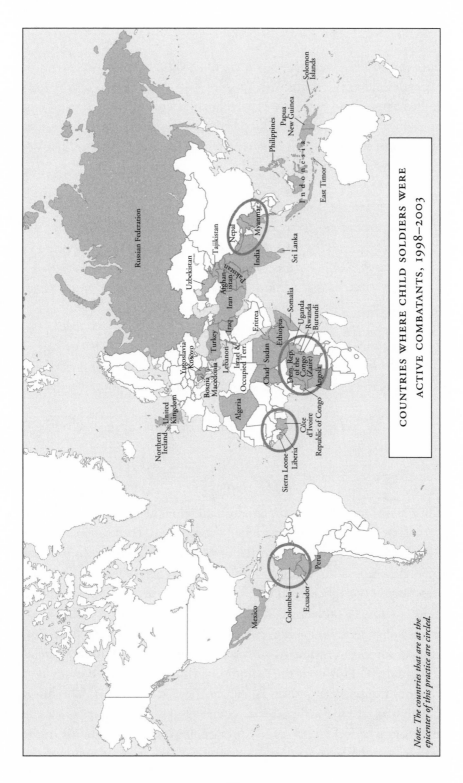

COUNTRIES WHERE CHILD SOLDIERS WERE
ACTIVE COMBATANTS, 1998–2003

Note: The countries that are at the
epicenter of this practice are circled.

17

2001 the FARC even released a training video that showed boys as young as eleven working with missiles.[18] In turn, some government-linked paramilitary units are 85 percent children, with soldiers as young as eight years old seen patrolling.[19] There has also been cross-border spillover of the practice. The FARC recruits children from as far away as Venezuela, Panama, and Ecuador, some as young as ten.[20]

> *They bring the people they catch . . . to the training course. My squad had to kill three people. After the first one was killed, the commander told me that the next day I'd have to do the killing. I was stunned and appalled. I had to do it publicly, in front of the whole company, fifty people. I had to shoot him in the head. I was trembling. Afterwards, I couldn't eat. I'd see the person's blood. For a week, I had a hard time sleeping. . . . They'd kill three or four people each day in the course. Different squads would take turns, would have to do it on different days. Some of the victims cried and screamed. The commanders told us we had to learn how to kill.*
>
> —O., age fifteen (recruited by FARC at age twelve)[21]

Europe

On the European continent, children under eighteen years of age have served in both British government forces and their opposition in Northern Ireland and on all sides in the Bosnian conflict. As one former Bosnian child soldier, who was fourteen when he enlisted, describes of the fighting, "It was World War I style fighting. There were a lot of mortar attacks, howitzers, and tanks—a lot of armor got involved. Both sides took a lot of casualties from the minefields and snipers . . . I kind of quit after my dad was injured. I had to take care of my family."[22] However, the majority of child soldiers in Europe have fought in opposition groups farther to the east, serving in Chechnya, Daghestan, Kosovo, Macedonia, and Nagorno-Karabakh. For example, young teens fought in the Kosovo Liberation Army (KLA) in the war against the Serbs in 1997–98. Many children have since joined the other Albanian rebel groups attempting to break away bits of territory from Serbia and Macedonia, serving in both the Liberation Army of Presevo, Medvedja and Bujanovac (UCPMB) and the National Liberation Army. In Chechnya, Russian commanders are now wrestling with the fact that, as the war has persisted, they are faced with younger and younger opposition fighters. As one Russian colonel commented, "In the [separatist] bands there are more and more youths, ages 14–16. They place the mines; they fire at the checkpoints. An adolescent does not even understand what he is being killed for . . . I think that we will have to create youth labor camps, put them there so they can learn at least something about civilized forms of existence."[23]

It is in Turkey, though, where the most child soldiers in Europe are found, in the Kurdish Workers' Party (PKK). In 1994 the PKK began the systematic recruitment of children. It even created dedicated children's regiments. In 1998 it was reported that the PKK had three thousand underage children within its ranks, with the youngest reported PKK fighter being an armed seven-year-old. Ten percent of these were girls.[24] The PKK is also known to have recruited children abroad, for example targeting Kurdish émigré kids who were attending schools and summer camps in Sweden.[25]

Africa

Africa is often considered to be at the epicenter of the child soldier phenomenon, with the Sierra Leone case being the most instructive. Armed groups using child soldiers cover the continent and are present in nearly every one of its myriad of wars. The result appears to be an almost endemic link between children and warfare in Africa. For example, a survey in Angola revealed that 36 percent of all Angolan children had either served as soldiers or accompanied troops into combat.[26] Similar patterns hold for children in Liberia, which has seen two waves of wars over the last decade. First, Charles Taylor seized power at the head of a mainly youth rebel army in the early 1990s. By the end of the decade, Taylor faced new foes in the LURD and MODEL, rebel groups that also used child soldiers to eventually topple him in 2003. The United Nations estimates that some twenty thousand children served as combatants in Liberia's war, up to 70 percent of the various factions' fighting forces.[27] Of particular note in Africa is the Lord's Resistance Army in Uganda (LRA), renowned, or rather infamous, for being made up almost exclusively of child soldiers. It has abducted more than fourteen thousand children to turn into soldiers. The LRA also holds the ignoble record for having the world's youngest reported armed combatant, age five.[28]

Don't overlook them. They can fight more than we big people . . .
It is hard for them to just retreat.
                    —Liberian government militia commander[29]

The areas where child soldiers have been present read like a master list of the continent's worst zones of violence. In Somalia, boys fourteen to eighteen regularly fight in warlord militias. In Rwanda, thousands of children are thought to have participated in the 1994 genocide. For example, one rehabilitation camp alone housed some 486 suspected child *genocidaires*. The boys were all younger than fourteen when they allegedly took part in the mass killings of thousands.[30] Across the border, in the ongoing fighting in Burundi, up to fourteen thousand children have fought in the war, many as young as twelve.[31] Indeed, at the start of the war, Hutu rebel groups sent between three thousand and five thousand children to training camps in the Central African Republic, Tanzania, and Rwanda. Since then, refugee and street children in these countries and Kenya have also been recruited for the fighting in Burundi. Similar practices prevail in fighting to the east in Congo-Brazzaville and Côte d'Ivoire (three thousand estimated child soldiers), while to the north, large numbers of Ethiopian youths fought in their country's war with Eritrea. Despite Ethiopian government claims that it had no child soldiers, hundreds of its POWs taken by the Eritreans were found to be between fourteen and eighteen. At the same time, the Ethiopian government faces an internal rebellion from the Oromo Liberation Front, which is also alleged to have recruited children. Two twenty-two-year-old members of the OLF recently testified that they had been fighting in the organization since they were eleven years old.[32]

Child soldiers have also become a common feature of the continent's largest conflict, the war in the Democratic Republic of the Congo (DRC). The fighting in what used to be Zaire began in 1996 with the revolt led by Laurent Kabila. His army had some 10,000 child soldiers between the ages of seven and sixteen.[33] As the war spread, it involved armies from eight different countries and a multitude of rebel groups. It continues today. Estimates are that there are presently between 30,000 and 50,000 child soldiers in the DRC—as much as 30 percent of all combatants.[34] In Bunia district, a particularly nasty war zone where European peacekeepers were deployed in summer 2003, they make up between 60 and 75 percent of the warring militias (8,000 to 10,000 in the Ituri to win alone).[35]

Congolese child soldiers were known as *kadogos,* "little ones" in Swahili. They have been so prevalent that they even served in Kabila's Presidential Guard. Indeed, when Kabila was later assassinated in January 2001, many held his unruly *kadogos* responsible. The ultimate blame fell on a boy serving as his bodyguard, who was shot during the ensuing firefight.[36]

The Middle East and Central Asia

The Middle East is another area where child soldiers have become an integral part of the fighting. Children today are engaged in fighting in Algeria, Azerbaijan, Egypt, Iran (as part of rebel groups now fighting against the regime), Iraq, Lebanon, Sudan, Tajikistan, and Yemen. These include children younger than fifteen serving in a number of radical Islamic groups. Young teens are also at the center of fighting in Palestine, making up as much as 70 percent of the participants in the intifada. The response by the Israeli military has been to change its rules of engagement. As one army sharpshooter stated, "Twelve [years] and up is allowed. He's not a child anymore. That's what they tell us." The outcome is that more than 20 percent of those killed in the intifada have been seventeen and under.[37]

The first modern use of child soldiers in the region was actually during the Iran-Iraq war in the 1980s. Iranian law, based on the Koranic *sharia,* had forbid the recruitment of children under sixteen into the armed forces. However, a few years into the fighting, the regime began to falter in its war with its neighbor, Saddam Hussein's Iraq. So it chose to ignore its own laws, and in 1984, Iranian president Ali-Akbar Rafsanjani declared that "all Iranians from twelve to seventy-two should volunteer for the Holy War."[38] Thousands of children were pulled from schools, indoctrinated in the glory of martyrdom, and sent to the front lines only lightly armed with one or two grenades or a gun with one magazine of ammunition. Wearing keys around their necks (to signify their pending entrance into heaven), they were sent forward in the first waves of attacks, to help clear paths through minefields with their bodies and overwhelm Iraqi defenses. Iran's spiritual leader at the time, Ayatollah Khomeini, delighted in the children's sacrifice and extolled that they were helping Iran to achieve "a situation which we cannot describe in any other way except to say that it is a divine country."[39]

While the child-led human wave attacks were initially very successful, they soon bogged down as the Iraqis adjusted by developing prepared defenses and using chemical weapons. All told, some 100,000 Iranian boy soldiers are thought to have lost their lives. The story of those who did not die is equally tragic. Several hundred Iranian boys were captured. However, when the Red Cross tried to arrange a repatriation program, the Ayatollah Khomeini sent a chilling message that made it clear that all the Iranian boy soldiers were meant to die. In rejecting the Red Cross's proposal to return the boys home, he stated, "They are not Iranian children. Ours have gone to Paradise and we shall see them there."[40]

Iraq, in turn, enrolled child soldiers in that conflict, and more recently, under Saddam Hussein, built up an entire apparatus designed to pull children into conflict. This included the noted *Ashbal Saddam* (Saddam's Lion Cubs), a paramilitary force of boys between the ages of ten and fifteen that was formed after the first Gulf War and received training in small arms and light infantry tactics. More than eight thousand young Iraqis were members of this group in Baghdad alone.[41] During the recent war that ended Saddam Hussein's regime, American forces engaged with Iraqi child soldiers in the fighting in at least three cities (Nasariya, Karbala, and Kirkuk).[42] This was in addition to the many instances of children being used as human shields by Saddam loyalists during the fighting.[43] A number of anti-Saddam paramilitary groups that emerged in the country also utilized children. For instance, the Free Iraqi Forces that were linked to U.S.-backed exile leader Ahmed Chalabi also recruited children as young as thirteen.[44]

The implications of this training and involvement in military activities by large numbers of Iraqi youth were soon felt in the guerrilla war that followed. Beaten on the battlefield, rebel leaders sought to mobilize this cohort of trained and indoctrinated young fighters. A typical incident in the contentious city of Mosul provides a worrisome indicator of the threat posed by child soldiers to U.S. forces. Here, in the same week that President Bush made his infamous aircraft carrier landing heralding the end to the fighting, a twelve-year-old Iraqi boy fired on U.S. Marines with an AK-47 rifle.[45] Over the next weeks, incidents between U.S. forces and armed Iraqi children began to grow, to the extent that U.S. military intelligence briefings began to highlight the role of Iraqi children as attackers and spotters for ambushes. Incidents with child soldiers continued into the guerrilla campaign that followed, ranging from child snipers to a fifteen-year-old who tossed a grenade into an American truck, blowing off the leg of a U.S. Army trooper.[46]

In the summer of 2004, radical cleric Muqtada al-Sadr directed a revolt that consumed the primarily Shia south of Iraq, with the fighting in the holy city of Najaf being particularly fierce. Observers noted multiple child soldiers, some as young as twelve years old, serving in Sadr's "Mahdi" Army that fought U.S. forces. Indeed, Sheikh Ahmad al-Shaibani, Sadr's spokesman defended the use of children, stating, "This shows that the Mahdi are a popular resistance movement against the occupiers. The old men and the young men are on the same field of battle.[47]

Last night I fired a rocket-propelled grenade against a tank. The Americans are weak. They fight for money and status and squeal like pigs when they die. But we will kill the unbelievers because faith is the most powerful weapon. —M., age twelve[48]

23

The overall numbers of Iraqi children involved in the fighting are not yet known. But the indicators are that they do play a significant role in the insurgency. For example, British forces have detained more than sixty juveniles during their operations in Iraq, while U.S. forces have detained 107 Iraqi juveniles in the year after the invasion, holding most at Abu Ghraib prison.[49] The U.S. military considered these children "high risk" security threats, stating that it had captured them while "actively engaged in activities against U.S. forces."[50]

Sudan has seen the largest use of child soldiers in the region, with estimates reaching as high as 100,000 children who have served on both sides of the two decades–old civil war. Since 1995 the Islamic government in the north has conscripted boys as young as twelve into the army and the paramilitary Popular Defense Forces. Homeless and street children have been a particular target. Poor and refugee children who work or live on the streets have been rounded up into special closed camps. Ostensibly orphanages, these camps instead have often acted as reservoirs for army conscripts.[51] The government has also targeted children in the towns it holds in the south to use against their kinsmen in the rebel Sudan People's Liberation Army (SPLA). Disturbingly, one report found that 22 percent of the total primary school population in Wahda province had been recruited into the Sudanese army or pro-government militias, the youngest being nine years old.[52]

The SPLA rebel group, in turn, has relied greatly on child fighters in its battle with the government. While it recently made a public relations gambit in demobilizing three thousand child soldiers, another seven thousand of its fighters (roughly 30 percent of its forces) are thought to be underage.[53] Actually, the SPLA began a practice of "warehousing" young recruits in the mid-1980s. It would encourage and organize young boys to flee to refugee camps located beside its bases on the Ethiopian border. At the boys-only camps, those past the age of twelve would be given full-time military courses, while those younger were trained during school breaks. These boys became the basis of what was known as the Red Army, and were even subcontracted out to the Ethiopian army while it was still allied with the SPLA.[54] Many of these boys later became the core of the famous Lost Boys of Sudan. When the Ethiopian regime allied with the SPLA fell in

1991, the refugees had to flee the camps on the Sudan-Ethiopian border. Thousands of boys had been separated from their families but were not yet incorporated into the SPLA. For the next decade, the unaccompanied boys wandered from refugee camp to refugee camp. Eventually, those who were unable to be reunified with their families were resettled in the United States in 2001.[55]

Child soldiers are also present in a number of areas in the region where American forces were deployed in the wake of the 9/11 attacks. Indeed, it was in Afghanistan that a fourteen-year-old sniper killed the first U.S. combat casualty in the war on terrorism. On January 4, 2002, Special Forces Sergeant 1st Class Nathan Chapman was on a mission in Paktia province to coordinate with local fighters. As he stood in the flatbed of a truck directing his unit, he was shot without warning from several hundred feet away. Just a few months later, another Special Forces trooper, Sergeant 1st Class Christopher Speer, was killed by a fifteen-year-old al Qaeda member while operating in Khost province. The young boy, who was originally from Canada, was the sole survivor of a group of al Qaeda fighters that had ambushed a combined U.S.-Afghan force. This led to a five-hour firefight involving massive air strikes. When U.S. forces went to sift through the rubble, the young boy popped up, with pistol in hand, and threw a grenade which seriously wounded Speer. The young boy was shot down by Speer's comrades but survived his wounds. A few months later, he spent his sixteenth birthday at the U.S. detention facility at Guantánamo Bay. Three other juvenile detainees were already on-site: two were captured in raids on Taliban camps and one while trying to obtain weapons to fight American forces. By this time, however, Speer had died from his wounds. In a sad irony, Speer had risked his life just two days earlier by going into a minefield to save two injured Afghan children.[56]

The presence of child soldiers in the fighting in Afghanistan should not have been a surprise. Indeed, surveys have found that roughly 30 percent of all Afghan children have participated in military activities at some point in their childhood.[57] When the Taliban became a force in the Afghan civil war in 1994, they gained strength and numbers by recruiting among young refugees who were attending Pakistani madrassahs (Islamic schools).[58] As one Taliban fighter justified the practice, "Children are innocent, so they are the best tools against dark forces."[59]

I regret that I fought and hate the war. It took everything from us. I have studied [until] sixth class. If there was not war, I would have already finished school by now. —R., age eighteen[60]

Once in power, the Taliban's leader, Mullah Omar, declared that any followers who were too young to grow a beard (a definition of maturity in line with the Taliban's pre-Koranic doctrines) should leave the fighting. This decree was widely ignored, with many believing it was just for international consumption. For the last few years of the Afghan civil war, Taliban recruitment of children tended to be cyclical, coinciding with school holidays and major offensives or defeats. As a prelude to large-scale operations, the Taliban typically would truck in more than five thousand children from sympathetic madrassahs across the border in Pakistan. Many were under fourteen. These "temporary" child soldiers would then return to school after one or two months of fighting experience. The Taliban's main foe, the Northern Alliance, also used child soldiers in the fighting in Panjshir valley, but was not as reliant on them.[61] As late as 2003 some eight thousand child soldiers were thought to be still active in Afghanistan, participating in the fighting between the Afghan government, various warlords, and remnants of the Taliban and al Qaeda.[62] U.S. soldiers continue to report facing child soldiers in Afghanistan, with the youngest on the public record being a twelve-year-old boy. He was captured in 2004 after being wounded during a Taliban ambush of a convoy.[63]

Asia

The practice of child soldiers is also highly prevalent in Asia. Children are engaged in insurgencies under way in Cambodia, East Timor, India, Indonesia, Laos, Myanmar, Nepal, Pakistan, Papua New Guinea, the Philippines, Sri Lanka, and the Solomon Islands. In India, some seventeen different rebel groups are suspected of using child soldiers, including along the volatile Kashmiri border with Pakistan.[64]

We prefer to recruit children at the age of eleven or twelve.
——SYED SALAHUDDIN, supreme commander of Hiz-
bul Mujahideen (Kashmir-based militant group)[65]

Children have particularly been at the center of the explosion of
rebel groups and internecine fighting on the many islands of Indonesia,
such as in Ambon.[66] There, thousands of Muslim and Christian boys
have formed local paramilitary units that protect and raid against the
other community. As one local aid worker notes, "They [the boys] are
so proud of their contribution. It's a common thing for them to say
they've killed. Since the government can't seem to do anything, they
all say they have an obligation to protect their families and their
religion."[67]

It is estimated that Myanmar alone has more than 75,000 child soldiers, one of the highest numbers of any country in the world, serving
both within the state army and the ethnic armed groups pitted against
the regime. The army pulls in young children through its Ye Nyunt
(Brave Sprouts) camps. As many as 45 percent of its total recruits are
under age eighteen. Twenty percent are under fifteen, with some as
young as eleven. The various rebel groups are estimated to have another
six thousand to eight thousand child soldiers.[68]

The spillover effects of this recruitment of children were tragically
illustrated in January 2000. When the Karen National Liberation
Army rebel group began to collapse in the late 1990s, it broke up into a
number of new groups. One of these, the Christian Karen militia
"God's Army," was led by twelve-year-old twin brothers, the enigmatic
Luther and Johnny Htoo.

The group gained notoriety not only from the famous picture of
the two young leaders smoking cigars, but also when young members
of their group took hundreds of hostages at the Ratchaburi hospital in
Thailand. The fighters were subsequently killed in a commando attack
broadcast live on Thai TV, and the group's camps were overrun. Ultimately, Luther and Johnny were reunited with their mother in a Thai
refugee camp. The family has since applied for asylum in the United
States, and their whereabouts are no longer publicly known.

The Philippines is another nation where U.S. forces have deployed as part of the war on terrorism. Likewise, it has an array of rebel groups using child soldiers. The communist New People's Army (NPA) is thought to have around a thousand child soldiers, mostly in the age range of thirteen to seventeen.[69] The Moro Islamic Liberation Front (MILF), a Muslim rebel group, has recruited children from elementary schools as young as nine. Abu Sayyaf, a radical breakaway group from the MILF, is suspected of being linked to al Qaeda (Osama bin Laden's brother-in-law was a financier for the group). In turn, it is also known to have boy soldiers whose ages range from eleven to fifteen. Some are volunteers, while others were actually sold to the group by their parents.[70] These dynamics of multiple rebel groups with child soldiers have presented a terrible dilemma for Filipino military forces, who are now fighting the groups alongside U.S. military advisors. As one Filipino marine sergeant stated, "How does one know if the enemies are children? They have guns like us, they are in full uniform and they fight like any other soldier. But if you mean have I seen young dead enemies, most of the dead I saw were young."[71]

These examples provide only highlights of the extent of the spread of child soldiers, not its entirety. They demonstrate just how deeply involved children have become in contemporary warfare. The manner in which many groups go about creating military capability has changed. Moreover, child soldiers are a new feature of nearly every area at war in our world. When analysts write of the "pre-modern" zones of "anarchy," "chaos," and "turmoil" (to use some of the most common terms) that characterize the emerging geopolitical structure, they are talking of the areas where children now carry out warfare.[72]

While these examples speak volumes, the raw numbers are also telling. Of ongoing or recently ended conflicts, 68 percent (37 of the 55) have children under eighteen serving as combatants.[73] Eighty percent of these conflicts where children are present include fighters under the age of fifteen.

In turn, this means that children are increasingly present in the various armed organizations that cover the globe (that is, both state militaries and all armed non-state groups operating in a politico-military context). Indeed, more than 40 percent of the total armed organizations around the world use child soldiers (157 of 366).

It is important to note that these are not just children on the borderline of adulthood, but include those considered underage by any cultural standard. Twenty-three percent of the armed organizations in the world (84 total) use children age fifteen and under in combat roles. Eighteen percent of the total (64) use children twelve and under.[74] While the exact average age of the entire set of child soldiers around the world is not known, it appears to be well below the eighteen years threshold. In one survey taken of child soldiers in Asia, the average age of recruitment was thirteen. However, as many as 34 percent were taken in under the age of twelve.[75] In a separate study in Africa, 60 percent were fourteen and under.[76] Another study in Uganda found the average age to be 12.9.[77] Indeed, many child soldiers are recruited so young that they do not even know how old they are. As one boy from Sierra Leone thought to have been seven or eight when he was taken tells, "We just fought. We didn't know our age."[78]

Seven weeks after I arrived there was combat. I was very scared. It was an attack on the paramilitaries. We killed about seven of them. They killed one of us. We had to drink their blood to conquer our fear. Only the scared ones had to do it. I was the most scared of all, because I was the newest and the youngest.

—A., age twelve[79]

The generally accepted estimate is that well over 300,000 children are currently fighting in wars or have recently been demobilized.[80] However, this figure is from a series of country case studies (twenty-six in all) and thus may be at the low end of the likely total, given the number of conflicts that were not included in the studies. To some, 300,000 is an immense number, while others might note that relative to the overall number of armed personnel in the world, it is a small percentage. However, when looking at the armed forces actually involved in conflict in the world at this time (as opposed to those at peace), it makes up just under 10 percent of all combatants.[81] What is more significant is that this number was near zero just a few decades ago.

Any debate over the numbers, though, belies the real issue at hand, the vast changes in war and breakdown in norms that these figures signify. Graça Machel, the former first lady of Mozambique and wife of Nelson Mandela, has served as a special expert for the United Nations on the topic. She perhaps said it best:

> These statistics are shocking enough, but more chilling is the conclusion to be drawn from them: more and more of the world is being sucked into a desolate moral vacuum. This is a space devoid of the most basic human values; a space in which children are slaughtered, raped, and maimed; a space in which children are exploited as soldiers; a space in which children are starved and exposed to extreme brutality. Such unregulated terror and violence speak of deliberate victimization. There are few further depths to which humanity can sink.[82]

Children of the State

Non-state actors such as armed rebel, ethnic, and political opposition groups are especially likely to use children as fighters. Sixty percent of the non-state armed forces in the world (77 of 129) use child soldiers. But children's use as soldiers is by no means limited to non-state actors or to armies actively at war. The United Nations estimates that, in addition to the 300,000 active child combatants, more than fifty states actively recruit at least another half million children into their military and paramilitary forces, in violation of both international law and usually their own domestic laws.[83]

> *An army recruitment unit arrived at my village and demanded two new recruits. Those who could not pay 3000 kyat [$400] had to join the army.* —Z., age fifteen[84]

In many countries, the children are incorporated through schools and armed youth movements, in which military training and indoctrination occur. These groups then form a valued reserve for the local regime to use to its own ends, particularly during a wartime manpower crunch.

Typically, states have larger and more formalized military apparatus able to incorporate more recruits. So, states' use of children often occurs in quite high numbers. For example, of the approximately 60,000 personnel in the El Salvadoran military during its civil war, ex-soldiers estimated that about 48,000 (80 percent) were less than eighteen years of age. Colombia's national security forces once included more than 15,000 children.[85]

Subject to the same military law as adults, children serving in state forces are often no better off than their compatriots across the lines. In Paraguay, for example, children as young as twelve are illegally recruited into the military. Many are then particularly targeted for ill treatment and punishment, which has resulted in several deaths of underage recruits.[86] Other case studies in Colombia, Ethiopia, Liberia, and Uganda all similarly report children being beaten or even shot for trying to escape government recruitment, or for disobedience or desertion (the use of the death penalty against children, though, is in contravention of international law; the Covenant on Civil and Political Rights prohibits capital punishment for persons less than eighteen years old).[87] In Russia, a number of army regiments have admitted boy orphans between the ages of twelve and seventeen who have nowhere else to go. In the words of one regimental commander, despite their youth, the boys can expect to be treated as regular soldiers. "Here they learn to be manly. No one licks them clean and no one pities them. Regardless of their age, they're treated as grown-up men, not as boys of their mental and psychological level of development."[88]

Girls with Guns

Another new wrinkle in the child soldier phenomenon is that the problem crosses gender boundaries. In the isolated instances in the past when children were used on the battlefield, they were exclusively boys. Now, while the majority of child soldiers are still male, there are significant numbers of girl fighters under the age of eighteen. Roughly 30 percent of the world's armed forces that employ child soldiers include girl soldiers. Underage girls have been present in the armed forces in fifty-five countries. In twenty-seven of these, girls were abducted to serve and in thirty-four they saw combat.[89]

Their numbers in these wars are equally significant. In the 1990s civil war in Ethiopia, as much as 25 percent of the total opposition forces were females under eighteen years; in turn, about 10 percent of the child soldiers in the PKK in Turkey are girls.[90] Similar percentages of female child soldiers (in the 10 to 25 percent range) also hold for the Shining Path in Peru, the FARC in Colombia, the LRA in Uganda, and in the fighting in Manipur, India. The LURD rebel group in Liberia (which later became part of the ruling government after it won the war) even organized a Women's Auxiliary Corps made up of young girls.[91]

> *I had a friend Juanita, who got into trouble. . . . We had been friends in civilian life and we shared a tent together. The commander said that it didn't matter that she was my friend. She had committed an error and had to be killed. I closed my eyes and fired the gun, but I didn't hit her. So I shot again. The grave was right nearby. I had to bury her and put dirt on top of her. The commander said, "You did very well. Even though you started to cry, you did well. You'll have to do this again many more times, and you'll have to learn not to cry."* —A., age seventeen[92]

The most significant user of girl soldiers, though, is perhaps the Liberation Tigers of Tamil Eelam (LTTE). Fighting in Sri Lanka since the mid-1980s, the group systematically recruits children. It has even gone so far as to establish the LTTE Bakuts, a unit known as the "Baby Brigade" made up of fighters sixteen and under. Estimates indicate that between 40 and 60 percent of its fighting forces are recruited below the age of eighteen, mostly in the ten to sixteen-year-old range. Roughly half of these LTTE troops are female, called "Birds of Freedom" by their fellow rebels. Many of these children have received specialized training as suicide bombers. The LTTE makes the startling claim that recruiting Tamil girls is its way of "assisting women's liberation and counteracting the oppressive traditionalism of the present system."[93]

To the north, the Maoist Lal Sena insurgency in Nepal has similarly been proud of its recruitment and employment of girl fighters. Since the group's emergence in 1996, more than five thousand Nepalese have died in the fighting, three hundred of them children; starting in 2002, the United States became involved in this conflict by giving the government tens of millions in military aid.) Lal Sena has recruited some four thousand child soldiers between the ages of fourteen and eighteen (around 30 to 40 percent of its total forces.[94] Its own propaganda highlights the fact that girls represent great numbers of this total and even describes the military activity of girls as "another bonanza for the revolutionary cause. That is, the drawing of children into the process of war and their politicisation."[95] Lal Sena is interesting in that it began to employ young girl and boy fighters after training and consultation with other rebel/terrorist organizations, including the Shining Path in Peru and Indian militant groups.[96] This indicates that there are teaching pathways by which the child soldier doctrine has been spread.

The fact that sexual abuse is often a common part of the child soldiering experience for these girls debunks any idea that their recruitment is somehow progressive. While they may be expected to perform the same dangerous functions as boy soldiers, many are also forced to provide sexual services or become "soldiers' wives." For example, the LRA in Uganda, a self-proclaimed "Christian" resistance group, specifically targets girls considered more attractive for abduction. They are then "married" to the organization's leaders as spoils of war. If the man dies, the girl is then given to another rebel. In Angola, girl soldiers were labeled by the rebel group as *Okulumbuissa*, a lower social category which sanctions a man to impregnate the girl without having to assume paternity and responsibility for the child.[97]

They picked me and took me away in the bush where I was forced to become a "wife" to one of the rebels. Being new in the field, on the first night I refused, but on the second night, they said, "Either you give in or death." I still tried to refuse, and then the man got serious and knifed me on the head. I became helpless and started bleeding terribly and that was how I got involved in sex at the age of 14 because death was near. —B., age sixteen[98]

Many of these girls then become pregnant. What happens next usually depends on the group's decision rather than the young mother's choice. For example, when a girl in the FARC in Colombia becomes pregnant, she often is forced either to have an abortion or give her baby to local peasants. When the child reaches thirteen, he or she is reclaimed by the FARC as part of the next generation of recruits.[99] In contrast, women in the LRA tend to keep their children. But in doing so, they become more wedded to the group, because their escape options are further limited. Observers thus report seeing young LRA girls in the midst of combat, fighting with babies strapped to their backs. These widespread abuses inevitably complicate attempts by former girl soldiers to reintegrate into their communities and families.[100]

PART II

The Process and Results of Child Soldiers

CHAPTER 3

The Underlying Causes

The child soldier is the most famous character of the end of the 20th century. —AHMADOU KOUROUMA, *Allah n'est pas obligé*[1]

The recruitment and employment of child soldiers is one of the most flagrant violations of the norms of international human rights. Besides being contrary to the general practices of the last four millennia of warfare, there are a number of treaties that attempt to prohibit it today.

At the international level, these treaties have been codified into law. They include the 1948 Universal Declaration of Human Rights, the Geneva Conventions of 1949, the 1977 Additional Protocols to the Geneva Conventions, and the 1989 Convention on the Rights of the Child. Additionally, the UN Security Council, the UN General Assembly, the UN Commission on Human Rights, and the International Labor Organization are among the international bodies that have condemned the practice. There has also been a global grassroots efforts against it, embodied in the Coalition to Stop the Use of Child Soldiers, an umbrella group of nongovernmental organizations based in more than forty countries. At the regional level, the Organization of African Unity, the Economic Community of West African States, the Organization of American States, the Organization for Security and Cooperation in Europe, and the European Parliament have also denounced the use of child soldiers.

In May 2000 the UN General Assembly adopted a new "optional protocol" to the 1989 Convention on the Rights of the Child, further illustrating the growing global sentiment against the use of child soldiers. This measure specifically targeted the phenomenon by formally raising the minimum age of recruitment and use to eighteen (the old convention limit was fifteen, which most armed groups would still be in violation of anyway). It has since been signed by more than a hundred states.

Unfortunately, the growing and global practice of using child soldiers illustrates just how extensively this long list of conventions and laws is ignored. The recruitment and use of child soldiers is a deliberate and systematic choice currently being made the world over. Simply put, children fighting on the battlefield has become normal practice in current warfare. Thus, rather than compliance, these prohibitive norms have been turned inside out. That is, going by actual behavior, the new standard is child soldiering, not the banning of it.

The underlying causes behind these deliberate violations of international standards are complex. They involve three critical factors that form a causal chain: (1) social disruptions and failures of development caused by globalization, war, and disease have led not only to greater global conflict and instability, but also to generational disconnections that create a new pool of potential recruits; (2) technological improvements in small arms now permit these child recruits to be effective participants in warfare; and (3) there has been a rise in a new type of conflict that is far more brutal and criminalized. These forces have resulted in the viability of a new doctrine of how to operate and succeed in war, particularly in the context of weakening or failed states. Conflict group leaders now see the recruitment and use of children as a low-cost and efficient way for their organizations to mobilize and generate force.

The Lost Generation

The desperate position in which many children around the world find themselves is almost unimaginable. While positive in some terms, the developments of globalization that dominated the last quarter century have left many behind, as well as rending many traditional societies and mores. The developed world saw great prosperity from the opening of economies, but this certainly did not produce a homogeneous world economy or culture with affluence for all. Indeed, three billion people, roughly half the world's population, currently subsist on $2 or less a day.[2]

The ensuing magnitude of global human insecurity is stunning in all its measures:

SECURITY: More than 1 billion live in countries in civil war or at high risk of falling into civil war.

INCOME: More than 1.3 billion in developing countries live in poverty, 600 million are considered extremely poor; in industrial countries 200 million live below the poverty line.

LITERACY: More than 900 million adults are illiterate.

HOMES: More than 1 billion rural people are landless or near landless; more than 400 million in developing countries live on degraded, ecologically fragile land. Another 1 billion live in urban slums.

WATER: More than 1.3 billion in developing countries lack access to safe water.

FOOD: More than 800 million in developing countries have inadequate food supplies; 500 million are chronically malnourished.[3]

Each of these measures of quality of life and hopes for the future is worsening.

The brunt of these socioeconomic problems has fallen on the youngest segments of the population, as we are now in the midst of the largest generation of youth in human history. Unprecedented numbers of children around the world are undereducated, malnourished, marginalized, and disaffected. Almost a quarter of all the world's youth survive on less than a dollar a day. As many as 250 million children live on the street, 211 million children must work to feed themselves and their families, 115 million children have never been to school.[4] A third of all children in Africa suffer from severe hunger. By 2010, this figure may rise to as many as half of all African children.[5]

These desperate and excluded children constitute a huge pool of labor for the illegal economy, organized crime, and armed conflicts. In describing the concurrent risks, Juan Somavi, secretary general of the World Social Summit, notes, "We've replaced the threat of the nuclear bomb with the threat of a social bomb."[6]

As the world population continues to swell from the present six billion to nine billion by 2025, these pressures will worsen. With the depletion of nonrenewable energy stocks, high-quality agricultural land, water resources, and fisheries, resource scarcities are growing at the same time demand is rising by greater amounts. For example, estimates are that, by 2025, two thirds of the world's population will face severe shortages of water.[7] As these social, economic, environmental, and political problems come together, some analysts worry that the problems will feed off each other. They fret about a cascading breakdown of our increasingly complex ecological, political, and economic systems, and have even come up with a new term for it, "synchronous failure."[8]

While this may be the ultimate nightmare scenario, it is clear that the disconnect between growing population needs and supplies sharply increases the general demands on state and society, while simultaneously decreasing their ability to meet them. Research indicates that the result is invariably socioeconomic fragmentation, a weakening of the state's legitimacy, and ensuing violent conflict.[9] Indeed, one survey found that countries with poor environmental scores are more than twice as likely to sink into civil war.[10] Conflict groups are well aware of these gaps and sometimes seek to exploit them. They can widen the gap by intentionally undermining social stability or even seek to gain strength and support by serving as surrogates for the social services that healthy societies and capable governments would normally be able to deliver. For instance, in war-ravaged Lebanon, the Hezbollah group offers the entire realm of social services, from running hospitals to schools. It not only aids its popularity but also creates a reliance on the armed group.

Other catastrophes, such as famine and disease outbreaks, under-score this broad trend of disconnection and distress among growing numbers of youth around the world. Of particular worry is the endur-ing nature of the AIDS epidemic in the developing world, particularly sub-Saharan Africa. Not coincidentally, this is where the centrum of the child soldier phenomenon lies.[11] The disease, currently infecting 4.8 million people a year, is altering the very demographics of the region, with terrifying consequences for both stability and security.

AIDS does not strike with equal weight across age-groups. In a "unique phenomenon in biology," the disease actually reverses death rates to strike hardest at mature, but not yet elderly adults.[12] The con-sequence is that population curves shift (eliminating the typical middle-aged hump), almost in direct opposite to the manner of previous epidemics. Such a shift in demographics is fairly worrisome. Recent research has found a strong correlation between violent outbreaks, ranging from wars to terrorism, and the proportion of young males to the overall population.[13] Once the ratio of young males grows too far out of balance, violent conflict tends to ensue. AIDS will likely cause this in several states already close to this dangerous threshold.

This process is known as "coalitional aggression." Young men, who are considered psychologically more aggressive, naturally compete for social and material resources in all societies. When outnumbering other generations, however, there are inevitably more losers than win-ners among the youth in this process. Moreover, the typical stabilizing influences of elders are lessened by the overall mass of youth. These lost youths are more easily harnessed into more pernicious activities that can lead to conflict. For example, demagogues, warlords, crimi-nals, and others all find it easier to recruit when a large population of angry, listless young men fills the street. Riots and other social crises are also more likely. In a sense, it is conflict caused from the bottom up, rather than the top down. While such a correlation is certainly a simplistic explanation of violence, the disturbing fact is that the pat-tern has held true across history. Outbreaks of violence from ancient Greek wars and the Hundred Years' War to recent societal breakdowns in Rwanda, Yugoslavia, and the Congo (DRC) were all presaged by similar demographic patterns.[14] Indeed, during the 1990s, countries with these population patterns (40 percent are of adolescent age or below) were 2.3 times more likely to experience an outbreak of civil conflict than those with lower proportions.[15]

There is also a more direct way in which the new demographics of AIDS can heighten security risks. The disease is gradually creating a new pool of orphans, a group especially susceptible to being pulled into child soldiering. By 2010, more than 43 million children will have lost one or both of their parents to AIDS, including 33 percent of all children in the hardest-hit countries (the normal percentage of children who are orphans in developing countries is 2 percent). Among them are 2.7 million in Nigeria, 2.5 million in Ethiopia, and 1.8 million in South Africa.[16] India alone already has 120,000 AIDS orphans. That only six of the forty countries hardest hit by AIDS have any plans to assist orphans makes the situation only worse.[17]

This cohort represents a new "lost orphan generation."[18] Both the stigma of the disease and the sheer number of victims will overwhelm the communities and extended families that would normally look after these orphans. Their prospects are heartrending, and dangerous. Besides being malnourished, stigmatized, and vulnerable to physical and sexual abuse, this mass of disconnected and disaffected children is particularly at risk of being exploited as child soldiers. Having watched their parents die and been forced to fend for themselves, many will consider they have nothing to lose by entering into war.

At the same time, the factors that disconnect the children from the structure of society also debilitate the very institutions needed to solidify the state and prevent conflict. For example, estimates of HIV infection rates among regional armies in Africa include 50 percent in the Democratic Republic of the Congo (DRC) and Angola, 66 percent in Uganda, 75 percent in Malawi, and 80 percent in Zimbabwe.[19] This devastates their ability to maintain the peace or resist new rebel and warlord groups. Similar hollowing-out is occurring in many other government agencies and parts of the economy in AIDS-hit regions.

Added to these socioeconomic trends is the continuing prevalence of global conflict; the result is an often dangerous mix. While many hoped for a "new world order" after the end of the Cold War in 1989, the real order that came about was embodied in the quip of "peace in the West, war for the rest."[20] A particular outgrowth was the dramatic increase in the number of internal conflicts. The incidence of civil wars has doubled since the Cold War's end, and by the mid-1990s was five times as high as at its midpoint. The broader number of conflict zones—that is, places in the world at war—has roughly doubled since the Cold War, with the present number holding firm over fifty.[21]

About half the ongoing wars in the world are entering their second generation of prospective fighters. In such extended conflicts, children have grown up surrounded by violence, and often see it as a permanent way of life. These children are also valued as a potential source of new recruits. For example, the head of a Karen rebel training camp in Myanmar describes how he brought his own twelve-year-old son into the fight. "I took him out of school in the third grade to turn him into a military man. I thought that if he studies now, he'll just have to fight later. Better to fight now, and learn later when there is time for it."[22]

In addition to witnessing fighting and bloodshed, children who grow up in the midst of war usually lack basic necessities (schools, health care, adequate shelter, water and food), face disrupted family relationships, and even experience increased patterns of family violence.[23] The totality of this environment makes it difficult for communities to foster healthy cognitive and social development. A weakened social structure is then generally unable to steer their children away from war.

Children are also typically forced from homes and stable environments during fighting. The UN High Commissioner for Refugees estimates that there are some twenty-five million uprooted children in the world, having become either cross-border refugees or internally displaced persons (IDPs). Each day, five thousand more children become refugees.[24] Children tend to remain in this situation an average of six or seven years, making them highly vulnerable to recruitment.[25]

The situation in Angola encapsulates the hopelessness that many children face. Over the course of its twenty-five-year war, some 300,000 children served in either the government army or with UNITA rebel forces. About one million children lost one parent and 300,000 lost both parents to the war. Seventy percent of Angolan children of school age are illiterate, and UNICEF judges the broader population to be at great risk of death, malnutrition, abuse, and development. That 45 percent of the population is less than fifteen years old only raises further worries for the long term.[26]

The perils of growing up during war are in no way unique to Angola. For example, surveys in Sri Lanka reveal similar dynamics. In the provinces where conflict has taken place, 40 percent of children between the ages of nine and eleven reported that either their houses had been attacked or shelled or that they had personally been shot at, beaten, or arrested. Fifty percent reported that a family member had been killed, abducted, or detained. The effects on children can be traumatic. Of this survey group of children, 20 percent exhibited symptoms of post-traumatic stress disorder.[27]

It is estimated that one out of every two hundred of the world's children suffers from a war-related psychological malady.[28] The impact of this is only starting to be understood. War is thought to have an all-encompassing impact on child development. It envelops children's attitudes, relationships, moral values, and the framework through which they understand society and life itself.[29] Having been exposed to horrible violence during key developmental stages of their life, many children come to accept it as a perfectly normal part of their existence. As one child in northern Uganda describes, "If you are under 20 and living here, you have known virtually nothing else your whole life but what it is like to live in a community enduring armed conflict—conflict in which you are a prime target."[30]

All this gives a new meaning to the moniker "the lost generation." The overwhelming majority of child soldiers are drawn from the poorest, least educated, and most marginalized sections of society, who have been forced to grow up in what one writer aptly termed a "roving orphanage of blood and flame."[31]

I don't know where my father and mother are. I had nothing to eat. I joined the gunmen to get food. . . . I was with the other fighters for eight months. There was nothing good about that life.

—M., age twelve[32]

Children who are forcibly recruited are usually from special risk groups: street children, the rural poor, refugees, and others displaced (those most vulnerable to efficient recruiting sweeps). Those who choose to enlist on their own are often from the very same groups, driven to do so by poverty, propaganda, and alienation. The combination of unimaginable misery many children face and the normalization of violence in their lives can lead them to search for a sense of control over their chaotic and unpredictable situations. Research on child development indicates that they will then be more likely to seek out and join armed groups that provide protection or adhere to ideologies that provide this sense of order, regardless of the content.[33] Those who find themselves to be victims often construct their identity along such lines. Such "victim motivation" can also become a motivation to commit acts of violence of their own, in a bid for pre-emptive protection or revenge.[34] The tragic result is that these coping strategies further place children in danger and feed cycles of violence.

New Toys for Tots

Concurrent with this global trend of socioeconomic disconnection has been the proliferation and technological advancement of personal weaponry. This development is a key enabler, without which the earlier trend would not matter. Technological changes are what allow this broadened pool of potential recruits to be turned into able soldiers.

When thinking about military operations, we typically focus on the most complex and expensive weapons systems, such as missiles, tanks, and aircraft carriers. For most conflicts around the globe, however, this picture is inaccurate. Instead, the weapons that shape contemporary warfare are the ones that are the simplest and least costly.

These "small arms," or "light weapons," include rifles, grenades, light machine guns, light mortars, land mines, and other weapons that are "man-portable" (a term often used by the military). Even though they represent less than 2 percent of the entire global arms trade in terms of cost, small arms are perhaps the most deadly of all weapons to society.[35] They are the weapons most often used both in battle and in

45

attacks on civilians and have produced almost 90 percent of all casualties in recent wars.[36] In just West Africa alone, more than two million people were killed by small arms in the last decade.[37] Indeed, modern small arms can rend the fabric of civil society like no other weapon; with them, a small, relatively weak group can easily turn a peaceful country into a man-made humanitarian disaster.

Technological and efficiency advances in these weapons now permit the transformation of children into fighters just as lethal as any adult. For most of human history, weapons relied on the brute strength of the operator. They also typically required years of training to master. This was obviously prohibitive to the effective use of children as soldiers. A child who was not physically matured could not bear the physical burdens of serving in the phalanx of the ancient Greek hoplites or carrying the weight of medieval knight's armor, let alone serve as an effective combatant. Even until just a few generations ago, personal battlefield weapons such as the bolt action rifles of World War II were heavy and bulky, limiting children's participation.[38]

However, there have been many recent improvements in manufacturing, such as the incorporation of plastics. This now means that modern weapons, particularly automatic rifles, are so light that small children can use them as easily and effectively as adults. They are no longer just "man-portable" but are "child-portable" as well. Just as important, most of these weapons have been simplified in their use, to the extent that they can be stripped, reassembled, and fired by a child below the age of ten. The ubiquitous Russian-designed Kalashnikov AK-47, which weighs 10½ pounds, is a prime example. Having only nine moving parts, it is brutally simple. Interviews reveal that it generally takes children around thirty minutes to learn how to use one. The weapon is also designed to be exceptionally hardy. It requires little maintenance and can even be buried in dirt for storage (something guerrilla groups often do, as a sort of insurance policy, in case a cease-fire breaks down).

Along with these improvements in simplicity and ruggedness, vast strides have been made in the lethality of personal weapons. The weapons that children can now fire with ease are a far cry from the spears of the phalanx or the single bolt rifle of the GIs. Since World

War II there has been a steady and multiplicative increase in the destructive power of small arms. With just one pull of the trigger, a modern assault rifle in the hands of a child can release a burst of thirty bullets that are lethal more than four hundred yards away. Or they can shoot off a rocket-propelled grenade (RPG) whose explosions can tear down buildings or maim tens at a time.

Thus, a handful of children now can have the equivalent firepower of an entire regiment of Napoleonic infantry. When targeting unarmed civilians, the results are doubly devastating. Hence, with only a few hours' training, a youngster can be taught all he or she needs to know in order to kill or wound hundreds of people in a matter of minutes.

When we arrived at their base, the rebels trained me on how to use a gun. They showed me how to dismantle a weapon and put it back together again. They showed me how to fire the gun and how to clean it. They taught me how to make sure I didn't get injured when it recoils. —P., age twelve[39]

Not only have these weapons become easier to use and far more deadly, but they have also proliferated, to the extent that there is almost a glut on the market. There are an estimated five hundred million small arms on the global scene, one for every twelve persons on the planet.[40] The consequence is that the primary weapons of war have also steeply fallen in price over the last few decades. This has made it easier for any willing organization to obtain them and then turn children into soldiers at a minimal cost.

The irony is that this proliferation of small arms partially resulted from the Cold War's "peace dividend." After the fall of the Berlin Wall, millions of weapons were declared surplus. Instead of being destroyed, however, it was cheaper to dump them on the world market. For example, when the two Germanys combined in 1990, the vast majority of the weapons stock of the East German army was auctioned off, much of it to private bidders. The result was literally tons of light weapons available at cut-rate prices. Light machine guns went for just $60, land mines for $19, and pistols for $8.[41] These stocks were added to the masses of weapons that had already been given to superpower proxies during the Cold War. Moreover, many ended up in the hands of arms brokers and gunrunners who had no compunctions about their final destination or use. The result is that as much as 40 to 60 percent of the small arms around the world are now in the hands of illicit organizations.[42]

Even with this dump of weaponry, however, manufacturing has continued apace for the last few decades, as weapons industries, particularly in the former Soviet bloc, have tried to stay afloat. The result is that there is no place around the globe where small arms are not startlingly cheap and easily accessible. More importantly, they tend to be concentrated in the most violence-prone areas. This phenomenon was so particularly evident with the Soviet AK-47–type assault rifle and its knockoffs that one analyst even coined the phrase "Kalashnikov Age" to describe how the 1990s saw its spread around the world and influence on global conflict levels.[43] For example, in just postwar Mozambique, there were around six million AK-47s for a population of roughly sixteen million.[44] For a period, they were even used as a form of currency.[45] In Uganda and Sudan, an AK-47 can be purchased for the cost of a chicken; in northern Kenya, it can be bought for the price of a goat (the equivalent is about $5).[46] In South Africa, AK-47s are just slightly more expensive, valued on the market at $12 each.

The outcome of this proliferation is that not only can any group readily obtain the arms necessary for war, but also that the general presence of combat weapons is now a pervasive part of daily life in many parts of the world. The effect is a militarization of many societies, which further places children at risk of being pulled into the realm of war. As one Afghan warlord lamented, "We have young boys that are more familiar with a gun than with school."[47]

While the weapons themselves are not the direct cause of conflict, their proliferation and cheapening is an enabler. It allows any local conflict to become a bloody slaughter. Moreover, an abundance of arms within society takes away certain barriers to civil war. The range of politically relevant actors literally multiplies and any sort of dissent within society can now easily become violent.

This dynamic also reworks the leadership structures within many societies—to dangerous ends. Power and control over the tools of war once tended to accrue with age. In many cases where weaponry has become pervasive, though, it has begun to devolve to what are called "youth elders." These are often impetuous, armed children, no longer constrained by the age groupings that limited who could participate in warfare and who gained the rewards that went with it. Instead, these youths now dictate the rules to the former heads of their tribes by the sheer dint of their new weaponry. This new authority has come without responsibility, and violence levels have risen. As one Kenyan analyst describes the alteration of tribal warfare in Africa, "Somehow, the seat of authority has moved from the elders to the youth, and that has some very, very bad consequences for managing conflict."[48]

Finally, this trend is representative of the general weakening of the state.[49] States' control over the primary means of warfare was once key in their formation.[50] With the proliferation of small arms and their centrality in much of warfare, this is lost. Small groups can not only mobilize disaffected children, but also turn them into a force that can quickly overwhelm the capacity of many states in the developing world. Thus the easy availability of inexpensive small arms has the potential to rework the local balance of power and further the risks of failed states. Even after the fighting has ended, the very presence of these weapons also makes it harder for war-torn societies to recover and war easier to reinitiate.[51]

Postmodern Warfare

The context in which these developments have occurred matters as well. The decision whether to implement a doctrine that uses children now takes place within a period of historic transformation in warfare. In many of the ongoing wars around the globe, the traditional political and strategic rationales behind the initiation, maintenance, and continuation of war are under siege (what earlier was termed a breakdown in the "Warrior's Honor").[52] While the large-scale military operations carried out by the Western powers have become more technological, this is not the only face of warfare. At the same time, in the majority of conflicts carried out in the developing world, warfare has become messier and criminalized. In many cases, the private profit motive has become a central motivator, equal or greater to that of political, ideo-logical, or religious inspirations.[53] Or, as one military analyst puts it, "With enough money anyone can equip a powerful military force. With a willingness to use crime, nearly anyone can generate enough money."[54]

Today, the fighting in a number of conflicts around the globe lacks any sort of link to a broader political or religious cause. Instead, they are driven by a simple logic of appropriation, from seizing mineral assets and protecting the drug trade to simple looting and pillaging. As World Bank expert Paul Collier writes, "The key characteristics of a country at high risk of internal fighting are neither political nor social, but economic."[55]

While many of these wars are fueled by new conflict entrepreneurs and local warlords that emerged in the 1990s in their individual coun-tries, the broader end of the Cold War also played a part in this shift. When outside superpower patronage ceased, the calculus of many ide-ological guerrilla groups, including those once motivated by Marxist doctrine, took a more market-oriented direction. Rather than stop fighting, the withdrawal of outside support just made them realize that their war economies had to change. The new rule of insurgency is that if conflict groups want to survive, they have to find their own financial resources.[56]

In many cases, there is a direct link between the fighting and ready commodities that groups can sell directly. These provide willing con-flict entrepreneurs with the incentive to quickly seize what they can.[57] In Sierra Leone, the key matter in the ten-year war was not over who was in place in the capital, but who had control over the country's dia-mond fields. Similarly, in the war in the DRC, foes and allies alike have battled over coltan mines. Coltan, a little known mineral that is drawn from mud, is a key ingredient for the circuit boards used in almost all cell phones, laptops, and pagers. In short, as one local observer noted, "People are fighting for money. Everything that happens, it's about money."[58] This stands in sharp contrast to the traditional understand-ing of war. The classic military philosopher Clausewitz, writing in the early 1800s, thought "Politics is the womb in which war develops."[59]

Today, for much of contemporary warfare, economics plays at least as much a part in nurturing and shaping conflict.

Therefore, whether the groups evolved from Cold War organizations or were new entrants into conflict, income generation (pure plunder, the production of primary commodities, illegal trading, etc.) is an essential activity in many wars. And a particularly lucrative area has been the international drug trade. For example, 70 percent of opposition groups' funds in Tajikistan are from drug income. The estimates are even higher in Colombia, where 90 percent of the cocaine sold in the United States originates. The rebels and their paramilitary opponents are thought to pull as much as 80 percent of their funding from the cocaine trade. Of this estimated $800 million a year, only 10 percent goes to the war effort, while the other 90 percent enriches the individual commanders.[60] Other activities are utilized as well. In the Philippines, Abu Sayyaf funds itself through kidnapping, while the Tamil Tigers in Sri Lanka run a worldwide shipping conglomerate. In Uzbekistan, Kosovo, and Afghanistan, militant groups profit by running protection rackets for opium traffickers.[61]

Many of these bands continue violent activities long after the original rationale for their formation has lost meaning.[62] While they may have started out with some ideological or popular goals, often related to the Cold War, that has fallen by the wayside as they struggle to survive. Far from being irrational or a breakdown in a system, war then becomes an end, not a means. As such, warmaking serves as an "alternative system of profit and power."[63] In such cases as Angola, Sierra Leone, and the DRC, winning the war by defeating the enemy became a secondary goal; instead, the groups ended up competing to profit from the general chaos brought about by the war. The combination of these criminal goals and increasingly less professional, "soldier-less" forces also leads to a variation in strategies toward civilians. Traditional insurgency strategy is to "swim among the people as a fish swims in the sea" (as elucidated by Mao Zedong, the Chinese communist leader and master of guerrilla warfare). These new or reconstructed groups aim at terrorizing and pillaging the population rather than winning hearts and minds.

In short, while economics has always played a role in conflict, the last two decades have seen a new type of warfare develop, one centered around profit-seeking enterprises. Conflicts around the globe are increasingly characterized not as temporary outbreaks of instability but rather as protracted states of disorder. Within these wars, resource and population exploitation, rather than mass production, drive the new "economy of war."[64] It may be organized mass violence, but it also involves the blurring of distinctions between traditional conceptions of war, organized crime, and large-scale violations of human rights.[65]

The New Child Labor Problem

These trends of socioeconomic dislocation of children, technologic simplification of weaponry, and the broader changes in the nature of much of contemporary warfare were necessary factors to the emergence of child soldiers as a global phenomenon. They not only created the mass availability of child recruits, but also the new possibility that they could indeed serve as effective combatants. They also underscored their utility in the changing context of warfare. In conflict after conflict, this has led to the implementation of a new doctrine of war, one that prescribes the recruitment of children and their use on the battlefield. The key is that this is not something that just happened, but has repeatedly involved deliberate choices among the leaders of local armed organizations. Children would not be used as combatants if the organizations they fight within did not see them as useful.

The strategy of using children as an alternative source of fighters has proven appealing to many groups, not only because it is cheap and easy to implement, but also because the costs are outweighed by the benefits so far. It provides an easy means for organizations, even the most weak and unpopular, to generate significant amounts of force with almost no investment. On the other side of the equation, the costs of using children in this manner are considered quite low. Moral opprobrium is the only major risk to a group that uses child soldiers. However, any group that contemplates using children as fighters has already shown itself unwilling to be limited by prevailing moral codes.

The lesson from this is that prohibitive norms are quite weak whenever they are not underscored by substantive penalties for violating them.

It is within this changing context of warfare that the perception of children and their role in warfare also has begun to change. With their ready availability and easy transformation into combatants, children now represent a low-cost way to mobilize and generate force when the combatants do not generally care about public opinion. This creates the doctrine of child soldiers, a new way of enacting violence that prescribes the methods and circumstances of children's employment in battle.

This new doctrine is particularly well suited for weak or failed states, which have become ever more prevalent because of the trends described earlier. During the Cold War, state failure was not as much of a problem, as the two superpowers competed to prop up their weaker allies and undermine their opponents. However, this created the precursors to today's problems. Fragile post-colonial structures never solidified, and by the end of the period many Third World countries were states in name only. They lacked any semblance of good governance and were instead shells of what a functioning government should be. In general, they were underdeveloped, financially fragile, patriarchially structured, and without proper systems of accountability and civil-military controls.[66] Despite outside aid, most developing militaries remained notoriously weak and brittle, incapable of carrying out any sustained military operations. Their forces were also comparatively small in relation to their overall populations.[67]

Thus, by the end of the Cold War, maintaining internal order became a near-impossible task for many of these weak states. It is no coincidence that many of the client states, which had received massive amounts of small arms, were the very states that then failed when their patron's support evaporated.[68] As these countries degenerated into violence, often ethnic scars reopened, and state assets went up for grabs. An opening was created for new conflict actors who could hijack the chaos.

Many of the warlords and "conflict entrepreneurs" that emerged had no great political or military background, but were distinguished only by their willingness to break old norms and mobilize force to their own ends. Foday Sankoh in Sierra Leone was a former cameraman; Charles Taylor in Liberia was an escaped convict; Joseph Kony in Uganda was just an unemployed young relative of a tribal shaman; and Laurent Kabila in the DRC was a little-known guerrilla leader who had been irrelevant outside his province for the previous thirty years. However, these men, and many like them, realized that arming children could serve as a means to gaining military capacity. Their comprehension of this not only sucked children into war, but also led to the spate of civil wars and state failures that shaped much of global politics after the Cold War.

Highly personalized or purely predatory armed groups, such as warlords, which are focused on asset seizure, are particularly dependent on this new doctrine of using children. Small fringe groups that would have found it impossible to mobilize—and thus been marginalized in the past—now can vastly expand their power by using children. In short, they can make children into soldiers and thus transform an insignificant force into an army. As an illustration, the Lord's Resistance Army in Uganda has a central cabal that numbers as few as two hundred men and enjoys no popular support among the civilian populace. But through the abduction and transformation of fourteen thousand children into soldiers, the LRA has been able to engage the Ugandan army in a bloody civil war for the last ten years.[69]

Regardless of the ideology behind a conflict, in wartime situations there is always some motivation to assemble added military force. It may be for political or strategic reasons or simply because of the high attrition rates among soldiers fighting in tough situations, such as in disease-ridden jungles. Children now provide a new alternative to adult recruiting pools. State regimes that are fighting unpopular wars, such as in El Salvador or Guatemala, or rebel or ethnic groups that are highly outnumbered or do not enjoy broad support, such as in Myanmar or Nepal, both find this new pool particularly useful. They often first seek to tap it when the adult pool runs dry. In Sudan, for example, it was after a recruiting drive for adult males fell flat on its face that the Khartoum regime began targeting children. For two years (1993–95) it tried to conscript all young men between the ages of eighteen and thirty-three. However, because of the unpopularity of the war the regime was fighting with the south, only 26,079 of the nearly 2.5 million men in that age bracket turned up for training. As a result, the government began to recruit street children to fill out its forces.[70] Likewise, the LTTE in Sri Lanka began using children in the nine-to-twelve age range after it faced a manpower shortage in battles against the Indian peacekeeping force in the late 1980s and could not pull in enough adults because it had lost local support.[71]

An added incentive is that children are recruits who come on the cheap. While adults usually desire to be paid for their roles, even if they believe in the cause, children rarely are. One survey of child soldiers in Burundi found that only 6 percent had ever received any sort of remuneration. In the eastern Congo (DRC), only 10 percent had ever been paid.[72] This can make children very attractive recruits, inducing a turn to child soldiering not just in emergencies but as an alternative, low-cost supply of recruits. For example, in the 1990s, the Colombian FARC group faced the rise of competitive paramilitary groups which paid its recruits $350 a month. Thus, the FARC (which paid no salary) had to find a means to keep pace in the recruiting wars. Its solution was to increase the role of children, and their numbers in the group doubled.[73]

The overall significance of all this is that children no longer enjoy any of the traditional protections stemming from their underage status. Instead, children are increasingly recruited because of the very fact that they are young. Groups that use child soldiers view minors simply as malleable and expendable assets, whose loss is bearable to the overall cause and quite easily replaced. Or, as one analyst notes, "They are cheaper than adults, and they can be drugged or conditioned more easily into violence and committing atrocities."[74]

Thus, the synergy of these three broad, and often interrelated, dynamics led to both the emergence and rapid growth of the child soldier phenomenon. Socioeconomic changes, technological developments, and base avarice within the changing contexts of war have created the circumstances, the opportunity, and the motivation for children to be turned into soldiers. Where once children and battlefield weapons were incompatible, now they combine to create a completely new pool of military labor. Stemming from the combined trends of socioeconomic disconnection and technological efficiency gains in small arms, children now represent an easy and low-cost way to mobilize armed force. The only remaining ingredients required are groups or leaders without scruples. They must be willing only to connect these trends and pull children into war. As the payoffs can be huge, many take this moral plunge. The result is what one analyst describes as a "systematic preference for children as soldiers" among warlords and other new military leaders of contemporary conflict.[75]

The classic example of the rationale behind using children as an alternate military labor source is that of Liberia. On Christmas Eve 1989, Charles Taylor, a fugitive from the Plymouth prison in Massachusetts, marched across the border with a self-styled "army" of 150 amateur soldiers with only small arms. His "invasion" to topple the Liberian government was barely noticed. Soon, though, he built his force into the thousands by the recruitment and use of child soldiers, most aged in the low teens. While Taylor once claimed that he enlisted children only to keep them "out of trouble," he was hardly so benevolent.[76] His growing forces terrorized the rural regions, exacted tribute, and seized any valuable assets they could lay their hands on. The invasion soon led to the collapse of the Liberian state, which had already been abandoned by its superpower patron. The civil war that ensued killed more than 200,000 people and left another 1.25 million as refugees. Within five years, Taylor was the richest warlord in the country, with "Taylorland" pulling in $300 million to $400 million a year in personal income through illegal trading and looting. A decade later Taylor was Liberia's president, demonstrating the potential payoffs of this new strategy of mobilizing force. Through child soldiers, he was able to use a small gang to gain a kingdom.

CHAPTER 4

How Children Are Recruited into War

I joined the Army when I was fourteen because, one, I was per-suaded that the only way to get my parents back or to stop that from happening was to be a part of the Army and kill those people who were responsible for killing my parents. But, you see, the thing that is very disturbing about this thing is that once I joined the Army and started fighting, I was also killing other people's parents and so I was creating a circle of revenge where I killed somebody else's parents, he's going to be persuaded by a different group, either the RUF or the Army, saying, "Okay. Join the Army and kill this person who killed your parents." So, it's a circle of revenge. And the disturbing thing about it is that it's kids that are killing kids.

—I., age fourteen[1]

Transforming a child into a fairly effective combatant is disturbingly simple. It begins with recruitment, either through abduction or "vol-untary" means. Recruitment is rapidly followed by cruel but straight-forward methods of training and conversion. Brutality and abuses of the worst kind underscore each stage, but these lie in part behind the overall program's usual effectiveness. The ultimate aim of the process is to foster a child's dependency on an armed organization and inhibit escape.

Forced Recruitment

Case studies indicate that in the majority of conflicts, a primary method of recruitment of children is through some form of abduction. Typically, recruiting parties are given conscription targets that change according to the group's need and objective. For example, the UPC/RP, a militia led by Thomas Lubanga in the eastern Congo, has a policy that each family within its area of control must provide a cow, money, or child to the group.[2] Often, the groups develop practices that are quite efficient. For example, the LRA sets numeric goals for child recruits and sends raiding parties into villages to meet them.[3] Other groups, such as the LTTE, reportedly maintain sophisticated computerized population databases to direct their recruiting efforts.[4]

All children are not automatically taken in such operations, but only those who meet certain criteria decided by the groups' leaders. The main standard is physical size, with the ability to bear a weapon being the normal cutoff point. Literally, recruiters will place a weapon in the child's hands to see if he or she is yet strong enough to hold it.[5] Other groups use alternative proxies to measure physical development. The SPLA, for instance, uses the presence of two molar teeth to determine whether the child is ready to serve.[6]

These standards not only illustrate the young ages often pulled in, but also how child recruitment is often a meticulously planned process. Those children who are judged too small to carry weapons or looted goods will either be set free or killed in order to intimidate both the local populace and the new recruits. Similarly, if the plan is to seize girls as attendants to more senior members of the group, only those considered more attractive might be taken. These goals are taken quite seriously, and failure to meet them risks punishment from superiors.[7]

The decision of where groups carry out their operations to find their recruits is also based on planned efforts to maximize the efficiency of their efforts. Both state armies and rebel groups typically target the places where children will both be collected in the greatest number and are most vulnerable to being swept in. These range from stadiums and buses to mosques and churches.

The most frequent targets are secondary schools or orphanages, where children of suitable size are collected in one place, but out of contact with their parents, who would try to spirit them away. Indeed, the LTTE even took to setting up a unit formed exclusively of orphans, the elite Sirasu Puli (Leopard Brigade).[8] The Congolese Rally for Democracy–Goma (RCD–Goma) and Rwandan Patriotic Army (RPA) are two other groups that also target schools almost exclusively, using kidnapping or coercion to pull in kids. Another common target area is the marketplace. For instance, during the Ethiopian fighting in the 1990s, a common practice was that armed militias would simply surround the public bazaar. They would order every male to sit down and then force into a truck anyone deemed "eligible." This often included minors.

Homeless or street children are at particular risk, as they are most vulnerable to sweeps aimed at them, which prompt less public outcry. In Sudan, for instance, the government set up camps for street children, and then rounded up children to fill them in a purported attempt to "clean up" Khartoum. These camps, however, served as reservoirs for army conscription.[9]

Other groups that are at frequent danger are refugee and IDP (internally displaced persons) populations. In many instances, families on the run become disconnected. Armed groups then target unaccompanied, and thus more vulnerable, minors.

The international community can even become unintentionally complicit in the recruitment of children, if it is not careful in its own practices. For example, in the Sudanese civil war, unaccompanied minors living in the UNHCR refugee camps were housed in separate areas from the rest of the refugee population. As the camps had no security, the SPLA easily targeted the boys. Indeed, certain rebel commanders even sought to have camps placed near them, not for humanitarian reasons, but so that they could maintain a reserve of recruits close at hand.[10]

I was abducted during "Operation Pay Yourself," in 1998. I was 9 years old. Six rebels came through our yard. They went to loot for food. It's called "jaja"—"get food." They said, "We want to bring a small boy like you—we like you." My mother didn't comment; she just cried. My father objected. They threatened to kill him. They argued with him at the back of the house. I heard a gunshot. One of them told me, "Let's go, they've killed your father." A woman rebel grabbed my hand roughly and took me along. I saw my father lying dead as we passed. —A., age fourteen[11]

Even national borders can fail to provide protection. In numerous instances, rebel groups target foreign villages just across the borders, which heretofore might have been considered outside the danger zone. In the Liberian war, for example, it was not uncommon to come across a child from Sierra Leone who had been abducted into the fighting. Similar cases hold in the Myanmar war with Thailand, the Colombian war with Peru, and all the nations surrounding the Democratic Republic of the Congo (DRC).

In many ways, these tactics of abduction and impressment into service echo the naval press gangs of the Napoleonic era. The difference is not just the lower ages, however, but that the present-day abduction raids are not only about building one's force, but are also instruments of war in and of themselves. Forced recruitment of children is often just one aspect in a larger campaign carried out by an armed group, designed to intimidate local civilian communities. Having already crossed one line of propriety, armed groups that abduct children for soldiering are also inclined to go on rape and looting rampages while in the villages.[12] Likewise, the children of certain ethnic groups might be targeted, in particular if there is a chance to use child soldiers against their co-ethnics on the other side. This was the case in Guatemala, where government recruitment of minors usually focused on the children of ethnic groups that had been in the political opposition. The indigenous Mayans called the theft of their young "the new genocide."[13]

It was an unbelievable and unreal event when the rebels arrested me and my family. We were told to carry their loads on our heads. We did so for some time and my sister cried out in pain to tell them she was sick and wanted to rest. The rebels asked us if we all wanted to rest, not knowing that after telling them we wanted to rest, they had planned something else for us.

We were left seated there for a while and they came back with cutlasses and a log of wood. We knew too well what these things mean, because we have heard that with these things they cut off the hands and feet of people. Now we were in a hideous state—they killed my parents in front of me, my uncle's hands were cut off and my sister was raped in front of us by their commander called "Spare No Soul." After all this happened, they told us, the younger boys, to join them. If not, they were going to kill us. I was in place to die with my parents because I felt like killing them myself—but they had something which I did not: a gun. I and my sister were left in a traumatized state. We had no parents any longer, and my sister was in pain after having been raped, and my own toe was cut off.

—R., age unknown[14]

For those children who are forcibly taken, it is often "a journey into hell."[15] Abduction is by definition an act of violence that rips terrified children from the security of their families and homes. Killings, rapes, and severe beatings often accompany it. Once caught, children have no choice; usually they must comply with their captors or die.

A Less Than "Voluntary" Recruitment

Not all children are forced into soldiering, though. Many may choose to join an armed group of their own volition and thus the groups that use them often claim they broke no moral codes. The rough trend line seems to be that roughly two of every three child soldiers have some sort of initiative in their own recruitment. For example, estimates are that 40 percent of the FARC's child soldiers are forced into service, and 60 percent joined of their own volition.[16] Another survey in East Asia found that 57 percent of the children had volunteered.[17] Finally, a survey of child soldiers in four African countries found that 64 percent joined under no threat of violence.[18]

To describe this choice as voluntary, however, is greatly misleading.[19] Children are defined as such, not only because of their lesser physical development, but also because they are judged to be of an age at which they are not capable of making mature decisions. By contrast, to go to war and risk one's life in an act that has societal-wide consequences is one of the most serious decisions a person can make. This is why the previous four thousand years of leaders left this choice to mature adults.

But how can a child volunteer? Because if I volunteer, maybe I don't know what I am doing, but you, the grown-up, should know. And you should stop me from volunteering being a soldier. It wasn't my choice. It wasn't the choice I had to become a soldier.

—C., child soldier from age nine to fifteen[20]

The most basic reason that children join armed groups is that they are driven to do so by forces beyond their control. A particularly strong factor is economic. Hunger and poverty are endemic in conflict zones. Children, particularly those orphaned or disconnected from civil society, may volunteer to join any group if they believe that this is the only way to guarantee regular meals, clothing, or medical attention. As one young boy in the DRC explained, "I joined [President Laurent] Kabila's army when I was 13 because my home had been looted and my parents were gone. As I was then on my own, I decided to become a soldier."[21] Indeed, surveys of demobilized child soldiers in the DRC found that almost 60 percent originally joined armed groups because of simple poverty.[22] The same ratio was found in a separate survey of child soldiers half the globe away in East Asia, indicating a broader international trend.[23]

The military was in need of people to increase their number. All the boys in the village were asked to join the army. There was no way out. If I left the village I would get killed by the rebels who would think that I was a spy. On the other hand, if I stayed in the

village and refused to join the army, I wouldn't be given food and would eventually be thrown out, which was as good as being dead.
—I., age fourteen[24]

There are no hard-and-fast rules. However, poorer children are typically more vulnerable to being pulled into conflict and are overrepresented in child soldier groups. Not only is their desperation typically higher, but also there is a higher correlation between family dysfunction (an additional driving force) and lower socioeconomic status.[25]

To be fully understood, these decisions must therefore be read within the environment in which they take place. In Afghanistan, for instance, boys growing up over the last decades are likely to have never known running water or electricity, and many will have lost one or more parents to the fighting. By the age of ten, most forgo school and are simply trying to find a way to support themselves. One report tellingly illustrated how a set of Afghan boys were so desperate that they literally had to choose between following a cow around to scoop up its excrement to sell as fuel or joining one of the armed factions. The choice of war may be more dangerous, but it at least provides free clothes, food, and some modicum of respect.[26] Or, as one Congolese child soldier similarly described, "I heard that the rebels at least were eating. So, I joined them."[27]

The same factors may also drive parents to offer their children for combat service when they cannot provide for them on their own. In some cases, armies pay a minor soldier's wages directly to the family. Other case studies tell of parents who encourage their daughters to become soldiers if their marriage prospects are poor. As one study done in Sierra Leone described, "Many mothers have remarked on the joy of seeing their ten-year-old dressed in a brand-new military attire carrying an AK-47. For some families the looted property that child soldiers brought home further convinced them of the need to send more children to the war front to augment scarce income."[28]

More perniciously, some parents may see material advantages in their children's death. In Sri Lanka, parents within LTTE-controlled zones who lose a child are treated with special status as "great hero families." They pay no taxes, receive job preferences, and are allocated special seats at all public events.[29] This type of familial prompting toward children's participation in terrorism and the cult of martyrdom has been a great concern in the Israeli-Palestinian violence, and will be discussed in further detail in Chapter 7. Parents may also drive children into war indirectly. A good portion of girl soldiers who join as "volunteers" cite domestic abuse or exploitation as the underlying reason.[30]

Structural conditions in the midst of conflict may also oblige children to join armed organizations for their own protection. Surrounded by violence and chaos, children may decide they are safer in a conflict group, with guns in their own hands, than going about by themselves unarmed. In one survey of child soldiers in Africa, nearly 80 percent had witnessed combat around their home, 70 percent had their family home destroyed, and just over 59 percent had a family member become a casualty of war.[31] As one child in Liberia (whose nickname was "Colonel One More War") noted of why he joined an armed faction, "We can't sit out. People are killing some of our friends. Can't die for nothing, so I took gun and fight. Thanks God I survived."[32]

Many children may have personally experienced or been witness to the furthest extremes of violence, including massacres, summary executions, ethnic cleansing, death squad killings, bombings, torture, sexual abuse, and destruction of home or property. Thus, vengeance can also be a particularly powerful impetus to join the conflict.[33]

Often, child soldiers are the survivors of family massacres. They experience what is known as "survivor's guilt," and are often filled with anger and desire for revenge.[34] Indeed, a number of child soldiers are motivated to join warring factions by the seemingly noble belief that they are helping to prevent other children from losing their parents. Only afterwards do they reflect that they may end up creating the same cycle for other children.

However, such victimization need not always be directly personal for the child to feel its power. The violence may have happened to a family member, a friend, a neighbor, or even some member of a group that the child feels a part of and thus experiences the incident almost as deeply.[35]

My father, mother, and brothers were killed by the enemy, I became angry. I didn't have any other way to do, unless I have to revenge. And to revenge is only to have a gun. If I have a gun I can revenge. I can fight and avenge my mother, father and brothers. That is the decision I took to become a soldier. The day my mother and father and brothers were killed, the enemy came by surprise. They attacked the village, they gathered the people and after that they took all the cows, and they burned all the houses, even all our clothes were burned inside the houses. We remained naked, without food, and we were suffering, from hunger even. Nakedness was also a problem. Then I decided what to do. I thought I'd better join the army [SPLA].   —M., age sixteen[36]

This aspect of revenge is particularly strong within what anthropologists refer to as "shame cultures." In these cultures, which often have clanlike social structures, the desire to preserve honor or avoid shame is so strong as to shape or override all other principles.[37] As such, a child who has experienced some type of loss in such a setting, particularly of a blood relative, will not see him- or herself to be of worth until the loss is avenged. For example, young Kosovar Albanians, within whom this ethic is quite strong, repeatedly cited it as their obligation to join the local rebel groups. Similarly, Afghan boys cite how they cannot become a "man" until they exact revenge upon those who killed a parent.[38]

When I was fighting, I enjoyed it—killing and destroying. I killed human being, many; young, old, anyone. The first one, an old lady, I shot from far away. I was very angry, so I shot her. Their families killed my people.   —M., age unknown[39]

Lastly, some groups may take deliberate advantage of the fact that adolescents are at a stage in life where they are still defining their identity. Conflict groups offer what are perceived as glamorous or honorable roles (soldier, hero, leader, protector), as well as membership and acceptance in a group. These messages are particularly seductive in areas where children feel the most powerless or victimized. As essayist Roger Rosenblatt notes, "War allows boys to look like men. This seems a shallow benefit, but it is no small thing for a teenage boy to have something that yanks him out of his social floundering and places him, unlaughed at, in the company of heroes."[40] One survey of child soldiers in Africa found that 15 percent volunteered because they were simply fascinated by the prestige and thrill of serving in a unit and having a gun.[41]

Indeed, the vulnerability of young children compared to adults is illustrated by the deliberate practices that many conflict groups utilize to take advantage of children's innocence. They often involve extraordinary or impossible promises to which only gullible children would give credence. In Sierra Leone, for example, the RUF promised poor rural children that fighting would help them escape the poverty and misery many of them had known all their lives. As one child fighter describes, "They told us we'd all have our own vehicle. They told us they'd build houses for us. They told us many things."[42] In Liberia, Charles Taylor promised that every child fighting for his group would get a computer if he won the war.[43] In Iran, young boys were promised that as long as they were wearing a key around their neck when they died in battle, it would unlock their way into heaven.[44] Other times, the promises can be quite simple for groups to fulfill, but equally illogical as a cause to fight in war. In Sri Lanka, for example, a number of young LTTE child fighters were convinced to join because the group promised to teach them how to drive tractors or motorcycles.[45]

> I was placed in a three-month political formation course. We learned how to "educate the masses" and to recruit more kids. They chose pretty girls and handsome boys to do the recruiting, because the kids would fancy them. We used to lie to potential recruits. We'd say that we'd pay them and that life was good . . . Most were fourteen or fifteen. The commanders preferred minors because they learn better and are healthier. The ideal recruit is about thirteen, because then they can get a full political education.
>
> —C., age eighteen (recruited at age thirteen)[46]

Conflict groups may also use education systems to glorify war, in order to induce children to identify with and join their organization. For example, in the late 1980s and early 1990s, the Education Center for Afghanistan was located in Peshawar, Pakistan, and was operated by Afghan mujahideen. It produced a series of children's books that became the basis of primary education across the country when the Taliban took power. Across the board they promoted to youths the concept of violence for the sake of Islam. These ranged from teaching the alphabet to first graders through warlike examples (such as "*Jim* [is for] *Jihad*") to illustrating mathematics to third graders with militant word problems ("One group of Mujahideen attack 50 Russian soldiers. In that attack 20 Russians were killed. How many Russians fled?"). Ironically, these textbooks were paid for by U.S. government grants.[47]

The speed of a Kalashnikov bullet is 800 meters per second. If a Russian is at a distance of 3,200 meters from a mujahid, and that mujahid aims at the Russian's head, calculate how many seconds it will take for the bullet to strike the Russian in the forehead.
—Word problem from fourth-grade Afghan textbook[48]

Propaganda and media distortion also can play a role. The aim is both to spread lies and stories that dehumanize the opponent and to create a meaning and direction that might otherwise be lacking among their youth audience. In Rwanda, for example, the Hutu government used radio to spread hatred of the Tutsis. The Tutsis were demonized as murderous outsiders, despite the fact that they had lived in the country for centuries. This helped induce disaffected Hutu children to join the youth militias and prepare them for their roles as killers in the 1994 genocide.[49]

In the end, children may join such groups simply because they are kids, and the slightest of whims or appeals may suffice to impel them to enter war. Observers report that many child soldiers in the Karen militia groups in Myanmar joined in search of some excitement in their lives. They simply found the daily grind of life in the refugee camps across the border in Thailand to be boring.[50] Other conflict groups will

intentionally hold parades and conduct training near schools or send
patrols through villages. The aim is to spread a happy, popular image
and use this to gain volunteers. Even if the recruits do not join immediately, these sorts of tactics create a legacy that can pay off as the children later grow.

> *I joined the army when I was young [at age fifteen] without think-*
> *ing much. I admired soldiers, their guns and crisp, neat uniforms.*
> *I just wanted to fight the way they did in the movies and so I*
> *joined the army.* —H., age twenty-one[51]

Peer pressure may be used as well. For example, LTTE recruiters
would visit schools and screen films of the government's depredations
and their own successful attacks (teachers risk death if they try to prevent this access). The recruiters deliberately boss around teachers and
force school bands to play at funerals for the dead of the group. In
doing so, they show who is at the head of the social order, at least within
a society at war. Then, child soldiers already in the group, wearing natty
new uniforms and shiny boots, would be presented to the class. They
would ask for a show of hands for whoever supports the cause of independence. Upon this, all those with hands raised would be driven to the
LTTE training camps.[52] Likewise, a number of groups teach songs or
poems that ridicule children who are not part of the cause.

> *Stop! O Younger brother*
> *Even if I weigh and sell you*
> *I can sell you for a good price even tomorrow.*
> *It is not for tying ten palmyrah trees and chopping them*
> *You are growing fat in your youth and idling.*
> *Why does hair grow on your face and body?*
> *Younger brother, you must be brave.*
> *Go! You are the cyclone*
> *Rise and Fight.*
>
> —"Poem to the Young Boy,"
> a LTTE recruitment song[53]

It is also important to note that, when growing up in a war zone, children will often experience an essential militarization of their daily life. The threat of death becomes a normal occurrence and their regular experiences will be shaped by the omnipresence of combatants around them. It is in this "amoral vacuum" that groups seeking child soldiers offer a voice that can appeal to lost children.[54] Some groups even try to reinforce this omnipresence by surrounding children's homes and schools with further images of war. These range from the typical wall murals that dot nearly every conflict zone to the LTTE's unique practice of building "memorial parks" for its "martyrs." These memorials are actually playgrounds designed to entice children to become soldiers. They even have militarized playground equipment such as seesaws that have toy automatic weapons mounted on the handles.[55]

CHAPTER 5

Turning a Child into a Soldier

*I was attending primary school. The rebels came and attacked us.
They killed my mother and father in front of my eyes. I was 10 years
old. They took me with them . . . They trained us to fight. The first
time I killed someone, I got so sick, I thought I was going to die.
But I got better . . . My fighting name was Blood Never Dry.*
                                                        —D., age sixteen[1]

The act of joining an armed group is only the first step in a child's path
to war. Becoming a child soldier is a longer process, involving indoctrination, training, and then battle.

Indoctrination and the Utility of Violence

Indoctrination is the act of imbuing a child with the new worldview of
a soldier. Traditionally, this opening step is key in the process for turning any civilian into a soldier. It provides what analysts call "sustaining
motivation," the collection of factors that keep soldiers in the army
despite the risks and rigors of the campaign. It also provides the "combat motivation," the factors that keep soldiers on the field in the heat of
battle.[2] Children are obviously not the prototypical recruit, so their
indoctrination is a critical determinant to the overall success of any
putative child soldier doctrine.

Historically, armies have had three general types of motivators to offer their soldiers: coercive motivators, based on physical punishment; remunerative motivators, based on the promise of material rewards; and normative motivators, based on the offer or withdrawal of such psychological rewards as honors and group acceptance.[3] Each of these is intended to keep the soldier in the army and lead him to take risks and commit acts of violence that he would likely not do otherwise.

Coercive motivation has been the most commonly applied technique for professional armies across history. For example, Frederick the Great believed that a soldier must be "more afraid of his officers than of the dangers to which he is exposed."[4] Similarly, British armies in the eighteenth and nineteenth centuries made frequent use of the lash to discipline soldiers for desertion, straggling, and cowardice; sentences of a hundred to two hundred lashes were not uncommon.[5] Other common practices were to force a soldier to "run the gauntlet" (be beaten by a line of his messmates) or march with a cannonball chained to one ankle if he failed to follow orders without question. On occasion, soldiers were punished by death.[6]

This primary use of force in the initial act of indoctrination is equally characteristic of child soldiers. Few of the forces they join deign to offer children true remunerative rewards, while normative motivators require allegiances and relationships that build up only over time. This is often contrary to most conflict groups' motivation to use the children on the battlefield as rapidly as possible.

Therefore, whether they have joined a state military or a rebel group, the entire process of their indoctrination and then training typically uses fear, brutality, and psychological manipulation to achieve high levels of obedience. For example, in many state armies, children generally receive much the same treatment as adult recruits. When the target is a child, these often brutal training-induction ceremonies, which may involve beatings and humiliation, become acts of sadism. A typical case is in Paraguay, where government military trainers beat children as young as twelve with sticks or rifle butts and burn them with cigarettes, all with the intent of trying to turn them into soldiers. Those who resist or who attempt to escape are further beaten or even killed.[7] More than III underage conscripts have died in the Paraguayan army since 1989.[8]

Once children are locked within a military organization that has chosen to utilize child soldiers, thus already violating the law and common codes of morality, few constraints exist on what trainers might choose to do. In turn, child soldiers become quickly dependent on their leaders for their protection from capricious violence as well as their every need. Combined with liberal amounts of terror and propaganda, impressionable children can rapidly begin to identify with causes they barely understand.

The exact types of indoctrination vary by group, but all take place at a time at which the child is at his weakest emotionally and psychologically—disconnected from family, traumatized, and at a fundamental loss of control. The overall intent of the process is to create a sort of "moral disengagement" from the violence that children are supposed to carry out as soldiers.[9]

Typically, groups not only utilize threats of punishment against the children but also seek to diffuse any sense of responsibility among the children for future violence. These may include dehumanizing their victims, such as by creating a "moral split" that divides the world into an "us versus them" dichotomy. For example, young recruits in the LTTE are continually taught that those outside the cause are enemies and should be killed. They are also shown videos of dead women and children. This inures them to violence as well as creates a sense of righteousness in targeting outsiders, as the children are told that the group's enemies did it. The effect is that many children often emerge from such programs with weakened senses of remorse and obsessions with violence.[10]

Another indoctrination tactic is to attempt to realign the child's allegiances and worldview. This involves both traditional modes of propaganda and what many would term "brainwashing." Young members of the RUF, for example, were encouraged to call their leader, Foday Sankoh, "Pappy." Part of their indoctrination program was to declare that he was now their father. Sankoh was also compared in the program to Jesus and the Prophet Mohammed. Similarly, all LTTE recruits swear an oath of allegiance to the group's leader, Velupillai Prabhakaran, every morning and evening, and he is similarly described as a father figure.

Many groups also utilize the creation of alternative personas to neutralize the effect of the antisocial actions they are attempting to indoctrinate.[11] Across regions, child soldiers typically take on nicknames. Some of the names are simply juvenile, such as "Lieutenant Dirty Bathe" (because he never took a bath), while others are chilling, such as "Blood Never Dry." The renaming, sometimes called locally "jungle names," is termed "doubling" by psychologists.[12] The renaming not only seeks to dissociate the children from culpability for the violence and crimes they commit, but also is intended to indicate a complete split with their prior self. Some units of child soldiers in Sierra Leone even took to calling themselves "cyborgs," self-consciously denoting themselves as human killing machines with no feelings.[13]

> *It's like magic. I killed people and it doesn't stick to me. I still go to heaven.* —"Bad Pay Bad," age unknown [14]

There is also often a physical aspect of reidentification in the indoctrination process. Many groups, such as the LTTE, shave their children's heads (akin to joining a professional military). This not only inculcates a break in identity, but also makes escapees easier to identify.[15] Some organizations even go to the extent of branding their new child recruits with the group's name or insignia. Leaders of the Revolutionary United Front in Sierra Leone, for example, would carve "RUF" onto children's chest, arms, and even foreheads with anything from needles to broken glass. In doing so, the scarring became not only a part of indoctrination but also acted as a lifelong stigma intended to keep children from returning to communities where the RUF was hated. As one former child soldier sadly describes, "I was branded because they said I would run away and now I can't even run away from my own self. Evil is with me all the time, imprinted on my body."[16]

> *I was on my way to the market when a rebel demanded I come with him. The commander said to move ahead with him. My grandmother argued with him. He shot her twice. I said he should*

kill me, too. They tied my elbows behind my back. At the base, they
locked me in the toilet for two days. When they let me out, they
carved the letters RUF across my chest. They tied me so I wouldn't
rub it until it was healed. —A., age sixteen[17]

The ultimate method of indoctrination, though, goes beyond these crimes. A popular tactic among the groups most dependent on child soldiers is to force captured children to take part in the ritualized killing of others very soon after their abduction. The victims may be POWs from the other side, other children who were abducted for the sole purpose of being killed in front of the recruits, or, most heinous of all, the children's own neighbors or even parents. The killings are often carried out in a public manner, such that the home community knows that the child has killed, with the intent of closing off any return.[18]

In some countries, including Colombia, the Democratic Republic of the Congo (DRC), Peru, and Mozambique, child soldiers have been forced to perform ritualistic acts of cannibalism on their victims, such as eating the victim's heart.[19] This is also calculated to instill contempt for human life. Any recruits who balk risk becoming the victims themselves, forcing the most terrible of choices upon a child.

I don't want to go back to my village because I burnt all the houses
there. I don't know what the people would do, but they'd harm me.
I don't think I'll ever be accepted in my village.
—I., age sixteen[20]

Former child soldiers typically cite this as the defining moment that changed their lives forever. Designed to break down resistance to the group's authority and destroy taboos about killing, the effect of the killing is to not only terrorize the children, but also implicate them in the worst acts of violence. Having crossed the ultimate moral boundary, they are made anathema to the only environment they knew and thus are even more reliant on their new organization. Their only two anchors in life become their guns and their fellow fighters. After this, their compliance to orders will often be near total. As Corinne Dufka of Human Rights Watch describes the practice, "It seemed to be a very organised strategy of . . . breaking down their defences and memory, and turning them into fighting machines that didn't have a sense of empathy and feeling for the civilian population."[21]

It's easier the second time. You become indifferent.
                                                          —L., age fifteen[22]

Whatever the means, the typical result of the indoctrination process is a moral and psychological disconnection that allows children to engage in what would normally be considered depraved actions. The effectiveness of these programs is heightened by the fact that many of the children who grow up in a climate of war may already lack the internal constraints against violence that ordinarily develop. Many will never have had exposure to positive role models, a healthy family life, the rewards for socially constructive behaviors, and the encouragement of moral reasoning. However, the effect is not limited to those of any particular background. These indoctrination techniques even have their parallel in all sorts of initiation processes across cultures (from street gangs to fraternities). As one psychologist notes of his time spent trying to rehabilitate child soldiers, "It was sobering to think that under certain conditions, practically any child could be changed into a killer."[23]

Training

The typical process of turning a civilian into a soldier involves recruitment, indoctrination, and then training in basic and later specialized military skills. However, some children were recruited to fill out such support roles as cooks, porters, or unarmed sentries. Thus, these kids are given little to no skills instruction, but set right to work. Children can also play certain uniquely valuable roles in guerrilla warfare. Local officers frequently note how children can move about more freely than adults, and are not instantly suspected of spying or supplying.[24] These secondary functions still entail great risk and hardship, though.

SAMPLE CHILD SOLDIER TASKS AND DUTIES

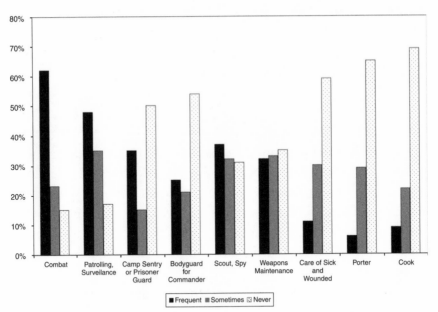

Source: International Labour Office, "Democratic Republic of the Congo Survey," in *Wounded Childhood: The Use of Children in Armed Conflict in Central Africa* (Geneva, 2003), p. 39.

I worked as a spy. They gave me cigarettes, groundnuts and other things to sell. While I was selling, I'd get information. I'd find out where the rebels had stored their weapons, what type of weapons they had, and where their base was located so we could attack them. If the base was not too far away, I'd just spend the day and go back to our base. If it was far away, I'd have to stay for a day or two before reporting back to my base. I was a good spy because all the information I gathered was used to launch attacks. Most times we were successful, so I think I was a good spy.

—I., age twelve[25]

In the end, though, the majority of children are primarily recruited to fight, and most are quickly trained to this task. Thus, while it is often claimed that child soldiers rarely fight, research indicates that the majority of child soldiers do participate in combat. In one global survey 91 percent of child soldiers had served in combat.[26] Another survey carried out in Colombia among FARC, ELN, and AUC child soldiers found that 75 percent had been in combat at least once, with multiple interviewees taking part in more than ten battles.[27] A third survey in Africa found that 87 percent had served on the front lines.[28] In Liberia, approximately 80 percent of the child soldiers were involved in direct combat.[29]

The typical training pattern is that the children are given short instruction in the most basic infantry skills: how to fire and clean their weapons, lay land mines, set an ambush, etc. There are also frequent attempts at instilling some form of basic discipline and esprit de corps, such as forced marches and parades. Training can range from a day to up to eleven months (the longest being in the RCD–Goma conflict group in the DRC). The training might either take place all at the start or, in some cases, with a period of brief training, then deployment and return for more advanced training after gaining combat experience. This variance is usually situationally dependent. For example, LRA members were run through formalized and much longer training programs before 2002, while the group had safe base camps in Sudan. Once the group was forced on the run by the Ugandan army, the training became far more sporadic. In either case, training levels are generally well short of the common standards of Western professional armies in both skills and duration, but are usually enough to learn how to kill effectively.

States' training of child soldiers is typically highly institutionalized, consisting of running them through formal training programs that mimic those given to adults. Children in state units are also often supplied with uniforms, regular rations, and even pay.

One example of the state-structured approach toward child soldiering was that of Iraq under the rule of Saddam Hussein. Over the past decade, the regime laid the groundwork for child soldiers by running a broad program of recruitment and training. Since the mid-1990s there were yearly military-style summer "boot camps" organized by the regime for thousands of Iraqi boys. During these three-week sessions, boys as young as ten were run through drills, taught the use of small arms, and provided with heavy doses of Ba'athist political indoctrina-

SAMPLE TRAINING PROGRAMS FOR CHILD SOLDIERS

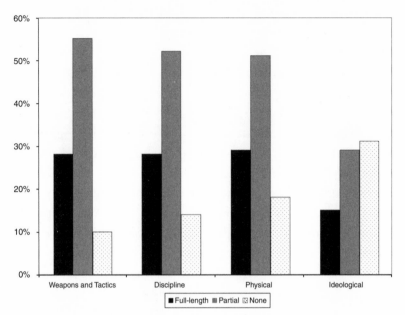

Source: International Labour Office, "Democratic Republic of the Congo Survey," in *Wounded Childhood: The Use of Children in Armed Conflict in Central Africa* (Geneva, 2003), p. 39.

tion. The military training camps were often named after resonating current events, to galvanize recruitment and bolster political support (for example, the 2001 summer camp series was named for the "Al Aqsa Intifada"). In addition, starting in 1998, there were a series of training and military preparedness programs directed at the entire Iraqi population. Youths as young as fifteen were included. The preparedness sessions, which generally ran for two hours a day over forty days, mandated drilling and training on small arms.

The Iraqi regime also worked to train specialized child soldier units, most notably the *Ashbal Saddam* (Saddam's Lion Cubs). This organization was formed after Iraq's defeat in the 1991 Gulf War, when the regime's hold on power faltered. The Ashbal Saddam involved boys between the ages of ten and fifteen who attended military training camps and learned the use of small arms and infantry tactics. The camps involved as much as fourteen hours per day of military training and political indoctrination. They employed training techniques intended to desensitize the youth to violence, including frequent beatings and deliberate cruelty to animals (the recruit might be asked to strangle a chicken or shoot a dog).

Rebel groups' training of child soldiers is typically less institutionalized and tends to be shorter. Their instructors may even be other child soldier "veterans." Of rebel groups, the Tamil Tigers may have the most developed child soldier training program, mimicking many of the drill techniques used by professional militaries. Developed in the early 1990s by the LTTE's military leader Wedi Dinesh, it was designed to make the LTTE's child soldiers more capable and daring than its adult fighters had been.[30] All links between the children and their families are broken, and the children are trained for four months in the jungle. Sleep and food are carefully regulated to establish control and build endurance. Each day the children wake at 5 a.m. and are put through physical training for two hours. They then spend the rest of the morning learning the use of their weapons, small unit tactics, parade drill, and other specialized skills such as rope climbing, codes, and map reading. The afternoon is divided between political indoctrination, including the reading and memorization of LTTE party literature, and more physical and skills training. During the evenings adult LTTE leaders deliver lectures. The topics vary—communication, explosives, and intelligence techniques—covering the child soldier equivalents to professional development programs. In all areas, risk-taking is highly extolled, including even screening movies that show a daredevil approach to battle prevailing.

This pattern holds for the other child soldier groups. Indeed, one of the few noticeable differences between the LTTE's training program and that of the FARC in Colombia is that FARC child soldier trainees typically begin their day at 4:30 a.m. rather than 5 a.m.[31]

Harsh discipline and the threat of death continue to underscore the training programs of almost all child soldier groups. In the LRA, for example, recruits' physical fitness is assessed and then built up by having them run around the camp's perimeters while carrying stones on their shoulders. Those who spill the stones or collapse are killed.[32] Those who disobey during marksmanship training risk having their fingers cut off.[33] In LTTE training classes, the first child to voice an interest in going home is beaten in front of the other children, effectively deterring others. Quitting during training activities is punished by sentences of harsh labor, including breaking stones or digging bunkers.[34] In the FARC and ELN, minor transgressions, such as consuming alcohol without permission, are punished by tying the child by their hands and neck to a pole for five days.[35] State armies are often equally harsh. In the Myanmar army, boys who arrive late for their tasks or refuse to eat their food are beaten by the other recruits with bamboo sticks. In some cases, officers literally rub salt in their wounds.[36]

Action

Once minimally trained, most new recruits are set very quickly out on the battlefield; to not use them as soon as possible goes against the very rationale for their recruitment. Moreover, their participation in operations can bind them tighter to the organization. At the same time, new child soldiers can be used to seize more children and build the group's numbers.

Despite their negligible training, the often cruel indoctrination and training programs mean that young children can be turned into the fiercest of fighters. Weakened psychologically and fearful of their commanders, children can become obedient killers, willing to carry out the most dangerous and horrifying assignments. When they do take on other armed forces rather than civilians, young children rarely fully appreciate the dangers of the battlefield. The result is that in the midst of combat they often get overly excited and take undue risks, sometimes even failing to take cover. Or, as one rebel commander in the DRC commented, "Children make good fighters because they are young. . . . They think it's a game, so they're fearless."[37]

Many believe that this fearlessness derives directly from the very state of childhood—that is, children are simply not as capable of understanding the consequences of their actions as adults. There are both psychological and physical explanations for this difference. Children, most particularly those in the pre-adolescent years, tend to have what is known as an "underdeveloped death concept." Children's psyches often have not yet developed a sense of their own mortality (death is a meaningless concept). Thus, children are generally psychologically incapable of weighing all the possible consequences of their actions in realistic terms.[38]

Researchers are beginning to believe that there may be an underlying physical basis for this difference. The prefrontal lobe is the part of the brain that some scientists speculate plays a crucial role in inhibiting inappropriate behavior. It does not reach its full development until as late as the age of twenty.[39] This provides an explanation for why children do not simply act like little adults, as well as further reasons as to why children are not morally equivalent actors in the realm of war.

I don't know why I killed these people. I killed them at a distance and at close range. I killed many. We didn't kill civilians if we were attacking a village and there were no enemies. The people we sent on reconnaissance would tell us who the enemy was. If there were enemies, we'd kill civilians. We had to kill our brothers too. If one of us committed a crime, our commander would tell us to beat him to death. One time, I had to beat and kill one of the other rebels. During an ambush, he'd fired when he wasn't supposed to, and we were discovered. I started beating him, but I didn't have the strength. So an older rebel beat him to death.

—I., age twelve[40]

A number of groups also try to reinforce this natural fearlessness by having the children take drugs or alcohol. The type of drug tends to depend on availability. The most common are cocaine, barbiturates, and amphetamines. Local concoctions are also highly favored. In Liberia and Sierra Leone, for example, a favorite was "brown-brown," cocaine or heroin mixed with gunpowder to make it stronger, while khat, a strong stimulant, is favored in East Africa. Initially, the child soldiers tend to be forced to take these drugs. Where needles were not available, group leaders make incisions around the child's temple and arm veins, pack the drugs in, and then cover the wound with plaster or a bandage. RUF child soldiers report that if they refused (called "technical sabotage" by rebel commanders), they would be killed.[41]

We smoked jambaa [marijuana] all the time. They told us it would ward off disease in the bush. Before a battle, they would make a shallow cut here [on the temple, beside his right eye] and put powder in, and cover it with a plaster. Afterward I did not see anything having any value. I didn't see any human being having any value. I felt light.   —A., age fifteen[42]

Later, as addiction grows, most begin to take the drugs voluntarily. By the end of the war in Sierra Leone, for example, social workers estimated that more than 80 percent of the RUF's fighters had used either heroin or cocaine.[43]

The outcome of this drug usage is that children become even more inured to violence and its consequences, almost operating on another plane of reality. In the words of the director of a child soldier repatriation camp, children "would do just about anything that was ordered" when on drugs.[44] As one boy soldier described the feeling, "I became stronger . . . They gave me a weapon and put some marks on my face. I was no longer human. I could do anything."[45] Another twelve-year-old noted how with drugs he was never afraid of going into battle: "After the injection, you just feel like doing any bad thing. You become a wounded man."[46] Canada's Lieutenant General Roméo Dallaire witnessed the effects while commanding the UN forces during the Rwandan genocide. He has an even more frank description: "Their brains are fried. On drugs, they will do anything."[47]

Regardless of what causes it, though, this tendency toward fearlessness is deliberately exploited by many child soldier organizations. Although some commanders have complained that child soldiers take excessive risks and can slow operations down through "misbehavior," many others actually prefer leading child soldiers to adults, because of this risk-taking and rote obedience.

My missions included diamond mining near Kono [Sierra Leone], drug purchasing, collecting ammunition in Liberia, looting villages and capturing civilians. I used to buy drugs at the Liberian border from a man called Papi. They forced us to take them. This is where they would cut and put the "brown-brown." [He shows a

raised welt on his left pectoral.] We would then inhale cocaine.
During operations, I sometimes would take it two or three times a
day. I felt strong and powerful. I felt no fear. When I was demobi-
lized I felt weak and cold and had no appetite for three weeks.

—Z., age fourteen[48]

Child soldiers are willing to follow the most dangerous of orders
without question. As one commander in Myanmar noted of his troops,
"Child soldiers are always very eager to go to the front lines."[49] A former child soldier in what was the RENAMO resistance group in
Mozambique explained that his group grew to "not use many adults to
fight because they are not good fighters . . . kids have more stamina,
are better at surviving in the bush, do not complain and follow direc-
tions."[50] Half the globe away, a Khmer Rouge commander in Cambodia similarly commented, "It takes a little time, but eventually the
younger ones become the most effective soldiers of them all."[51]

The general result is that, despite their smaller physical size and
development, child soldiers are serious players on the modern battlefield. As one report describes:

Children make very effective combatants. They don't ask a lot
of questions. They follow instructions, and they often don't
understand and aren't able to evaluate the risks of going to war.
Victims and witnesses often said they feared the children more
than the adults because the child combatants had not developed an understanding of the value of life. They would do anything. They knew no fear. Especially when they were pumped
up on drugs. They saw it as fun to go into battle.[52]

Child Soldier Tactics

For rebel groups, the standard unit tactic is to place child recruits
in small platoon-sized groups (roughly thirty to forty children) under
the command of a few adults. The children are most often grouped by
age. Units tend to stay on the move and operate as raiding parties. As

they are usually targeting civilians or ambushing much smaller opposition units or outposts, their effect can be devastating.

The use of child soldiers by state militaries is dependent on the context that led to the adoption of the child soldier doctrine. Typically, when these forces are fighting against guerrilla groups, children are mixed in with standard units of adult soldiers to maintain some form of control. In conventional wars, where they have often been brought in as stopgap measures, they are set out on their own in the front lines to act as cannon fodder or disrupt advancing enemy formations.

Many groups often attempt to break in their new child soldiers by first using them to attack "soft" targets such as villages or weakly defended military or police posts. This both ensures success and inculcates the child into the machine of killing. It also adds a powerful psychological aspect to the operations. The groups make examples of recalcitrant villages or areas, killing or pillaging with little mercy. However, they generally release just enough survivors to spread the story. Thus, terror becomes one of the groups' best weapons.

> *The first time we went out on patrol, we attacked a village and we killed so many people. I was afraid that first time. I don't know how many people I killed, because I was just shooting. I couldn't see anything. They just told me to shoot.* —L., age twelve[53]

> *I can never forget being in the battlefield for the first [time]. At first, I couldn't pull the trigger. I was lying almost numb in ambush watching kids my age being shot at and killed. That sight of blood and crying of people in pain, triggered something inside me that I didn't understand, but it made me past the point of compassion for others. I lost my sense of self.* —I., age fourteen[54]

However, child soldiers have also been proven to be quite effective even when facing regular adult troops. Their audacity, plus their sheer numbers and firepower, is sometimes able to make up for their relative lack of size, experience, and formal military training. It also helps that the adult troops of developing state armies are often even less trained than the child soldiers they face.

The tactics that are utilized then tend to vary by the situation and level of training. The use of human wave attacks by child soldier groups is quite common. The prevailing model is the brief use of preparatory fire, usually with mortars and rocket-propelled grenades (RPGs). This is quickly followed by a mass charge of the child soldiers, described by one Western soldier who witnessed the practice in West Africa as "yelling and screaming while blasting away on automatic. They generally overrun the objective with some ease, as the defenders are simply not much better."[55] An adult soldier in Myanmar recalled the terrifying experience of facing such a child soldier attack: "There were a lot of boys rushing into the field, screaming like banshees. It seemed like they were immortal, or impervious, or something, because we shot at them, but they just kept coming."[56]

The LTTE may be the most effective at this type of attack. In the battles over the northern peninsula of Sri Lanka, it faced a series of highly fortified Sri Lankan army bases.[57] It first deployed child soldiers against these in 1990, in an attack on the army camp at Mankulam. This attack was initiated by a suicide bomber driving a truck through the gate just before dawn, followed by a barrage of mortars, RPGs, and machine guns. Waves of LTTE fighters drawn from the Baby Brigade then followed and captured the fort by mid-afternoon.

Over the next decade the LTTE attacks gained in complexity and scale. By the mid-1990s the LTTE began to perfect its strategies, deploying a mix of Baby Brigade fighters with Black Tigers, which were specially trained suicide units. The LTTE provided the Baby Brigade units with new training in night combat, as well as boat handling and long-distance swimming to add an amphibious element. Reconnaissance and intelligence began to be emphasized and the forces even rehearsed on near-life-sized models of the attack objectives. The greatest victory came in 1996, when the LTTE launched Oyatha Alaikal (Operation Ceaseless Waves) on the Multavi military complex. Ultimately the attack involved more than five thousand LTTE troops and included both child soldier human wave attacks by land and amphibious assault troops and suicide bomb boats by sea.[58] To sow confusion, a number of LTTE leaders also dressed in Sri Lankan army uniforms. In the end, the force overran the complex and beat back a relief force. Out of a total defending force of 1,242 soldiers, the attackers killed 1,173 (roughly 300 were killed after being captured). The LTTE suffered casualties of around 300 killed and 1,000 wounded.

The Multavi operation illustrates that, despite their usual grouping in smaller platoon-sized units, child soldier forces can operate strategically. Their organizations are able to coordinate them into battalion-level or even larger operations. These larger operations tend to occur when their foe has been intentionally overextended and made more vulnerable. A series of prefacing feints and smaller attacks may be used to prompt this, intended to cause the opposition force to disperse to protect its supply lines. The group then cuts the supply lines, masses its own small units, and focuses an attack designed to overwhelm certain isolated units. During peacekeeping or coalition operations, child soldier forces have also been surprisingly savvy in targeting the politically weakest contingents. For example, this was a particular strategy used against the ECOMOG in Liberia and Sierra Leone. The result was that several of these lesser national contingents were pulled out, increasing the burden on the core state units (in this case, Nigeria).

Child soldier organizations have also demonstrated an awareness of the unique problems they present by putting children on the battlefield (covered further in Chapter 9). They often try to take deliberate advantage of the moral and operational dilemmas that result.[59] In a number of cases, including Colombia, Liberia, Sierra Leone, and the DRC, the youngest units (known as "small boy units") are used as the spearhead of assaults. Often, the children are sent forward naked, to create further sympathy and confusion among their opponents. Naked children are also believed to be imbued with magical powers in certain tribal cultures, adding to the disruptive effect.

The cover of children's assumed innocence is also often utilized to a force's advantage. In Iraq, rebel groups reportedly used children both as scouts and spies, particularly when targeting U.S. convoys. In other reported situations, they would deliberately move in front of U.S. convoys at traffic junctions, as if they were playing, whereupon the convoy, now stopped, would be attacked by accompanying forces.[60] In West Africa, seemingly unarmed children sometimes were left as "bait" in supposedly abandoned villages. Unsuspecting troops who went to their aid would then find themselves attacked by the children and a hidden force around them. Other common tactics included infiltration techniques, such as appearing to be playing games or attempting to trade with the opposing force as a cover for an ambush, as well as false surrenders.[61]

Over time, children gain combat skills and become shockingly proficient fighters—that is, if they survive their initial years of fighting. Those who know best often remark on the skills of these small but experienced soldiers. One retired Green Beret officer who worked with the child soldiers in the SPLA's Fifteenth Brigade in a private capacity described them as "the best soldiers I've seen in Africa." He estimated that roughly 50 percent of these were in the fourteen-year-old range and below. He also described the Colombian, Thai, and Filipino soldiers he had worked with in other contracts who were in the age range of fourteen to seventeen years old as "damn near as good as conscript-drafted Americans or Europeans in the use of NATO tactics."[62] Likewise, in Afghanistan, Northern Alliance commanders were quick to identify youngsters as among their best troops. In one report, an officer described a child soldier in his unit as the finest soldier he had ever commanded. The fifteen-year-old had been fighting since he was eleven and could hit a man in the head with an AK-47 from 200 meters (656 feet).[63]

> *Children make the best and bravest. . . . Don't overlook them. They can fight more than we people. It is hard for them to just retreat.*   —Liberian militia commander

Thus, as they build up combat experience, child soldier units can even coalesce into quite disciplined forces that can take on a professional force on their own terms. The elite of the entire LTTE force is the Sirasu Puli, or Leopard Brigade. Its members are children who have grown up in LTTE-run orphanages and have been taught from an early age to revere the group and its leaders. In December 1997 the Leopard Brigade fought a force of commandos from the Sri Lankan special forces, and was able to surround and kill nearly two hundred. This loss resonated further, demoralizing the entire Sri Lankan army, as these soldiers were the vanguard of the entire force.[64] Similarly, the Okra Hills battle in 2000 between the British SAS and the West Side Boys in Sierra Leone was a hard-fought engagement lasting more than six hours. The British special forces, who are considered among the best soldiers in the world, won, but at a cost of more than twenty-five wounded and one killed. These were somewhat high numbers, considering that the SAS came in with an edge in training, technology, and equipment, and even had the element of surprise.[65] As conflicts carry over for generations, child soldiers can grow up with the fighting. They can even form the nucleus of groups' long-term fighting capabilities. In Uganda, for example, the core of Yoweri Museveni's National Resistance Army was a unit of three thousand children, including five hundred girls, who had been orphaned by the government's earlier rampage in the Luwero triangle. They joined the rebels and were trained into one of its essential elements.[66] Over the next decade they helped tiny Uganda carry an outsized influence in the Lakes region of Africa, often bullying its much larger neighbors. Likewise, the Red Army that the SPLA established in the 1980s was one of the sustaining factors in its decades-long fight against the government.

Escape

The lives that child soldiers lead can be terrifying and rife with danger. Moreover, most did not choose to lead it. Thus, for those outside this realm, it is difficult to conceptualize why they would stay in these groups and run such terrible risks. However, the child soldier doctrine has its deliberate sustaining factors. The very processes of recruitment and indoctrination are designed to bind the children to the group and, if this is not successful, prevent escape. The induction works to disconnect children from their old lives and commit them to the cause. Even if they want to leave, many may have no homes to return to or feel that they will not be welcomed back because of the violent acts they have committed. The physical tags, such as cropped hair, tattoos, or even scarring and branding, also make escapees easier to identify and recapture.

A sad reality is that many child soldiers do not want to leave their new lives. The general threshold appears to be a membership of one year or longer in the organization.[67] This holds true even among abductees, who at the onset tend to define themselves as victims. After a period, though, the doctrine's dark processes win out and the children's own self-concept becomes entwined with their captors. The conditions are so adverse and indoctrination so persistent that the children can come to view themselves as members of the group. Some grow physically and psychologically addicted to the drugs their adult leaders supply. Others gain a sense of identity within the small units or even, somewhat surprisingly, develop the bonds of combat that keep them from deserting their fellow child soldiers.

> *I enjoyed the task of patrolling Kabul in a latest model jeep, with a Kalashnikov slung over my shoulder. It was a great adventure and made me feel big.* —M., age seventeen[68]

Researchers studying why soldiers stay in fights have often found that psychological factors are the most effective means of maintaining combat motivation and unit cohesion. A desire for acceptance from some community is often the one thing that holds soldiers together amid otherwise intolerable conditions. One of the most powerful of these is a sense of loyalty to one's comrades.[69] The same dynamic can happen even with child soldiers and lead them to stick with their groups.

Child soldier units can become bonded by their shared hardships and by the fact that they will have literally matured alongside each other. As one writer described an FMLN squad in El Salvador made up of thirteen- to nineteen-year-old girls and boys, "Together they are growing up. The common experiences they have had and the life they share now gives them a bond that is perhaps greater than if they were true blood siblings."[70] A reinforcing factor is that many of the children are orphans, meaning that their unit becomes their new family.

> *I had many friends in the bush. Whenever I fell behind during the fighting, they'd help me get back to my unit. One time, we were in the north, and we were attacked by the Kamajors [government-*

allied militia in Sierra Leone]. I was in a house, and I didn't know what was going on. When I came out, one of my friends killed the Kamajor who wanted to kill me. It was timely . . . timely intervention. My friend shot the Kamajor and he fell. I ran towards the gutter, and another friend launched an RPG at the enemy, so I managed to escape. Without those two friends, I'd be dead.

—I., age twelve[71]

Four of us decided to escape because we were missing our family. We finally ended up in Freetown [Sierra Leone]. The others, they stayed in Makeni. They refused to come with us. They were hooked on cocaine, and they were enjoying life there in the bush.

—P., age twelve[72]

However, the critical factor that binds children to the group is fear. Escape is quite difficult. Fellow fighters, including other children, almost always surround them. These other troops are equally fearful of what will happen to them if they do not turn in the escapees. There is also the risk that, even if they are able to break away from their own small unit, escaping child soldiers will still run into other units in the field. Indeed, because of the decentralized nature of many rebel groups, many child soldiers have gone through a cycle of abduction and escape across different units and even sides.[73]

Escape is particularly hard for adolescent girls. Not only are they highly vulnerable to being taken advantage of while on the run, but they often have become pregnant while in captivity. This creates a further impediment that can either lead them to stay or have a more difficult time in their getaway. The result is that escapee figures are often significantly lower among girl child soldiers. In the LRA, for example, young women make up 40 percent of its total abductees but only 10 percent of its successful escapees.[74]

Even the prospect of a successful escape still carries many risks and can be deterring. This is especially so during a battle or when opposition soldiers are on patrol. The soldiers may be on edge from the ongoing fighting or fearful that the escapee is part of an ambush. In either case, they may have a shoot-first attitude that endangers escapees.

Once past these initial risks, the now former child soldiers' ordeal is rarely over. Often, they find that they have nowhere to go. Their homes may have been destroyed; their parents may have been killed or may have fled to safer areas. Even those children who are able to find their homes or families may hesitate, fearing reprisals or ostracism by community members who blame the children for complicity in atrocities.

The underlying deterrent factor to escape, though, is the terrible punishment that will follow a failed escape attempt. Even for children within state armies, to flee is to commit desertion. Under most military codes of justice, this is punishable by long prison terms or even by facing a firing squad.

One boy tried to escape, but he was caught. His hands were tied, and then they made us, the other new captives, kill him with a stick. I felt sick. I knew this boy from before. We were from the same village. I refused to kill him and they told me they would shoot me. They pointed a gun at me, so I had to do it. The boy was asking me, "Why are you doing this?" I said I had no choice. After we killed him, they made us smear his blood on our arms. I felt dizzy. I felt so sick. They said we had to do this so we would not fear death and so we would not try to escape.

—S., age fifteen[75]

Rebel groups tend to use capital punishment more, as these groups are less bound by the law and need to send a stronger deterrent to maintain their numbers. The executions often are inclined to be ritualized and drawn out, as they present another opportunity for indoctrination. On the orders of their leaders, those children who attempt to flee and are caught are usually killed by other children. This is often carried out by as many as are present, to make all complicit. In most cases, the killing is done with handheld weapons to make it more personal for each executioner. The executioners are also typically forced to smear their arms and faces with the spilled blood of their victims.

Other frightening techniques are used as well. The LRA, for instance, has had escapees tied to trees and burned alive in front of its young troops. In other cases, young soldiers have had to carry around the decomposing corpses of other young fighters who were killed while attempting escape.[76]

Still, despite these overwhelming risks, vast numbers of child soldiers run at every opportunity. Some hate their new lives, some do it out of terror, and some just miss their families. Of the thousands abducted, there are also thousands who have escaped. The majority of child soldiers interviewed have tried to escape at least once.[77]

I grew tired of seeing so many friends killed. It was four lost years, four years without a family. —E., age seventeen[78]

We trained for five months in the training fields and were later taken to a place known as "Acholi" for further military training. As I was forced into the military [I coped with] whatever I was facing, but then I gave up hope and lost confidence in myself. [One night] I pretended to go to the latrine to defecate, and instead, I went directly into the bush. Some bodyguards fired at me, and I fell down and began rolling. They tried to confirm whether I was dead, but they didn't find me. When I got up, I managed to cross the road and I moved and moved. The journey took me ten days, and on the way, I ate like an animal. Reaching Uganda's border, I was assisted by a church leader, who gave me food and directed me to the UNHCR office. —S., age unknown[79]

I tried to escape, but I was far away from my village. I didn't know where I was. I made friends with another boy in my unit. He's the one who told me how to escape. We left at night. We walked the whole night. We spent two days in the bush to escape from the rebels. But when I got to a village, the people arrested me. They beat me. They were going to kill me because I was a rebel, but my aunt saw me. She saved me.

—D., age sixteen[80]

The circumstances of these escapes are varied. While a number of former child soldiers claim to have planned their escape well beforehand, the majority state that they were simply waiting for an opportunity. The hold their organization had on them was short term, dependent on the tight observation commanders were able to keep on them. They went along with the program, but fled whenever a sudden opportunity presented itself—often in the heat and chaos of a military engagement. As explored further in Chapter 9, this hold is potentially a center of gravity for child soldier groups that can be exploited. Its breaking can help defeat these forces while minimizing the loss of life among children.

CHAPTER 6

The Implications of Children
on the Battlefield

*If there is any lesson that we can draw from the experience of the
past decade, it is that the use of child soldiers is far more than a
humanitarian concern; that its impact lasts far beyond the time of
actual fighting; and that the scope of the problem vastly exceeds the
numbers of children directly involved.*
                                    —KOFI ANNAN, UN secretary general [1]

The rise of the child soldier phenomenon portends a number of
changes for both the manner in which conflicts are carried out and the
consequences that they will have. Unfortunately, none of these new
dynamics can be considered positive.

As a new source of fighters, children multiply the potential military
capacities of groups that choose to adopt the child soldier doctrine.
This eases the difficulties groups often face in force generation, thus
increasing the likelihood of rebellions and wars. Children's recruitment
also allows a proliferation of armed opposition groups with weakened
or nonviable ideological bases, which would have prevented their survival just a few decades ago. Moreover, the way in which child soldiers
are used means that those conflicts are inherently "messier," featuring
atrocities and attacks on civilians. At the same time, child soldier group

94

leaders consider children's lives cheaper. Subsequently, they deploy their recruits on the battlefield in a manner that leads to a higher casualty ratio.

The ultimate result is that, when children are present, violent conflicts tend to be easier to start, harder to end, and greater in loss of life. They also lay the groundwork for conflict recurrence in following generations.

More Wars

Children are targeted for recruitment because they represent a quick, easy, and low-cost way for armed organizations to generate force. Any organization willing to use children as fighters will usually be able to field a force well beyond what they would be able to do without them. With this, the balance of potential forces in a war is shifted. Equally, armed groups' calculus of when they should initiate or end a war is also altered.

In economic terms, the use of children lowers the "barriers to entry" into conflict. By lessening the costs of assembling a force, groups that would have been easily defeated in the past now can emerge as very real contenders. Organizations that would be little more than gangs become viable military threats.

It is no coincidence that 60 percent of the nonstate armed forces in the world today deliberately make use of child soldiers. For rebel groups, using the child soldier doctrine is a way to overcome their weak starting point as far as recruiting, organization, and other state-centered systemic barriers to their growth. Indeed, the practice becomes a model; the more armed factions in a conflict, the more likely that they will use child soldiers. One illustration was the rapid proliferation of armed groups in Liberia once children became a part of the fighting.[2] For smaller rebel groups, the gains from using children are a multiplication of their fighting numbers. The LRA, which used children to go from 200 core members to an army of 14,000 soldiers, is the classic example.

Child soldiers thus become one of the many forces lessening civil order and undermining weak state institutions, leading to what has become known as the "failed state" phenomenon. The rise of new armed groups in the context of weakening state institutions has repeatedly been the spark for coups, revolts, and other political and ethnic struggles to secure control over resources. As the recent collapse of the DRC illustrates, warlords, plunderers, and other violent actors then often emerge to fill the void left by a failing government. These groups all recruit children to help them build their personal power. That the child soldier phenomenon is concentrated in areas that are undergoing tenuous political transitions, such as Africa and Southeast Asia, only heightens its threat of instability and state failure.

It is important to add that, while the West often imagines itself able to stand aside from failed states, the realities of the global system no longer permit this. Since the 1990s more than eight million people have been killed in failed states like Somalia, Liberia, Sierra Leone, and the DRC (all where child soldiers were present) and millions more have become refugees. Within these countries, hundreds of millions more have been deprived of basic human needs, such as security, health care, and education, which then feed back upon the problem.[3] For many, the resulting scenes of chaos and tragedy create a moral imperative to take action.

These occurrences may create a strategic mandate to act as well. The failure of local states can destabilize entire regions, create refugee flows that wash upon our doorsteps, or sometimes even endanger valuable financial or political assets. Some claim that the United States, for example, has equal or greater economic investments in areas in Africa that are at risk than either in the Middle East or Eastern Europe. These include critical supplies of oil (roughly one fifth of all U.S. oil imports) and strategic minerals.[4]

More important than lost investments is that these weak or failed zones tend to become havens for transnational terrorist groups. The collapse of governance in Afghanistan may have mattered little to the United States in the late 1980s and 1990s, but it was an issue that came back to haunt us on September 11, 2001. As the UN Special Envoy Lakhdar Brahimi noted, the 9/11 attacks were "a wakeup call, [leading many] . . . to realize that even small countries, far away, like Afghanistan cannot be left to sink to the depths to which Afghanistan has sunk."[5] The decay of local law and order in these states gives outside extremist groups freedom of operation. These zones then become a magnet for global terror groups that are seeking to take advantage of the local void in governance. As al Qaeda's basing in Afghanistan illustrates, terrorism tends to thrive where failing or failed states are too weak to stamp it out.

Indeed, even state failures that are seemingly disconnected to this threat can still have dangerous consequences. For example, policymakers in Washington were unconcerned by Sierra Leone's collapse in the 1990s, as they saw little strategic value in the tiny country. Its state failure also had more to do with the child soldiers of the RUF than al Qaeda or any other terrorist groups. Nonetheless, the tiny West African country served as a critical node in the fund-raising efforts of Osama bin Laden's al Qaeda network. The group used the chaos of Sierra Leone's war to hide its own activities, including the conversion of al Qaeda cash into more easy to smuggle diamonds in the period just before the 9/11 attacks. In addition, three al Qaeda members reputed to have been involved in the 1998 bombings of the U.S. embassies in Kenya and Tanzania also took refuge in Charles Taylor's Liberia in the summer of 2001.[6] This illustrates that stability even in far away West Africa, which child soldier groups endanger, should be a concern of American national security.[7]

Longer Wars

The ease of force generation through a child soldier doctrine not only increases risks of more wars and state failures, but also affects how long these wars last. Organizations that use children are sometimes able to endure conditions that would break forces that do not. In turn, "as conflicts drag on, more and more children are recruited."[8]

Often state militaries will deploy massive numbers of child soldiers as a stopgap measure, in order to delay defeat or create valuable breathing space for their regular army to regroup and rebuild. The Ethiopians successfully utilized such a strategy in 1998 in their war with Eritrea. After their original operations against the Eritreans floundered, they placed recently recruited teenagers to act as a skirmishing force to break up Eritrean attacks. The Ethiopian army was able to recover and reconstitute its force, ultimately winning the war a year later. Similarly, whenever its fortunes were failing in the Afghan civil war, the Taliban would bus in madrassah students from across the Pakistani border and plug them into the front lines. Ultimately, this strategy gained them control of 95 percent of the country before U.S. intervention in late 2001 turned the war for its Northern Alliance opposition.

Likewise, rebel groups that depend on child soldiers can easily regenerate and rapidly replace battlefield losses. Many of the missions assigned to child soldiers do not require lengthy training and indoctrination. Quick turnover of personnel is possible, meaning that one advantage of using the child soldier doctrine is that only a small core of adult fighters is needed to maintain the organization. Thus, just when it seems that their fighting ability has been defeated, a rebel force can disappear into the bush and quickly build itself back up again. The RUF in Sierra Leone was completely routed in two separate instances in 1995 and 1997, first by the South African private military firm Executive Outcomes and later by the West African ECOMOG force.[9] Each time, however, it used abducted children to return back to strength and carry on the war. Likewise, just when the power of the LRA in Uganda had seemingly been broken by the army's Operation Iron Fist in summer 2002, the group was able to reconstitute its forces through the abduction of another 8,400 children over the next twelve months.[10]

The result is that outright victory over child soldier groups appears to be harder to achieve. These groups will often find a way to persist despite attempts to stamp them out, sometimes for years. As long as they are able to maintain a small organizational foundation, they may never be strong enough to win, but they will also be more difficult to kill off.

The presence of child soldiers also can create added difficulties for any peace process, as illustrated by the repeated breakdown of settlements in places ranging from Sri Lanka to Sierra Leone. Their ability to help conflict groups rapidly return to the field makes promises of disarmament and demobilization less tenable. These commitments, though, are often the key to successful negotiated settlements of war.[11] In short, children make wars easier to start and harder to end.

Wars Without the Ideology

Besides the increase in the amount and persistence of conflicts, the use of children means that a group's agenda becomes less important to its ability to generate force. That is, the connections between the group's purported cause, the underlying motivations of the group's leaders, and its likely success in fielding a combat organization are broken. By pulling in their recruits through abduction or indoctrination, groups that have causes that enjoy no grassroots support are still able to mobilize. They are also less likely to die out because of their unpopularity. For instance, the RUF in Sierra Leone had no discernible popular following and no real social program.[12] This, however, did not prevent it from launching a vicious civil war that lasted for almost a decade. Instead, it acquired child combatants either by terror tactics or by appealing to disenfranchised youth.

By using children as fighters, the philosophy behind an organization becomes almost irrelevant. Most child soldiers are not motivated by any internal belief in the rightness of their cause. Interviews with child soldiers typically reveal that they are unable to articulate any specific program their group stands for. Some organizations are even notable for their very lack of ideological training. In fact, many child soldiers are beaten or threatened with death if they begin to question the tenets of their group too closely.[13]

I don't know what I was fighting for. The rebels just told us that we were fighting for the people. I don't know what the war was all about because at the time, I was not really old enough to understand these things. —L., age twelve[14]

With this change, there is also less of a need for payoffs and bargains between leader and followers. Adults might balk at the proposition of risking their lives at no gain to themselves in order to win diamond mines for a warlord. But the very processes that put child soldiers in that position prevent them from doing so. The groups, in turn, have less incentive to establish systems of good governance, as they do not depend on the prosperity or compliance of their host communities.[15] Instead, they become more predatory and destructive.

Such agendas also make it more difficult for a society under siege to respond appropriately. The lack of agenda or political demands by a rebellion often offers no negotiated solution. As one local journalist described the beginning of the fighting in Sierra Leone, "From the taxi driver to the government minister, nobody seemed to have a clue of what the fighting was all about. Nobody knows what the rebels wanted."[16]

The result is that, with children present, political ideology is less necessary to the maintenance of warfare. Indeed, many conflicts fueled by child fighters have been simply about personal greed and the seizure of valuable mineral assets. When Foday Sankoh, a failed commercial photographer, took over the RUF, he first killed off its original political theorists, then he operated the group with an essentially gangland mentality. There was a focus on making money by seizing diamond mines, looting villages, and exacting protection money, but there was little effort to cultivating popular support or enacting social change.

Similarly, fringe religious movements and cults that would have been marginalized in the past can now use child soldiers to become quite powerful forces. These include even the most bizarre and internally inconsistent. The result is that within weak states, cult leaders on par with a Jim Jones or David Koresh can now present serious dangers to societal stability.

For instance, the leader of the LRA in Uganda, Joseph Kony, first emerged at the age of twenty-eight claiming to be possessed by the Christian Holy Spirit. With a few loyal followers, he took to the bush and launched his war. Allegedly, his group is fighting to bring back respect for the biblical Ten Commandments. Under his interpretation, however, this includes the abduction, torture, rape, and killing of children, the use of sex slaves, and the prohibition of living near roads or riding bicycles.[17] Kony also has allowed himself to have sixty-seven wives, because, as he says, King Solomon had more than six hundred.[18] Ironically, the LRA's closest ally has been the militant Islamic government of Sudan, so it once even amended its "Christian" doctrine to include the requirements that prayers be made toward Mecca and that pig farming be banned.[19]

At face value, such a group would appear to lack any sustainability. And unlike rebel groups of the past, it has not even bothered to create a political wing, let alone a discernible ideology or program of any sort. Yet, by using child soldiers, Kony has been the force behind a ten-year civil war that has killed more than 100,000 and left another 500,000 as refugees.[20]

The Mess That Children Make

Thus child soldiers allow groups lacking clear, popular agendas to thrive. This not only mutes the possibility of any positive political change emerging from war, but also can exacerbate the violence that takes place within conflicts. In most cases, such conflicts tend to quickly degenerate into rapacious affairs that concentrate their violence on civilians. Regardless of the groups' motivations, though, the presence of children on the battlefield generally adds to the confusion and chaos of war, increasing both the levels of atrocities and killing. This higher level of bloodshed, in turn, makes the conflict more difficult to end and more likely to recur.[21]

The use of children as combatants is a violation of the laws of war in and of itself. However, the doctrine behind the use of child soldiers institutionalizes heightened levels of violence and atrocities. While mass killing, rape, and torture have certainly been used by groups without child soldiers, the manner in which children are recruited, trained, and deployed makes these violations an inherent part of the conflict. Additionally, this violence is not just directed outwards at the opposition, but directed inwards as well, at the children within the force.

The intrinsic methods of recruitment and indoctrination involved in child soldiering entail massive violations of the laws of war. Armies, militias, and rebel groups must often use brutish methods to forcibly recruit children and break down community resistance to their conscription. Atrocities also play a central role in the methods used to turn children into soldiers. Children are often forced to commit heinous acts against POWs, fellow soldiers, their neighbors, or even their own family, such that the child is stigmatized and implicated in the violence.

> I was forced to do amputations. We had a cutlass, an ax and a big log. We called the villagers out and let them stand in line. You ask [the victims] whether they want a long hand or a short hand [the amputation at the wrist or elbow]. The long hand you put in a different bag from the short hand. If you have a large number of amputated hands in the bag, the promotion will be automatic, to various ranks.   —A., age sixteen[22]

Children's presence as fighters also affects the norms of good behavior in war. The protections typically afforded to wounded soldiers and prisoners of war are often ignored in lieu of indoctrination needs. Rebel groups with child soldiers tend not to take prisoners. Instead, they typically kill the POWs on the spot or bring them back to camp to kill as instructive victims. Likewise, even the force's own wounded children are subject to being executed by their fellow fighters, as leaders see them as needless drains on the organization and easily replaced. One survey in Colombia found that more than a third of former child soldiers admitted to having directly participated in out-of-combat killings. Another third volunteered that they had not been personally involved, but had witnessed others carry out such killings (indicating that the figure may be even higher).[23]

Other aspects of traditional laws of war, such as respect for neutral humanitarian groups, international organizations, or reporters, are also generally ignored. Multiple child soldier groups are also endemic users of antipersonnel land mines, considered illegal by international law. For example, the FARC and AUC in Colombia both include mine laying in their child soldier training programs.[24]

On the other side, treatment of captured child soldiers by opposition forces is often brutal. They are considered to be criminals, traitors, or terrorists and held in military prisons. Captured child soldiers of both sexes are often subjected to abusive interrogation procedures, torture, isolation, rape, and death threats.

Because we're in the bush and there was no food. And on top of that we were made to kill the enemy, the officers we captured, the government. But the most bad thing is that we were told to hate. We were told that if we touched these people they can't feel pain. They were different from us.

—C., served age nine to fifteen[25]

A related concern is that the active participation of some children in a war carries a wider risk for other children in the conflict zone. It exposes any child to the suspicion that they, too, are involved in the conflict. Identifying who is a threat and who is not is a particularly hard dilemma in civil wars, where rebel forces tend not to wear uniforms in order to blend into the civilian population. This makes all children potential targets for attack, interrogation, or other harassment.[26] The resulting mistakes can be quite tragic. A typical example occurred in Colombia in August 2000. A group of elementary school children age six to ten were walking along a trail guarded by a Colombian army unit. Wearing backpacks, they were mistaken for a FARC guerrilla unit. The soldiers laid an ambush and six of the children were killed before the confusion was sorted out.[27]

In general, civilians tend to bear the brunt of the atrocities committed by child soldiers. They are targeted because they are less likely to offer substantial resistance and thus represent softer targets for inexperienced fighters. However, there are also a number of institutionalized reasons for why organizations with child soldiers target civilians. Child soldier groups are often unpopular or predatory in nature. Thus, terror aimed at local communities prompts acquiescence or can be used to punish any communities that have been reluctant to provide assistance. In these cases, refugees will sometimes be deliberately allowed to escape in order to spread the message and inculcate further fear among the populace and opposition forces. Lastly, civilians are targeted for reasons of organizational growth. Their communities represent a ready source of additional recruits. These effects often spiral outwards, creating massive flows of refugees and internally displaced persons. In Uganda, for example, nearly half the population (over 200,000) has fled their homes in the Gulu district, where the LRA is active.[28]

There is also a higher level of sexual violence caused by child soldiers' presence in wars. For instance, a shocking 53 percent of all women who came into contact with the young fighters of the RUF in Sierra Leone experienced rape or some form of sexual violence. About 33 percent were gang-raped.[29] Not even the highly organized ethnic cleansing campaign of the Bosnian Serbs, which even included rape camps, ever reached this level of disturbing efficiency.

Sexual abuse has a long history in warfare. However, in these cases it is no longer incidental to the conflict or carried out by soldiers against their commanders' orders. Instead, it is utilized as a strategic and indoctrinating weapon, specifically planned by the organization. Sex abuse offers a means for the groups to terrorize civilians and further bind their soldiers to the organization.[30] Many child soldier groups have also used rape as a sort of reward to young pubescent soldiers who have been inculcated into a culture of violence. For example, one RUF operation in Sierra Leone was even called "Operation Fine Girl." Its specific aim was to find and abduct pretty girls, especially virgins, the younger the better.[31]

> *When we attacked a town, we would rape people. When we saw a lot of girls, we'd rape. Even I had a woman. I was 12 at the time. She was about 15. Our commanders said that all of us had to have a woman. If we didn't, they'd kill us.*
>
> —D., age sixteen[32]

> *So, on our way to be killed, we were taken to a house with about 200 people held in it. My older cousin was sent to go and select 25 men and 25 women to have their hands chopped off. Then she was told to cut off the first man's hand. She refused to do it saying that she was afraid, I was then told to do it. I said I'd never done such a thing before and that I was also afraid. We were told to sit on the side and watch. So we sat. They chopped off two men's hands. My cousin couldn't watch and bowed her head down to avoid the sight. Because she did that, they shot her in the foot. They bandaged her foot and then forced her to walk. We left the two men whose hands had been cut off behind.*

We were then taken to a mosque in Kissy [Sierra Leone]. They killed everyone in there. . . . They were snatching babies and infants from their mother's arms and tossing them in the air. The babies would free-fall to their deaths. At other times they would also chop them from the back of their heads to kill them, you know, like you do when you slaughter chickens. . . . One girl with us tried to escape. They made her take off her slippers and give them to me and then killed her . . . one time we came across two pregnant women. They tied the women down with their legs eagle-spread and took a sharpened stick and jabbed them inside their wombs until the babies came out on the stick.

—K., age thirteen[33]

In addition to these atrocities aimed outwards, there is a prevalence of such crimes committed against girl soldiers by their own compatriots. For example, in the RUF, rape was often used as a punishment for military failure.[34]

A number of rebel organizations, such as the LRA, RUF, and in Angola, UNITA, even treat young female soldiers as commodities and force them to serve as the "wives" of adult leaders. Often given as rewards to successful commanders, the girls are then traded by the organization if the first recipient is killed. Documents seized from an LRA camp reveal that Kony even kept a written record of his "presents."[35] Beatings, rapes, and often pregnancy ensue. When this is not in line with the group's plans, some organizations, such as the FARC, force young female child soldiers to have abortions or use contraceptives, often by ordering an intrauterine device inserted regardless of the girl's wishes.

You have to use birth control, even if you are not part of a couple. The nurse inserts an IUD. It's painful. Every eight days they check it. Eight days after I arrived, they inserted one in me.

—M., age fourteen[36]

This broad range of atrocities breaks almost all the age-old norms of approved behavior in warfare. However, the involvement of children in these extreme acts of violence is a deliberate method used to desensitize them to the suffering of others. Many are taken at such a young age that they do not know the basic moral codes of right from wrong. Such experiences further disconnect them from their moral base. Add the presence of drugs and the fear of being killed by their own leaders or the enemy and it all makes children more likely to commit such acts in the future.

The result is that when children are present in a conflict, experience has shown that they are among the most vicious combatants in the war. As one UNICEF worker put it, "Boys will do things that grown men can't stomach. Kids make more brutal fighters because they haven't developed a sense of judgment."[37]

Indeed, the younger child soldiers are, the more vicious they tend to be. In Sierra Leone, in fact, teenage rebel units were often scared of younger "small-boy units." These units were considered far more cruel and unpredictable, such that elder child soldiers would often steer clear of them.[38]

> Sometimes, when I was angry, I'd kill some of my fellow rebels. If we fell into an ambush and these bigger boys made a mistake, we'd kill them.   —P., age twelve[39]

The Cheapening of Life

Child soldiers are deliberately recruited by groups for the very reason that their lives are considered to be of less value than fully trained adult soldiers. Child soldiers are thus "spent" by commanders in that vein. They are typically used in ways that subject them to risks above and beyond the normal dangers of war.

The first use of child soldiers that heightens their casualties is the exploitation of children as shields. They are deployed in such a manner to protect the lives of organization leaders and better trained, and thus considered more valuable, adult soldiers. This makes child soldiers particularly vulnerable to being charged with tasks that entail greater hazard. For example, when children are present in an organization, they are most often the personnel used to explore suspected minefields, usually through simple trial and error. In fact, this was the original motivation behind the use of children in the Iran-Iraq war, to clear paths for follow-on assault forces.[40] In Guatemala, underage soldiers were even termed "mine detectors." The results of these tactics are damning, as a principal cause of death and injury of minors in conflicts is land mines.[41] In Cambodia, for instance, 43 percent of all the land-mine victims in military hospitals had been recruited as soldiers between the ages of ten and sixteen.[42]

In other cases, commanders use children as direct shields at checkpoints or when ambushes or battles loom. The children are exposed at the front to test whether there is a real threat or not, while their commanders remain safely hidden in the rear. At times, the children are deliberately ordered not to take cover, and are beaten or killed if they attempt to duck or crouch behind trees or buildings.[43]

The second scenario is the use of children as cannon fodder. For the same reason as their use as shields (their relative cheapness to recruit and utilize, compared to adults), they are also commonly employed in what are termed "human wave" attacks. The tactic is designed to overpower or wear down a well-fortified opposition through sheer weight of numbers. The very value of children is that they are extra targets for the enemy to deal with and expend ammunition upon. In Uganda, new LRA recruits are forced to the front lines, regardless of whether they are armed or not. In the words of one commander to his child fighters, "Even if you don't have a gun, you must go and take part in the fighting by making noise."[44] Those who do not run in the direction of gunfire are beaten or killed. Similar situations are reported in the DRC. There, unarmed child soldier units have been ordered to advance on opposition forces while beating trees with sticks to make their presence known. Their aim is to distract the enemy from the real attack coming from another direction. Their ensuing losses are obviously high.[45]

Some commanders view children as mentally predisposed for such duty in that they do not have the same awareness of the full consequences. In other cases, as in Sierra Leone, Sri Lanka, and Myanmar, child soldiers were often given drugs, such as amphetamines and tranquilizers, to blunt fear and pain.

While they may not be the most sophisticated of tactics, these attacks can often be quite effective in overwhelming even a well-prepared and fortified force. As noted in Chapter 5, the LTTE Operation Oyatha Alaikal (Ceaseless Waves), aimed at the Multavi military complex, proved prophetic in its name. Assault waves of children were able to overrun a key strategic site in Sri Lanka.

At the same time, though, these tactics entail massive casualties. Ceaseless Waves left over three hundred LTTE child soldiers dead and more than a thousand injured.[46] In most cases, though, commanders see children as expendable resources whose losses do not destroy and may even benefit the cause. One KLA officer in Albania bluntly described his own poorly trained teenage troops: "They are cannon-fodder. In the bush, they would not survive more than 48 hours."[47]

The results are often terrible losses among child soldiers, much higher in proportion to equivalent adult units. Almost 70 percent of young KLA recruits referred to above were killed when they tried to go from Albania to Kosovo. Since 1995 about 60 percent of LTTE personnel killed in combat in Sri Lanka have been children age ten to sixteen. Roughly 20 percent of the total were girls less than sixteen.[48] In Mozambique, children were around a quarter of the combatants, but roughly 60 percent of the total casualties.[49]

These losses are particularly high in conventional battles, when the children face professional opposition units. One seventeen-year-old Ethiopian who was forcibly recruited at the age of fifteen, describes how his unit was used in a stopgap measure in a 1999 battle with Eritrean army forces. Equipped with just small arms that they had minimal training on, they were ordered to hold a trench line while the regular army forces pulled back to regroup. "It was very bad. They put all the 15- and 16-year-olds in the front line while the army retreated. I was with 40 other kids. My friends were lying all over the place like stones. I was fighting for 24 hours. When I saw that only three of my friends were alive, I ran back."[50]

Child Soldiers and the Conflict Merry-Go-Round

The added tragedy of child soldiers is that the doctrine's implications do not stop at the conflict's termination. Rather, the use of underage combatants lays the groundwork for future violence and instability. The experiences that children come away with from participating in war can have a devastating effect both for them and for the broader society. The cumulative effect of these traumatic experiences will color and inform their choices, opinions, and perspectives for the rest of their lives.

By exploiting youth for political purposes, child soldiering violates the most fundamental rights of a child. It exposes them to the dangers of conflict while plunging them into a system where killing is sanctioned, at a time when they are mentally and morally unprepared to deal with the consequences. It inculcates a culture of impunity that is hard to reverse. Plainly put, children who have grown up fighting often find it difficult to imagine exactly what peace is and how they should function in it.

This may be perhaps the most pervasive effect of soldiering on children, though it is never identified as a violation in any international treaty and certainly not mentioned in security studies. In pediatric psychology, it is known as the "Destruction of Childhood."[51] While hard to define in exact terms, it is best characterized by the losses a child faces when he or she is thrust into the realm of war. These may be loss of self, of family, of community, of health, of security, of recreation, or, perhaps most important of all, of future.

The results for the broader social order are dangerous as well. It is becoming apparent that the past use of children in war breeds the conditions for future war. As one psychologist writes, "A society that mobilizes and trains its young for war weaves violence into the fabric of life, increasing the likelihood that violence and war will be its future. Children who have been robbed of education and taught to kill often contribute to further militarization, lawlessness, and violence."[52]

In a sense, the phenomenon of child soldiers feeds upon itself. Each round of fighting creates a new cohort, traumatized by the war and bereft of hope and skills, who then become a potential pool and catalyst for the next spate of violence. Indeed, in some areas, such as Sudan, we are even seeing children of child soldiers becoming soldiers.[53] In Liberia, social workers described the thousands of ex–child soldiers from the first war who received no psychological counseling as "ticking time-bombs."[54] The result in 2001 was that thousands of street children who had fought for Charles Taylor just a few years earlier switched sides and went to war on behalf of the new LURD opposition group. Thousands more were remobilized and fought for the regime. Others worry that, given the large numbers of former child soldiers, the same type of instability will plague Sierra Leone for decades to come. In describing the child fighters of the RUF, one local observer commented, "You won't believe how isolated they are, how little they know of the outside world and how many of them know nothing outside of war. They are asking what will happen to them if there is peace. They don't know life without a gun."[55]

This dark aftermath of the child soldier doctrine is not constrained by sovereign borders. Often child soldiers are recruited from second countries, among refugee communities or ethnic diasporas, and trafficked across borders. For example, children from Angola, Burundi, Kenya, Rwanda, and Uganda have fought alongside their adult sponsors in the civil war in the DRC. Children have also been recruited from global diaspora communities by Kurdish and Kosovar armed groups. In each case, the impact of violence in one country then reverberates back to their homelands.

In fact, as a look at the map on page 17 demonstrates, there are geographic clusters of wars where child soldiers are located, perhaps indicating cross-border regional spreading of the instability. The legacy of the peace agreement in Liberia, for instance, was an outflow of fighting into Sierra Leone, also carried out by children. The fighting there soon spilled over into Guinea. The Guinean government directly blamed the clashes, which left almost five hundred dead, on "lost defrocked soldiers, fearing neither God nor man, a rebellion that has become, for many youths of the region, both a way of life and a means of survival."[56] Soon after, Côte d'Ivoire was the next neighbor to succumb to child soldier–led chaos. Roughly three thousand underage recruits reportedly participated in the fighting there. Many of these young fighters spoke English, indicating that they were from Liberia and Sierra Leone (the local dialect in Côte d'Ivoire is a form of French).[57]

Indeed, the presence of child soldiers may mean that a neighbor's peace agreement, which used to be good news, could portend a direct threat of war. For example, the fighting in the DRC created literally thousands of socially disconnected youths who have known only a life of killing and looting. These semi-literate boys and girls did not care for whom or where they fought. Many have simply moved on into other countries, in search of the next war to fight. The outcome is that cease-fires in the DRC later led to outbreaks of violence in the Central African Republic and Congo-Brazzaville.[58]

Part of why the legacy of child soldiering is so dangerous is that, in many ways, children bear greater burdens from war than their adult counterparts. Many child soldier veterans have physical disabilities and/or psychological scars that are heightened by their youth. Most have special rehabilitation needs. Or, because they were removed from school at an early age, they may have no skills other than killing and being able to fieldstrip weapons.

The very nature of their use means that child soldiers are more likely to have been injured or disabled in war. The most frequent permanent injuries they suffer are loss of hearing, blindness, and loss of limbs. Health care for wounded child soldiers is always problematic, particularly as the countries where most of them are found are least likely to have top medical facilities. At times, the only medicine available is herbal.

Disease rates are also much higher among ex–child soldiers, due to the stresses and malnourishment that they often face. Drug addiction is a common affliction as well, with resulting implications for their future health and development. Even the process of withdrawal from the addiction can be a grueling experience.[59]

A particular problem is sexually transmitted disease (STD). The prevalence of STDs is thought to be far higher among child soldiers than the general population or their adult soldier equivalents. While the data is limited (testing is often unavailable and sometimes discouraged, as it can create a lifelong stigma for children), what we do know from isolated testing is highly disturbing. At repatriation camps in Uganda, 70 to 80 percent of the female child soldiers and 60 percent of the male child soldiers tested positive for one or more STD.[60] Likewise, 70 to 90 percent of rape survivors in Sierra Leone tested positive for STDs, while roughly 50 percent were positive for HIV, indicating high rates among male child soldiers, who are thought to be among the prime transmitters.[61] In Mozambique, where there are more than one million AIDS cases, the provinces where child soldiers were deployed have the highest concentration.[62] This feeds back into the security problems that the epidemic presents down the line.

These physical maladies carry greater emotional, psychological, economic, and social disadvantages for children, which endure for the rest of their lives. For example, a land-mine explosion is likely to cause greater damage to the body of a child than to that of an adult. For those children who do survive, the medical problems related to amputation are far more severe than for adults. The limb of a child grows faster than the surrounding tissue. It thus requires repeated amputation. Children also need new prostheses regularly, about every six months for those in puberty. Such injuries, in particular the loss of sight, hearing, or limbs, can also present severe obstacles to a child's social and educational development, particularly if occurring in communities that lack the resources to aid handicapped people in rejoining society.[63]

I would like my arms and hands to be mended. I am in great agony and a terrible situation. I don't have hands. I can't eat my food, I have to be fed by someone else. I would like to see my hands working. I want peace and the war to be stopped. I want to go to school and get an education. If the hospitals were working I would like my hands to be treated. If it was up to me, I would say that no child of my age should ever lose his hands. I would like to say to the militia, look what you have done, you have destroyed my hands. Please don't continue to blow off children's hands. Please stop the fighting. —S., age twelve[64]

The doctrine of child soldiers also creates many of the same problems among the wider population, who will have suffered from their atrocities. It thus has additional wider social effects, hindering economic and social development for years to come.

For instance, the inherent nature of child soldier recruiting and activity will damage the future educational prospects of not just individual children who were soldiers but also children in the wider region where they fought. Attacks on schools are an efficient way for groups to abduct many children at once. Additionally, many groups specifically target schools and teachers as potential points of resistance to their programs. The result is that formal education completely stops in susceptible regions, often for years, and is difficult to restart once the war is over. In Uganda, for example, more than seventy-five schools were burned down and 215 teachers killed during the LRA rampages—in just one province, in just one year.[65] The same pattern holds in other areas, such as health care and refugees. In Sierra Leone, for example, 62 percent of the rural health units were so destroyed by the war that two years later they were still not functioning.[66] In the LRA regions in Uganda, more than 70 percent of the population (1.2 million) has been driven into refugee camps, with tens of thousands more children "night commuting" (they sleep in protected towns to avoid recruiting and abduction raids in the rural areas at night).[67] Thus, future life prospects are dimmed not only for the children who were fighters but also for their entire generational cohorts.

The final long-term consequence of the use of the child soldier doctrine is how it disrupts children's psychological and moral development. Child soldiering is a form of child abuse, which we do know has potential neurobiological effects on brain development and long-term distress to the child's personality, sometimes leading to antisocial behavior.[68]

The numbers that underlie children's experiences in war illustrate just how devastating the practice can be on the individual level. For example, in one survey of child soldiers in Africa, 77 percent witnessed someone being killed, 63 percent were abducted from home, 52 percent were seriously beaten, 39 percent killed someone else, 39 percent helped abduct other children, 35 percent were sexually abused, 6 percent saw their parents or sibling being killed, and 2 percent had to kill a family member.[69]

Thus, the cumulative involvement of children in the violence of war can be destructive on numerous psychological levels. It desensitizes them to suffering and often eliminates the sense of empathy. This may occur either from witnessing horrible scenes of violence or from having been participants. In either case, the effect is to "harden" their psyches.[70] Their new moral code is dominated by fear of further violence or aggression from those around them. This makes it difficult for them to disengage from the often violent behavioral norms they established as child soldiers.

The modes of their recruitment, transformation, and use in warfare make children not only more likely to commit severe acts of violence during the fighting, but also afterward. The experience can create deep emotional and psychological scarring. "The child's understanding of power may become distorted. Survival becomes equated with aggression, with a sense of control over other people. The social modeling these children received for months or years is one of fear and brutality. The children may still have difficulty facing the consequences of their actions."[71]

Most worrisome is that childhood is the period of identity formation. Childhood is meant to be a period of development that involves interaction with family and establishment of interpersonal networks that enhance children's understanding of their social surroundings and how to act within them. The use of violence during this stage can become a central element of a child's sense of self and even carry over into adulthood, long after any of the original motivations or contexts behind that behavior have disappeared.[72] While the scarring is not necessarily permanent, it certainly creates great difficulties both for the children and their interface with society.

This is complicated by the fact that many former child soldiers find that any return to their pre-recruitment lives is often highly problematic. The modes of recruitment and indoctrination often meant that children were forced to commit atrocities against their own families and communities. Others may have fought on the losing side. In either case, their home communities often consider them beyond redemption. It is very difficult to convince family and community members who witnessed the children taking part in the destruction of their towns and villages that they must now be forgiven.

Thus, gaining back a lost childhood is difficult. The result is a potential mass of disaffected children, often disconnected from society, who have but one viable job skill: killing.

There is no work for me. I have few skills except using a gun and it's easy money . . . I used to be FRELIMO [the government army], then joined RENAMO [the rebel army], then joined FRELIMO. I have played war for both. Now I work for myself and my group. . . . We try not to kill people, but accidents can happen during confusion.

> —A., age nineteen (describing his turn to crime in postwar Mozambique, years after his military service)[73]

These tendencies toward further violence contribute to the difficulty that many countries—and outside peacekeeping forces—face in post-conflict situations, particularly when trying to integrate formerly hostile groups into a united society. One former British peacekeeper described it as a "nightmare scenario." His unit found it nearly impossible to try to keep order in such situations, surrounded by "savage little hooligans with no sense of right or wrong or value for life . . . armed with high velocity rifles and . . . normally high as kites on cannabis, cocaine, or palm wine—usually all three."[74]

Thus, even after the initial conflict ends, the use of child soldiers can haunt societies for generations to come. Although child fighters are far from the only ones who are afflicted as a result of their experiences in war, they suffer the most and have the least capacity to recover. "Reviled by their families and communities, traumatised by the memories of the atrocities they committed, thousands of former child soldiers . . . are being left to their own devices. And many complain of being hungry. These are all potential ingredients for a new war."[75]

CHAPTER 7

The New Children of Terror

I will make my body a bomb that will blast the flesh of Zionists, the sons of pigs and monkeys. I will tear their bodies into little pieces and cause them more pain than they will ever know.
—A., age eleven[1]

Terrorism, it is said, is the "weapon of the weak." Thus, it should be no surprise that children also participate in this dark domain of modern warfare. As on the world's battlefields, children are increasingly present in terrorist groups. Many of these groups have long had youth wings to provide broader support in the populace, but now these youths are being used in actual operations to strike at targets behind the battle lines. This is for the same fundamental reasons that children serve now on the battlefields: they offer terrorist group leaders cheap and easy recruits, and provide new options to strike at their foes.

With the United States now involved in a global war on terrorism, children's role in this aspect of war should take on added importance to Americans. Captured al Qaeda training videos reveal young boys receiving instruction in the manufacture of bombs and the setting of explosive booby traps. The result is that at least six young boys between the ages of thirteen and sixteen have been captured by U.S. forces in the war on terrorism.[2] They were housed in a special wing of the detainee facility at Guantánamo Bay, Cuba, called "Camp Iguana."[3] In addition, several more in the sixteen-to-eighteen-year range are thought to be held in the regular facility for adult detainees at Camp X-Ray.

Perhaps the most disturbing aspect of contemporary terrorism is the growth in suicide bombing over the last few years, particularly emanating from the Middle East. Here, too, children are present. Radical Islamic groups like Palestinian Islamic Jihad and Hamas have recruited children as young as thirteen to be suicide bombers and children as young as eleven to smuggle explosives and weapons. At least twenty-nine suicide-bombing attacks have been carried out by youths since the fighting between the Israelis and Palestinians sparked up again in 2000.[4] Perhaps the most tragic example was a semi-retarded sixteen-year-old whom Hamas convinced to strap himself with explosives. He was caught by Israeli police in the town of Nablus just before he was to blow himself up at a checkpoint.[5]

But Palestine is not the only locale in the Middle East to see this practice emerge. In Morocco, thirteen-year-old twin sisters, who had been recruited by al Qaeda–linked groups, were caught in summer 2003. They were in the process of trying to suicide-bomb a Western business and local government building.[6] Likewise, U.S. Army intelligence reports claimed that in late summer 2003, the insurgent forces in Iraq began to copy this tactic and give young children explosive vests to suicide-bomb coalition forces.[7]

It is important to note, though, that neither terrorism nor children's roles in it are a uniquely Muslim phenomenon. Just as there are a variety of terrorist groups across the world whose members represent nearly all religions, so, too, is there a broader set of terrorist groups that seek to mobilize children. For example, the Real IRA, a coalition of dissident IRA terrorists in Northern Ireland, began to recruit boys in the fourteen to sixteen-year-old range in the late 1990s.[8] The youngest reported terrorist was a nine-year-old boy who was sent by the ELN in Colombia to bomb a polling station in 1997 (a ten-year-old was later used by the FARC to bomb a military checkpoint in 2003).[9] Likewise, when Muslim terrorist groups began to use child suicide bombers, they were not actually breaking any new ground. Instead, they were following the lead of the Tamil LTTE in Sri Lanka, which has consistently been one of the most innovative terrorist groups. The LTTE, which has utilized suicide bombers to kill both the Indian prime minister and the Sri Lankan president, is a master at the technique. It even has manufactured specialized denim jackets designed to conceal explosives. Some are even tailored in smaller sizes for child suicide bombers.[10]

Why Terrorists Recruit Children

Terrorist groups choose to utilize children for reasons that mimic those of rebel groups. Children are a relatively low cost way to build their forces, as their youth brings certain distinct advantages to operations.

The thinking behind using children may have both tactical and strategic rationale. For example, the Real IRA began to pull in children at the low point of its recruiting efforts in the late 1990s. The group faced opposition from other competing Irish nationalist groups and thus had a strategic rationale to expand its recruiting base. Additionally, many of its activists were also well known to the British authorities. The recruitment of young "clean skins" (as they were called by British intelligence) was thus an operational response by the group as well. These boys had no police or intelligence records and allowed the group to raise its membership numbers with less fear of infiltration.[11]

Similarly, two factors have led Palestinian groups to use children during the intifada. The first was strategic, in that having children take part in the violence (whether it be burning tires or throwing Molotov cocktails) was a way to attract the television cameras needed to keep the Palestinian cause on the world's screens. The second was tactical. Israeli troops had a standing order not to shoot live ammunition against children under the age of twelve. So Palestinian gunmen began to work in tandem with the children, using their efforts to draw out Israeli troops, as well as provide a screen for their sniping.[12]

This same rationale also holds for why groups recruit children for suicide bombing. Suicide bombing is an efficient method for weaker forces to strike at an otherwise well-prepared opposition. Even if they lack the technology for guided missiles or other "smart bombs," the inclusion of the human element allows groups to create a thinking bomb that can adjust to changing circumstances. As one leader of Hamas commented, "We do not have tanks or rockets, but we have something superior—our exploding Islamic human bombs. In place of a nuclear arsenal, we are proud of our arsenal of believers."[13]

By the standards of typical costs of guided weaponry, the human bomb is also stunningly cheap. All that is needed to make an effective bomb suit for the terrorist is a nine-volt battery, a light switch, a short cable, mercury (readily obtainable from thermometers), acetone, gunpowder, and some form of homemade shrapnel such as nails or screws. Palestinian experts note that the total cost of a typical operation is about $150, with the most expensive part often being the bus fare to get the bomber in place. Add in a young terrorist and the bomb is then able to kill or wound all individuals within a twenty-five- to fifty-meter (80 to 164 feet) radius.[14]

The suicide bomb also is an effective attempt to step around or wear down the common means of defense. Deterrence plans fail, as the terrorist doesn't care about the consequences. Likewise, guards have greater difficulties in screening, particularly if the terrorist is willing to die and take the guard with him. By including children among the set of potential attackers, the scope of defenses must be even wider. As the mother of one suicide bomber in Palestine commented, "This is a girl who would never appear on a wanted list. She sat at home. She was not active in anything political. [Israeli president Ariel] Sharon can chase all the ones he says organize these operations, but he cannot chase away the will of young people to carry out these things."[15]

Thus there is an additional, distinctly psychological element to using child terrorists. The use of suicide bombers spreads wider fear than conventional terrorism. It presents the image of an unbending foe who will seek victory at any cost, including its own destruction. A child in this role heightens the hysteria terrorists seek to cause. To put it another way, if even children are a potential threat, then everyone is.

Why Children Join Terrorists

While it is easy to see why terrorist group leaders would see the appeal of children as operatives, *why* children would join terrorist groups, and be willing to sacrifice their lives in suicide bomb attacks, is more complex. The information is far from complete, and certainly varies by case. There are, however, some common threads that lead children into this pernicious form of violence. As with conventional child soldiers, many of these factors center on the combination of youth's inherent susceptibility to powerful influences and the harsh environments which can shape them.

The first factor that might lead children to join terrorist groups is the potential of religious motivation. While most religions are decidedly against suicide, they also tend to laud the concept of martyrdom, dying for one's faith. This is particularly so in Islam, where the concept of jihad, a personal battle to improve one's faith, has often been expanded by radicals to declare holy wars against other nonbelievers. Radical leaders frequently cite passages from the Koran that claim a *shaheed,* or martyr, will be immediately forgiven all his sins and even be married to seventy-two beautiful virgins in paradise. Additionally, martyrs are given the ability to admit seventy relatives to paradise, perhaps adding an element of motivation for family support of the faithful. For children who have known nothing but poverty and hopelessness, such visions for the future are highly enticing. As one Palestinian psychiatrist in Gaza noted, an important factor in suicide bombers is their sense of frustration with their surroundings, connected to the desire to go to heaven.[16]

However, it is noteworthy that the groups that use suicide attacks are by no means only radical, religiously motivated. As the appeal of the operations grew in Palestine, for example, Fatah and the Popular Front for the Liberation of Palestine, which were both highly secular militant groups, adopted the tactics.[17]

There is also the potential of economic motivations. While the majority of terrorist group leaders, such as Osama bin Laden of al Qaeda and Carlos Castaño of the AUC, come from relatively privileged backgrounds, they often target the youngest and the very poorest for their foot soldiers.[18] As one extremist leader in Pakistan explicitly notes, "We want their children."[19] The head of Laskar Jihad in Indonesia admits that he even likes to recruit "children as young as eight" to train in terrorist and suicide operations.[20]

The financial inducements that these groups are able to offer vary. One particularly powerful element for children is rewards that flow to the family. In this recruitment tactic, a group is able to promise poor youngsters that their family will be better taken care of in their absence. In Palestine, for example, suicide bombers' families were offered up to $25,000 from the Iraqi government of Saddam Hussein and by private Saudi donors to the "Martyr's Fund." The rate from Hamas was about $5,000, along with such staples as flour, sugar, and clothing.[21] Other groups, such as the LTTE in Sri Lanka and the Jamiat Islami in Pakistan, move young suicide bombers' families into nicer homes or provide them with first access to better jobs. Thus, their sacrifice is painted to the children as a means to be selfless and raise their family's lot in life. To do otherwise, then, when there are no better options, can be spun as an act of selfishness on the child's part.[22] These offers particularly resound with children growing up in conflict zones and refugee camps, who can visualize no other way to help their families out of their fate.

The institutions that a child interacts with, most particularly educational, might also play a role. In a number of areas, militant groups run schools that are then used as recruiting and training grounds for future terrorists. For example, LTTE-run orphanages in Sri Lanka even have shrines set up to honor suicide bombers.[23] In the border regions of Pakistan, approximately 15 percent of madrassahs provide some sort of training that prepares children for militant groups.[24] In the occupied territories of Palestine, Hamas has set up a series of schools that are highly politicized, even down to the pre-school level. The walls in these schools are labeled with posters such as "The children of the kindergarten are the *shaheeds* of tomorrow"; similarly, classes teach hatred along with reading skills.[25] As one Hamas leader, Sheikh Hasan Yusuf in Ramallah, commented of the bombers his group had trained, "We like to grow them from kindergarten through college."[26] One of his opponents, a leader in Shin Bet, the Israeli secret police, concurred. "You don't start educating a *shaheed* at age 22. You start at kindergarten, so by the time he's 22, he's looking for an opportunity to sacrifice his life."[27]

QUESTION: *What do you feel when you pray [for the souls of the martyrs]?*

SABRI: *I feel the martyr is lucky because the angels usher him to his wedding in heaven. . . .*

QUESTION: *Is it different when the martyr is a child?*

SABRI: *Yes, it is. It's hard to express it in words. There is no doubt that a child [martyr] suggests that the new generation will carry on the mission with determination. The younger the martyr—the greater and the more I respect him. . . .*

QUESTION: *Is this why the mothers cry with joy when they hear about their sons' death?*

SABRI: *They willingly sacrifice their offspring for the sake of freedom. It is a great display of the power of belief. The mother is participating in the great reward of the Jihad to liberate Al-Aqsa.*

—SHEIKH IKRIMI SABRI, the mufti of Jerusalem, appointed by the Palestinian Authority [28]

Other related institutions with which children have a deep contact can also motivate. For example, the Palestinian Authority ran a series of summer camps in 2000 that had a distinctly violent aspect. More than 25,000 campers learned everything from infiltration techniques and assembling AK-47s to the art of ambushing units and kidnapping leaders.[29]

Social motivations may also play a powerful role in inducing children to join these groups, often with their parents' approval. It is no coincidence that the majority of suicide bombings take place in what anthropologists call "shame societies." In such settings, young people are taught from birth that the acquisition of honor and avoidance of shame are the critical motivators of behavior. These beliefs take on an added power in settings that entail humiliation and subservience. Any act of retaliation, even one that has no realistic chance of recompense, can still be interpreted as heroic and cancels out the shame. Violence thus becomes as what psychiatrist Franz Fanon described as a "cleansing force," which releases youth to become fearless in their actions and use bloodshed to drive out their feelings of "inferiority," "despair," or "inaction."[30]

This can take place at the level of the individual or family unit or at the greater societal level. For example, most believe that the young fifteen-year-old al Qaeda member who killed an American medic in Afghanistan was brought into the realm of terrorism by his family. Not only was his father a noted terrorist financier, but his two older brothers were also members of the organization. As one cleric who knew the family while they were in Canada noted, "Ahmed Khadr made his boys into his own image—a fanatic driven by hate for the West and wrong ideas of Islam."[31]

> *My parents encouraged me to come here* [to Najaf, site of battle against U.S. forces in summer 2004]. *I would prefer to live and taste victory, but if not my death will be rewarded with spiritual gifts in heaven.* —M., age fourteen[32]

Palestinian society may be the best current example of how this individual-level phenomenon can build up to a broader national-level concern. In Gaza City, the heartland of Hamas, some 1.3 million refugees live in a 140-square-mile enclave of semi-permanent shelters; 70 percent are unemployed and 80 percent live in abject poverty.[33] Thus, the Israeli occupation, with its treatment of two generations of Palestinians as second-class refugees, followed by the near-complete decimation of Palestinian civil society in the violence over the last decade, has arguably backfired. Rather than a cowed Palestinian populace, its result has instead been broad youth rage expressing itself through the violence of the intifada and suicide bombers. Participating in violence has given many youths a sense of mission and control over their lives that they otherwise lacked while growing up in squalid, seemingly permanent refugee camps.[34] As one Hamas leader notes, he finds no shortage of willing recruits for suicide operations from this pool. "Our biggest problem is the hordes of young men who beat on our doors, clamoring to be sent. It is difficult to select only a few. Those whom we turn away return again and again, pestering us, pleading to be accepted."[35]

These social motivations can also be directed through the family. Some groups, such as the LTTE in Sri Lanka and the Jamiat Islami in

Pakistan, give young suicide bombers' families special recognition and honors in the community. Hamas in Palestine even celebrates the child's "martyrdom" with festivities, treating the event as if it were a wedding. The death notice will take the form of a wedding announcement in the newspaper.[36] Hundreds of guests congregate at the family's house to offer congratulations. Sweet desserts and juices that the youth outlined in his will are served. These joyful scenes and the idea that they might achieve similar renown in their home village resonate to other potential recruits and their families. Many parents whose children have died in the operations take it as a point of pride. Mothers have been seen to dance with joy at the occasion.[37] In turn, those parents who demur from providing their children can expect anything ranging from low-level harassment to condemnation in the local newspaper.[38]

> *Everyone treats me with more respect now that I have a martyred son. And when there is a martyr in the village, it encourages more children to join the jihad. It raises the spirit of the entire village.*
> —H., Kashmiri father[39]

The broader social environment can also help construct children's identity in ways intended to reinforce these tendencies. For instance, if martyrdom is taught as being a good and honorable deed on national TV, then it is more likely to become an unfortunate part of a national consciousness. For example, Palestinian television once even had a *Sesame Street*–like television program called the *Children's Club*. With its puppet shows, songs, and a Mickey Mouse character, the show definitively had a children's audience in mind. However, the substance of it was very adult and pernicious, celebrating violence. Its shows even included children's songs with such lyrics as "When I wander into Jerusalem, I will become a suicide bomber."[40]

Likewise, many worry about the effect that the repeated images of civilian casualties in Iraq will have in the Islamic world. The concern is that repeated airings of civilian casualties in the Arab media will motivate Arab youngsters to join groups like al Qaeda that target the United

---

The Songs of the *Children's Club*

I finished practicing on the submachine gun of return.
I trained my friends from among the children and the youths,
We swore to take vengeful blood from our enemies for our killed
  and wounded.

When I wander into the entrance of Jerusalem I'll turn into a
  martyr warrior,
In Battledress! In Battledress! In Battledress!
Thank you. Bravo, bravo, bravo.

On your life, I foresee my death and I rush towards it,
On your life, this is the death of a hero
and he who seeks the death of a martyr warrior this it
and I how I suffer the chains of the Jews.

The youth will be victorious
The youth will be victorious
We are ready with our guns
We are ready with our guns
Revolution until Victory
Revolution until Victory.[41]

States. As one seventeen-year-old in Syria noted of his response, "I was watching what was happening and I found myself cursing for the first time in my life. I felt I wanted to kill, not only curse."[42]

As explored in Chapter 4, these influences of society, family, and so on may not be the only environmental factors that are sufficient to lead a child into terrorist activity or its support. Further personal experiences might play a role. These include the loss of a relative or friend, or some other form of direct suffering from violence. A common experience is jailing or brutalization from local security forces. Rather than deterring the kids from radicalization, it often tends to place them under the influence of the leaders of the radical groups while in custody. Such children then want to use violence even more when they get out and are better prepared to do so.

It is important to note that while all these factors may provide an explanation for why children might join a terrorist group, they do not combine to offer any sort of justification. Terrorism is typically a highly communitarian, unspontaneous enterprise. The suicide bomber is, as terrorism expert Walter Laquer describes, "only the last link in the chain."[43] Few terrorist instances, and no suicide bombings to date, are the result of freelancing individuals. Instead, most are the result of careful planning by groups that recruit, indoctrinate, and train specifically for the purpose of killing defenseless civilians. In some cases, these groups are doing so with children in mind as both perpetrators and potential victims, making their actions even more distasteful.

Thus, while the motivations may vary by individual recruit, the underlying success of any effort by terrorist groups to recruit children is dependent on their having a recruiting pool at hand. This pool is shaped by both its environment and the permissiveness that society may or may not give to the group to access it. When children are disillusioned, humiliated, lack proper schooling, and see themselves with no viable future, they are more likely to take refuge in radicalism. For many, then, even killing themselves becomes interpreted as relief from a present life that they see as intolerable. In turn, society's willingness to sacrifice their youth may be generated by external political actions, such as an occupation, or by internal societal causes, such as an ethic of revenge.

In either case, the outcome is that children bear the costs of society's failures. It is particularly disturbing that an increasing number of radical Muslim clerics preach that Islam permits suicide bombings and that the child bombers are martyrs to be lauded. Their view is that Islam may forbid suicide, but that these cases are different because of the adversary. As one cleric in Kashmir put it, "If Jihad is undertaken according to the strict interpretations of the Koran, suicide missions can be allowed if they offer military or strategic advantage to the Muslim army."[44] Such individuals are then described as not taking their own lives, but rather as sacrificing themselves for the good of the community. These are highly controversial assertions—and, many respected Muslim clerics and scholars would argue, lack any merit in religious texts.[45] However, in the present context, such beliefs often go unchallenged and popular support for the practice is especially high among Muslim populations that see no other options available to them. For example, more than 70 percent of Palestinians approve of suicide bombings.[46]

That this practice is tolerated, let alone celebrated, is a terrible indictment of political and religious leaders in the region. As one Arab journalist put it, "What kind of independence is built on the blood of children while the leaders are safe and so are their children and grand-children? Are only the miserable destined to die in the spring of their lives? Those children who are killed may not, in their short lives, have enjoyed a fresh piece of bread, sleeping in a warm bed, the happiness of putting on a new piece of clothes, or carrying books with no torn pages to school."[47]

Training and Action

The training of children in terrorist actions varies as much as the techniques for recruitment. Indeed, the process is undergoing constant refinement.

It begins with the selection of children. In addition to their intelligence and enthusiasm, appearance in relation to potential targets is highly important. The ability to blend in or otherwise not raise suspicions among security forces allows the attackers to get closer to their targets. Thus, groups are careful to keep this in mind in selecting their operatives. For example, the LTTE uses cute young girls who are less likely to look suspect, while Palestinian Islamic Jihad often selects those who can pass for Israeli Jews.[48]

Once selected, the terrorist goes through an intense period of mental preparation. For suicide bombers, this often takes place in small cells made up of a training leader and two or three candidate bombers. This compartmentalization not only makes it harder for security forces to crack the organization, but also increases the intimacy and hold of the leader over the new recruits.[49] The cells are often named for resounding events or subjects, to increase their impact on motivation. Hamas suicide bombing cells, for instance, are usually given a name taken from a Koranic text or resonating event in Islamic history. There is also the use of pledges among the new members. For example, some radical Islamic groups pledge the *bayt al ridwan* (named after the garden in Paradise), which seeks to lock the group further together in a shared fate.

The training also often includes the concentrated study of texts that reinforce the notion of sacrifice, as well as tasks of memorization and visualization. Other indoctrination strategies include carrying out reenactments of past successful operations. Repetition is used to drive points home. A focus is also made on the ease of death. Its pleasures are extolled in contrast to a future life of sadness, sickness, and continued humiliation. Hamas, for example, even has its recruits lie in empty graves, in order to see how "peaceful" death will be. In turn, LTTE survivors tell of training drills in which they would rehearse what they would do if captured or wounded. Their coaches instructed them on how to bite into the cyanide capsules that they would wear in necklaces during operations. As one fourteen-year-old trainee tells, "It mixes with our blood, and within one second, we die."[50]

Rather than sadness at their coming fate, potential suicide bombers often describe this training and indoctrination as a period of great anticipation and happiness at their selection. As one young member of Hamas (who woke up from a coma a month after his attack) describes, "We were in a constant state of worship. We told each other that if the Israelis only knew how joyful we were they would whip us to death! Those were the happiest days of my life."[51] Trainers reinforce these feelings by extolling the coming triumph and celebration at their success. The candidates are even referred to by new honored titles, such as *al shaheed al hayy* (the living martyr), that afford them special status.

The final hours are often spent praying and making wills or farewell messages that are recorded on video or audiocassettes. These farewell videos and tapes not only are used for future recruiting, but also help make it harder for the bombers to back out, and thus risk public humiliation.[52] In the LTTE, young suicide bombers are given the honor of spending their last meal in camp with the leader of the Tigers.[53]

Once trained and indoctrinated, the terrorists are sent into action. Again, the intersection of the group's needs and the target's responses determine their use. Some operations may be highly targeted, such as the LTTE strategy of aiming at individual leaders, and thus require complex planning. They may even involve layers of infiltration to get bombers as close to their targets as possible. Other operations, whose intent is simply to strike wider fear in the opposition's public, may be aimed at collateral damage and thus less tightly designed. Hamas, for example, has a more ad hoc approach and typically lets the bomber choose the target. As one trainer describes, "We told them, 'Blow yourselves up any place where there are people.' They went wherever they knew to go."[54] These might include buses or former workplaces.

After the operation is carried out, groups are usually quick to claim credit. This is both an achievement of their wider goals to spread fear and an aid in their recruiting strategy. For example, Hamas and Palestinian Islamic Jihad typically notify the local media right after attacks and distribute copies of their attacker's final video or audio message. This is followed up by extolling the action in local organizations affiliated with the group, such as mosques or schools. These groups also might praise the heroism of the youth through posted leaflets and graffiti (usually depicting the bomber in paradise under a flock of green birds—referring to a belief that the soul of a martyr is carried to Allah upon the wings of a green bird of paradise). Calendars are even distributed that have illustrations of the "martyr of the month."

Conclusions

While there are multiple reasons for children to become involved in terrorist groups, none are simply coincidental or beyond the control of the groups themselves. Instead, they are usually the result of the combination of a harsh environment that leaves children with no good choices and a deliberate mobilization strategy by the group to pull children into terrorism. Sometimes this process is enabled by the parents' approval. This may be the saddest aspect of children's involvement in such groups. When a parent wishes that a child grow up to be a suicide bomber instead of a doctor or teacher and live to an old age, something is indeed wrong.

Chapter 8 will deal further with potential responses to deter and diminish the use of children by militant groups in general, but there are a few particular aspects in responding to the use of children as terrorists.

In attempting to defeat this practice, the key is to affect both the recruiting pool and the groups' willingness and ability to access it. A focus should be made on the underlying problem of hopelessness that often leads children (and/or their parents) to believe that they have no better future than involvement in terrorism and a likely early death. An essential problem to deal with is the surroundings of violence, humiliation, and lack of opportunity that underlie this desperation. As Charles Stith, the former U.S. ambassador to Tanzania (who served in the wake of the 1998 al Qaeda attack there), notes, "People who have hope tend not to be inclined to strap 100 pounds of explosives on their bodies and go into a crowd and blow themselves up."[55]

Many counter such claims by asserting that terrorism is an affair of the well-off elite from rich, stable countries; they usually point to those who perpetrated the 9/11 attacks as evidence. However, in doing so, they focus on the leadership (Osama bin Laden or Mohamed Atta) rather than the membership of the wider organization and the troops who make the operations possible. For instance, if we look at all of those who seized the planes on 9/11, prosperity was not one of their hallmarks. Indeed, a number of the hijackers were *alghamdi*—a name that indicates that they did not even have a respectable tribal origin, and thus were accorded a low social status in their countries. Equally, all came from countries with growing poverty and steeply declining standards of living, and had lessened job prospects. Moreover, while 9/11 shapes most Americans' understanding of terrorism, it does represent the whole.

Focusing solely on the leadership of terrorist organizations also misses the larger socioeconomic context of radicalism and terrorism, as well as how and where terrorists thrive. Successful terrorist groups are based in and thrive in zones of chaos, poor governance, and lawlessness. Indeed, it is the context that surrounds, nurtures, and protects a movement like al Qaeda that makes it such a magnified and continuing threat compared to a group like Baader-Meinhof or the Oklahoma City bombers that withered on the vine. Likewise, effective extremist groups rely on a division of labor between young and uneducated "foot soldiers" and ideologically trained and well-funded elite operatives.[56] Al Qaeda's use of this structure was further illustrated by the 2003 Morocco bombings. The operatives in these attacks were young men, some as young as seventeen, who were recruited from local slums. In short, elites certainly play a role in terrorism, but it is a broader, communal affair.

Two particular issues must then be resolved to undercut the present terrorist threat. The first is to affect the context. The seemingly permanent status of conflict and its dispossessed refugees in a number of war zones (including Israel-Palestine and Kashmir) is an obvious driving force behind children's participation in violence. This is heightened by failing educational systems and economic stagnation that hold back the realization of human potential across many regions. As Fadl Abu Hein, a psychology lecturer from Gaza, notes, "Martyrdom has become an ambition for our children. If they had a proper education in a normal environment, they won't have looked for a value in death."[57]

The second facet is to begin to undercut the institutions that assist terrorist groups in the mobilization and recruitment of children. Possible responses range from enlisting moderate religious leaders to speak out against the use of children, specifically by noting that the involvement of children in terrorism is counter to the true intent of religious texts, including the Koran, to establishing campaigns designed to reverse the social and economic rewards that accrue. Shutting down payment plans and punishing families for the actions of their children are other strategies. The overall key is to weaken the high regard that such terrorists are often given by society.

Finally, the cost-benefit analysis of terrorist groups must be altered. Presently, the downside for groups to use children is minimal. They have created a context in which neither local nor international support has been harmed by such a decision. Those that use children must be convinced that it is no longer in their best interest. When the institutions that influence children are controlled by groups that can be identified, such as the Palestinian Authority media, which extolled attacks by children, costs must be extracted. The programs must not only be shut down, but the group should also be made to fear the loss of something it values more, such as recognition by and interaction with international authorities. The ultimate intent of the pressure is to force the group into the realization that recruiting and using children for violence is not just an illegal and immoral strategy, but also a detraction from its long-term goals.

PART III

Responding to the Child Soldier Problem

Preventing Child Soldiers

It's a good start to write documents and stuff, but it's time to stop
theorising and start doing work to end this.

—I., age thirteen[1]

The use of children as soldiers raises both the frequency and savageness of conflict. It makes conflicts easier to start, tougher to end, and more likely to recur. Even worse, the trend appears set only to magnify in the coming years. What, then, is to be done in response—before, during, and in the aftermath of children's use as soldiers?

This chapter will look at potential ways to prevent and deter the practice of using child soldiers. In order to be effective, any effort against their use must seek to understand the doctrine behind it and see it for what it is. Child soldiering stems from a set of deliberate choices and strategies designed by leaders to gain from using children in war. By understanding the causes, as well as the resulting dynamics, more nuanced strategies can then be developed that attack the doctrine at its very heart.

Good Deeds Regardless

At the global level, the underlying causes behind the rise of child soldiers include such overarching problems as world poverty, the lack of economic and educational opportunity for many of the world's youth, and the spread of war and disease. There are powerful reasons for tackling these problems, regardless of the presence of child soldiers. However, their effect in pushing children into the realm of war makes serious action all the more important. Indeed, advocates working in these areas should contemplate linking their calls for action, now based exclusively on moral concerns, to the broader security concerns yielded by child soldiers. This will help them to make a more effective case.

To deal with all the varied issues of global distress requires both greater amounts of aid aimed at sustainable development and more effective and efficient responses by the recipients. The United States lags far behind the rest of the developed world in its aid to those less well off. It spends a far lower percentage of its budget on foreign aid relative to other prosperous states. Indeed, it gives the lowest in terms of the percentage of its national GDP of any industrialized country. Among the donors, the United States also has the worst record for spending its aid budget on itself; 70 percent of American aid is spent on U.S. goods and services. Finally, much of this aid is also directed at a limited number of strategic allies who are middle-income states, such as Israel, Russia, and Egypt, rather than to the worst-off areas of the world.[2] When aid does go to conflict zones, it often follows the headlines, rather than seeking any sort of balance. For example, sufferers from the war in Bosnia received an average $238 in aid per person. At the same time, the Democratic Republic of the Congo (DRC) was suffering from a far more traumatic (over three million more died in the DRC than Bosnia) but lesser covered civil war/humanitarian crisis. It received only $3 in aid per person.[3]

The result is that a number of critical global needs get short shrift from the U.S. government. For example, AIDS is a grave threat that threatens to kill tens of millions over the next decade and undermine entire societies. It also cannot be beaten back on the cheap. Estimates are that an annual war chest between $7 billion and $10 billion is needed to fight its global spread, primarily to fund prevention programs around the world. Yet the international community is nowhere near that goal. Despite all the rhetoric, the U.S. government's response has been insufficient, so far pledging under the Bush administration just around $500 million a year in actual funds to the battle.[4] Similar low levels encompass such issues as support for education, refugees, and other aid to communities in need. Pertinent to child soldiers, it wasn't until 2003 that the U.S. government made a dedicated effort toward this issue. Following a gala two-day self-promoting launch event held at a Washington, D.C. hotel ballroom, the Department of Labor helped fund a $13 million initiative along with the International Labor Organization, primarily targeting child soldier recruitment and rehabilitation in the DRC.[5] It is better than nothing, but clearly insufficient to the global task ahead.

On the opposite side of the equation, it is equally appalling that the vast majority of developing states still spend far higher percentages of their national incomes on their (usually ineffective) militaries than on their own people's critical needs in education and health. Many of these funds could be shifted toward the next generation of children and make a far greater difference in alleviating their social and economic problems.[6] Donors should make this a condition of their aid grants.

Another global initiative that mandates action is dealing with the proliferation of small arms. A far more prudent strategy must be developed to help dampen the global spread of cheap and deadly weapons.

Here, too, though, the Bush administration is out of step with international consensus.[7] While the international community has worked to clamp down on the *illegal* trade in light weapons, in recent years the United States worked at the opposite end. The saddest illustration of this was at the 2001 UN Conference on the Illicit Trade in Small Arms. Following intense lobbying by the National Rifle Association (NRA) leadership, the U.S. worked to counter any efforts to make international small arms sales more transparent (one doubts whether the group's core members, who are hunters and sportsmen, would be pleased to support the spread of AK-47s to children abducted by warlords).[8]

The administration and NRA lobbyists (the U.S. delegation even had NRA board member Bob Barr attending the UN conference) have conflated domestic gun control issues with those of international relations. This is completely inappropriate, as none of these global efforts would have had any effect in limiting U.S. citizens' constitutional right to legally own arms and serve in state militias, as laid out in the Second Amendment. Instead, these global efforts would have made the sale of machine guns and rockets to non-state actors, such as rebel and terrorist groups that arm children, more difficult. That the United States was joined only by China and the Arab League in this effort should have set off alarms to reassess this odd position.

In addition to helping make the international weapons trade more transparent and aboveboard, the United States and international community should make greater efforts to support (with both funding and technical assistance) local initiatives that seek to control or reverse small arms proliferation. One example is the setup of weapons collection programs in post-conflict states and those at risk of conflict. Such pilot programs have been fairly successful in Albania and El Salvador and could work elsewhere.[9]

However, problems of global development and violence are broader issues that merit their own library's worth of study. The issue of child soldiers warrants action along a number of more specific lines as well. In particular, the norms against child soldiering have been proven to be insufficient. While most efforts have focused on raising awareness of child soldier issues and bolstering the laws against it, they have yet to make a real dent against the popularity of the doctrine. Stigmatization of those groups that utilize children in this manner must be backed up with real punishments that change their leaders' calculations.

Talk Is Cheap

Recently, in the academic literature that studies international relations, many experts have written about the importance of beliefs about right and wrong in shaping policy. They claim that beliefs shape actions, even when they go against one's interests.[10] Such socially directed behavior is described as being guided by a "norm," or what anthropologist Paul Bohannan describes as "a rule, more or less overt, which expresses 'ought' aspects of relationships between human beings."[11]

This research about the power of beliefs extends into the military realm. Many have argued that "norms" about what is proper and improper behavior on the battlefield still matter today. They argue, for instance, that norms have limited the use of certain weapons that many states might find advantageous, but are horrific in consequences. Two examples are chemical and biological attacks, which might have been quite useful in recent wars, but were considered so horrible in World War I that the vast majority of nations have since held back. Most recently, activists have tried to harness this type of thinking by advocating the outlawing of such weapons as the anti-personnel land mine.[12]

The word "norm" can have two meanings, though. It can describe ethical beliefs about what is right behavior, but it can also describe the standard or most common practices of behavior, irrespective of ethics.[13] Thus, while people writing about norms in international relations have focused on the positives of how ethics direct people toward good behavior in warfare, they have ignored the second aspect. Little has been written about the darker side of social behavior in warfare, the buildup of new beliefs and most common practices. These new standards prescribe malicious behavior instead.

As discussed in Chapter 1, the past decades of warfare have seen the breakdown of moral codes that guided behavior in war. This has led to increasing savagery toward the innocents in war, ranging from civilians in general to children in specific. Yet little of the new literature on norms deals with what to do about it. Likewise, the role of non-state actors in developing norms that direct common practice has also been incorrectly assumed by most analysts to be only positive.[14] Being apart from the state is no guarantee of good behavior. For every positive non-state actor, such as the global campaign to eliminate land mines, there has been a non-state one that lacks a moral core, such as the Lord's Resistance Army that abducts and enslaves children.

As explored in Chapter 3, the most basic ethical injunctions against using children in war collapsed in a rapid fashion. Their failure was influenced primarily by technological and geopolitical changes, with the result that children are now regular actors on the battlefield. This indicates that the durability of ethical norms in the face of external forces is far less powerful than believed. If ethical norms are not self-sustainable, their power is limited. It also reinforces the argument that, while common behavioral practices are often grounded in moral principles, their strength is influenced by the very real contextual factors of their environment that determine their efficiency, risk, and reward.[15]

This weakening of constraints may be particularly strong for non-state armed groups; for them, moral norms are less likely to shape their interests. This is much in line with the camp of "realist" thinkers in the international relations literature, who feel that beliefs have no great role in politics. Instead, they believe that actions are always best explained by power and interests. However, there is one important caveat to this sort of argument. The irony is that, while the rise of norms may be due to the power and interests of the strongest actors in the system (whom the realists exclusively focus on), the normative breakdown in this case was due to the innovations of some of the weakest actors in the international system. In fact, it was because of their very weakness that such groups chose to violate the old norms against using children. Much like the way terrorist groups have brought back the possibility of chemical and biological weapons actually being used, so, too, with child soldiers have the weaker parties set a new standard of behavior in contemporary warfare.

Lost Norms and Child Soldiers

Regardless of where one falls in the debate over the influence of norms, there is no doubt that the practice of using child soldiers violates widely accepted international beliefs about proper behavior. The human rights abuses involved, which range from abduction and rape to torture and murder, shock the conscience. Moreover, they violate the most elementary principles of international humanitarian law. Hence, the challenge is to turn the international consensus against the use of children as soldiers into action; in a sense return a failing norm—the old belief that children had no place on the battlefield—to a reality.

The practice of the last four millennia of warfare, in and of itself, makes a strong case for customary international law's proscription against child soldiers. Furthermore, the twentieth century saw a range of treaties emerge that codified international law's standing against the use of children in combat. These include:

- 1924 League of Nations Declaration of the Rights of the Child;
- 1948 United Nations Universal Declaration of Human Rights;
- 1949 Geneva Conventions;
- 1950 European Convention on Human Rights;
- 1951 Convention and 1967 Protocol Relating to the Status of Refugees;
- 1966 UN Covenants on Civil and Political Rights and Economic, Social and Cultural Rights;
- 1969 American Convention on Human Rights;
- 1977 Additional Protocols to the 1949 Geneva Conventions;
- 1981 African Charter on Human and Peoples' Rights;
- 1984 Convention Against Torture and Other Cruel, Inhuman or Degrading Treatment or Punishment;
- 1989 UN Convention on the Rights of the Child;
- 1990 OAU African Charter on the Rights and Welfare of the Child.

Of these, the 1989 Convention on the Rights of the Child was perhaps the most notable, and certainly most representative of global consensus. Indeed, it was the most quickly and widely ratified international treaty ever, with more than 190 state signatories. In its article 38, the convention pushed governments to take all feasible measures to ensure that children have no direct part in hostilities.

Despite this deep body of international law against the practice, the child soldier doctrine spread widely in the 1990s, in all the ways outlined in the previous chapters. The response by the international community, though, was to condemn the practice and codify the use of child soldiers as a specific violation of the law. The United Nations also created an office of the Special Representative of the UN Secretary General for Children in Armed Conflict to investigate and lobby for children's rights in warfare. This position is now held by a former Ugandan diplomat, Olara Otunnu.

The major impetus behind these efforts was a group of concerned nongovernmental organizations (NGOs) from all around the world, united under the umbrella of the Coalition to Stop the Use of Child Soldiers. The coalition was formed in May 1998 by six leading NGOs: Amnesty International, Human Rights Watch, Save the Children–Sweden for the International Save the Children Alliance, Jesuit Refugee Service, the Quaker United Nations Office–Geneva, and International Federation Terre des Hommes. Over the next years it built up a global network of interested NGOs, aid agencies, research institutes, and other linked coalitions that were willing to stand against the use of child soldiers.

A major part of the coalition's strategy was to build a consensus and enact treaties against the practice of child soldiering from the state and regional level first. In this it was quite successful, eventually mobilizing campaigns in more than forty different countries. These efforts resulted in a series of regional agreements that encompass much of the globe, including:

- 1996 OAU Resolution on the Plight of African Children in Situations of Armed Conflicts;
- 1997 The Capetown Principles;
- 1997 Declaration by the Nordic Foreign Ministers Against the Use of Child Soldiers;
- 1998 European Parliament Resolution on Child Soldiers;
- 1999 Berlin Declaration on the Use of Children as Soldiers;
- 1999 Montevideo Declaration on the Use of Children as Soldiers;
- 1999 Maputo Declaration on the Use of Child Soldiers;
- 2000 OAS Resolution on Children and Armed Conflict;
- 2001 Amman Declaration on Child Soldiers.

In its push for international condemnation of the practice, the group met with great success. In 1999 the UN Security Council adopted Resolution 1261, which condemned the targeting of children in armed conflict, including their recruitment and use as soldiers. In 2000 the United Nations General Assembly adopted an Optional Protocol to the Convention on the Rights of the Child, which dealt with the involvement of children in armed conflict (see Appendix). This protocol amended the 1989 treaty significantly, in order to better deal with the child soldier issue. Its major aspects were to raise the age from fifteen to eighteen at which direct participation in armed conflict would be legally permitted (there was some dispute on this among the various treaties), ban compulsory recruitment of any child under eighteen, and explicitly include non-state actors under its coverage. With intense lobbying, the treaty was quickly adopted. By 2003, the treaty had been signed by more than 111 parties and ratified by 50.

Thus, as a result of the efforts of the Coalition to Stop the Use of Child Soldiers and other international actors, the ethical norms against child soldiering have been buttressed by a series of international regimes. The UN special representative, Olara Otunnu, has also made a direct attempt to get conflict groups to stop using children, meeting with rebel group leaders in more than twenty countries to negotiate their end of the practice. In January 2003 the treaty was followed up by UN Resolution 1460, which called on specific child soldier groups in five countries (Afghanistan, Burundi, DRC, Liberia, and Somalia) to halt the practice and provide the Security Council with a report on the steps they have taken.

Ethical norms are clearly important in providing the standards that are intended to guide behavior. Proponents of the legal effort against child soldiering point to five key strengths of this activism: (1) it established an international standard on the employment of child soldiers, (2) codified legal norms, (3) set minimum age requirements that are more difficult to fabricate, (4) encouraged states to implement the laws, and (5) raised public awareness, both in the West and in areas where the child soldier groups were active, potentially empowering greater activism.[16]

However, we should not confound ethical norms with actual behavior or enforcement. Unfortunately, all this international attention and condemnation of child soldiers did not translate into an end of the practice. Throughout the process, the use of child soldiers on an international scale did not diminish, but instead spread still further. Indeed, many of the same countries that signed the various treaties continued to flout their obligations. This is evidenced by the fact that while there are more than one hundred signatories, child soldiers are still present in roughly eighty-five countries. Indeed, some of the largest known users, such as the various child soldier groups fighting in Colombia, Myanmar, and Uganda, were not even on the specific Resolution 1460 list released by the United Nations in early 2003. When the UN Security Council took up the issue in January 2004, child soldiers in these and other conflicts (such as in Chechnya, Nepal, and Sri Lanka) were yet again not on the agenda.

Moreover, few of the rebel groups using child soldiers have been swayed by either the new protocol or by the meetings with Otunnu. The typical pattern is that, after some period of public denial, these groups would make a pledge to stop the use of child soldiers in an effort to garner international goodwill and aid. Their practices would be little altered, though. For example, despite multiple meetings with the United Nations and multiple public pledges to stop over the last decade, the LTTE has continued to conscript children seventeen and under. This continued even after a cease-fire took hold in Sri Lanka in 2003. Indeed, in the six months since the latest LTTE pledge not to use or recruit child soldiers, UNICEF received 1,370 complaints of child soldier recruitment, primarily from parents whose children had gone missing.[17]

Similar discrepancies between pledges made to the United Nations and ensuing practice have occurred with UNITA in Angola, the FARC and ELN in Colombia, ALIR in Rwanda, SPLA in Sudan, the Kamajors in Sierra Leone, Lal Sena in Nepal, the DRC government and its rebel opponents in the DRC, NPA and MILF in the Philippines, and the Taliban in Afghanistan, to name just a few. For instance, one rebel group in the DRC made a pledge not to use child soldiers in February 2001. Just a few weeks later, it had a ceremony to celebrate its recent military training graduates. More than eighteen hundred were between the ages of twelve and eighteen.[18] Over the next two years, the reported rate of child soldier recruitment picked up pace in some provinces of the DRC.[19] Likewise, among terrorist groups, both Hamas and Palestinian Islamic Jihad have publicly disavowed the use of children, only to later renege.[20]

Indeed, the only change for some groups as a result of this growing lobbying effort against child soldiers was simply to deny or try to better hide the practice. For example, when they first entered the Afghan civil war in 1994, the fundamentalist Taliban recruited mainly among young Afghan refugees attending Pakistani madrassahs. Following international pressure, the leader of the Taliban, Mullah Omar, issued a public decree in 1998 that any of his followers who had not yet grown a beard were too young and should leave the force, with any commander using child soldiers facing punishment. Just one year later, the United Nations reported that Taliban offensives were using between two thousand and five thousand children bused over from the religious schools, many pre-adolescent.[21] Likewise, RENAMO in Mozambique stead-fastly denied its use of children throughout its war with the government. At the war's end, though, many of its marchers in demobilization parades were children, including one sixteen-year-old who had been fighting since he was eight.[22]

Other groups play the public relations game and carry out child soldier demobilizations, but only in a token manner. For example, in 2001, the RCD–Goma group in the eastern Congo set up a "commission" on the demobilization and reintegration of child soldiers. However, only the most sickly or difficult recruits were released.[23] In 2003, it made another promise to the United Nations to release its estimated 2,600 child soldiers. However, when it came time to demobilize, only 104 child soldiers (4 percent) were released.[24] Most recently, the group has moved its training camps to less accessible regions to minimize even the token interference from outside observers. Similarly, the SPLA had a large public ceremony in 2001, releasing 3,500 claimed child soldiers to great fanfare in front of the UN and international media. Of course, most of the children were later reported to have not been child soldiers to begin with (the real underage fighters were elsewhere) and the organization soon admitted having close to another 10,000 still within its ranks.[25] Perhaps the most bizarre example of this denial strategy is the LRA. A group that almost single-handedly exists through its abductions and use of child soldiers created a Web site that denies the practice.[26]

The result is that, while at least most groups no longer publicly extol their recruitment of children, the doctrine behind child soldiers has continued to spread around the globe and children are more involved in warfare than ever. Hence, the efforts can be lauded on the awareness side, such that these groups' recruitment of children is no longer as much a point of pride (for example, the now defunct FMLN in El Salvador once complained that it was left out of an article in *Time* magazine about child soldier groups), but they are clearly lacking in their ability to alter actual practice.[27] As even the Coalition to Stop the Use of Child Soldiers writes, "Remarkably little progress has been made in ending the use of child soldiers and some violators have even increased their recruitment of children."[28] For those wondering why this is so, a useful data point might suffice: despite directly working on the issue since 1996, the United Nations and the broader international community have yet to take one single formal action beyond condemnation of known child soldier recruiters and users, including those who have directly lied about it. The axiom that talk is cheap was never more true than when it comes to child soldiers.

Turning Outrage into Action

There are a number of simple actions that can be taken to make the practice of using child soldiers more difficult. These include support for expanding the availability of birth records to help children and families become better able to document ages (many children are swooped up because they cannot legally prove that they are underage), and aiding local nongovernmental organizations and religious and community leaders, who can make appeals against the practice on the basis of local values and customs. Aid agencies and NGOs can also help distribute the aforementioned international agreements throughout child soldier zones, to help spread the word that the practice is illegitimate and that the international community condemns it. Another area is to reach out to particular at-risk groups, such as refugees and street children, to counter the propaganda that often tricks them into volunteering. However, these efforts simply to spread the news of treaties have been and will continue to be insufficient.

The crux of the problem is that groups deciding to adopt the child soldier doctrine have never been ignorant about whether it was the ethical thing to do or confused about what exactly was allowed under international law or norms of proper behavior. The codes against using children as soldiers have been around for thousands of years. Groups that have brought children into warfare know that they are violating a moral code. As just one illustration, the LTTE has one of the most systemized approaches in its execution of the child soldier doctrine. However, even this group makes a point to omit the dates of birth on the headstones of its child soldiers, knowing that the historic judgment of its use of these children would not be kind.[29]

Those who use child soldiers are, by definition, willing to ignore and transgress already long-standing ethical norms and will unlikely be swayed by new ones. Those who are willing to round up children, send them into battle, and often force them to commit rape and murder are simply unlikely to be persuaded by moral appeals. To put it another way, one cannot shame the shameless.

Governments and groups interested in preventing the practice of child soldiering must realize that the employment of children as soldiers reflects the use of a well-planned doctrine, resulting from conscious and deliberate decisions taken by adults. Unless the real calculations and conditions that led to this choice are altered, the prohibitions against child soldiering will be as empty and continually violated as the new, largely symbolic prohibitions against land mines. They will still be used in large numbers. In short, making laws is not the same as finding ways to enforce them.

This realization may be a splash of cold water on the global activist movement against child soldiering, but all is not hopeless. Indeed, there are a number of possible, and not overtly arduous, steps that can be taken to turn the ethical norms against child soldiers back into standard practice. Each represents true possibilities within the realm of policymaking; in general, they lack only the requisite level of attention and political will, each of which can be mobilized.

The first feature of a program to weaken the practice of child soldiers is that it must be smart and judicious. Any effort to stop a global practice inherently faces an uphill battle. Thus, it is better to try to make the biggest difference in children's lives where possible. One aspect of this is to focus on the worst abuses, as a shrewd use of the limited political capital and attention at hand. While all uses of children under the age of eighteen as soldiers are wrong, not all are equal.

The groups working to stop the use of child soldiers are motivated by noble ideals, but too often they have been distracted by other political agendas. Thus, they have often squandered their valuable energy and capital. This lack of focus has hampered efforts so far, and often backfired. As an example, while it is a positive that an international coalition has been built, anti-American prejudices are too often allowed to misdirect its underlying mission to stop the use of children as soldiers.

For example, the Coalition to Stop the Use of Child Soldiers has wasted its political capital by engaging in a long-drawn-out public relations war with the U.S. and British governments. If the group had been more strategic in its thinking, these global powers could have been among its leading supporters. The crux of the dispute was over the presence of a small number of seventeen-year-old recruits in their forces who had volunteered with parental permission (00.24 percent of the U.S. military). While this practice may not be agreeable to all the varied members of the coalition, all can agree that it is certainly not the same as the LRA abducting children and forcing them to slaughter their own families. Despite this, the group made it a focus of its lobbying efforts. Its annual report listed the two practices as equivalent abuses under the same heading.[30]

If the underlying intent is to aid those children most in need, such verbal jabs at the United States and Britain have been completely wasteful and generally backfired. The groups have created instant opposition among those in the policymaking establishment who can do the most to help, and wasted the limited political capital they have on the least egregious acts. The result was that the coalition developed an adversarial relationship with the U.S. government, in particular the Defense Department. It led to the United States delaying ratification of the treaty until the end of 2002, and, more importantly, cost the group the world superpower's potential influence on the cause's behalf.

Yet, the saddest part may be that this feud was all needless. At the end of the day, U.S. law is already so protective of children and parental rights that the various treaties changed little. For example, of the fourteen hundred U.S. military personnel who were under eighteen and assigned to active units in 2002, only forty-five were assigned to units overseas. The essential reason is that while seventeen-year-olds may join the U.S. military upon their high school graduation, by the time they make it through boot camp and then advanced skills training, they will be past eighteen.[31] A compromise has been worked out (these small numbers are prohibited from entering into combat), but valuable time was lost. Relations with the military community certainly need to be shored up as well, as there are many common interests.

Instead, the focus of groups working to stop the use of child soldiers should turn from standard setting and borderline issues to tackling the heart of the matter. If the advocacy community hopes to make an ultimate difference, it must enact a strategy toward changing the present practices of those most offensive abusers of children and deterring those who would consider so in the future. In order to accomplish this, it must move from moral excoriation to actually changing the political and economic calculations that lead to the use of children. In military parlance, if it wants to beat child soldier users, it must get inside their "decision cycle."[32]

Groups choose to use child soldiers not by accident or ignorance, nor are they motivated by pure malice. They have underlying interests, and have deliberately set up special processes for the recruitment, indoctrination, and utilization of child soldiers because they believe they will draw certain advantages from the practice. It is these calculations that must be altered if the overall doctrine of child soldiers is to be defeated.

One potential strategy is a program designed to criminalize the doctrine. The legal transgressions involved in child soldiering are almost too numerous to make an exhaustive list. They are so self-evidently against the laws of war, and have been so for over four millennia, that to claim otherwise is pointless. Indeed, as one expert notes of child soldier commanders in the DRC, "They know it's a war crime, but they seem to believe they'll never be brought to justice. There is a sense of rampant impunity."[33] The problem is that, so far, these commanders have been right.

Given the number of treaties and legal compacts that this practice violates, there is no need for additional international law in this area. Rather, what is needed is that the full measure of international law be applied to those leaders who adopt the child soldier doctrine. This would take away the overwhelming sense of impunity under which they now operate.

Two legal pathways offer hope in this area. They both entail treating the use of child soldiers as a war crime, in and of itself, and prosecuting the leaders behind the practice for the explicit recruitment and use of children. Their underlying rationale would be to set a legal precedent that connects the practice with punishment. The focus on the doctrine as a war crime, rather than the abuses that result, would also lower the bar for prosecution. That is, the widespread presence of child soldiers within an organization would be fairly easy to prove, compared to the current higher burdens of proof that leaders must be aware of acts of atrocity by their soldiers. For example, leaders of the RUF may be able to distance themselves from certain massacres by saying they were elsewhere or didn't know of the actions committed by their subordinates. But it would be impossible for them to claim ignorance of the fact that the majority of their soldiers were underage.

Moreover, the criminalization of the practice would make it binding on other states to turn over any leaders who have escaped across state boundaries. This would also apply to their assets, which might have been acquired as a result of using child soldiers. It is also important to note that non-state groups do not escape the jurisdiction of these laws either. Like all governments, they are both bound by the basic principles of international law and required to respect all four Geneva Conventions, even in internal conflicts.

The first means for carrying out such a program is through the ad hoc international tribunals that are often established in response to egregious conflicts. The most recent is the war crimes tribunal in Sierra Leone. Prosecuting former leaders of the RUF and the Civil Defense Force (CDF) who are now in custody, not just for various war crimes but for the specific crime of recruiting and using child soldiers would be an important first step. The means would then be as much of an offense as the ends. It would clearly establish the criminality of the practice and the costs that might follow. Some have argued that pro-government leaders such as Sam Hinga Norman should be granted immunity because they fought on the "right" side, but this does little to excuse their use of the wrong means, child soldiers.

As with many woefully underfunded international initiatives, these ad hoc courts also merit greater support from the donor community. The Sierra Leone court's budget has already been cut from its originally estimated needs of $114 million to $57 million. Funding for its future remains uncertain.[34] The donor community should increase its level of support, with the proviso that the court uses its special position as a mechanism to open new ground in the battle against child soldiers. The court may also consider its potential means to prosecute foreign facilitators of the child soldier practice in Sierra Leone. These include prosecuting now exiled Liberian leader Charles Taylor, as well as those who dealt with him, for using child soldiers. Any amnesty offers for such leaders in the interests of peace must be weighed against the signal of impunity in using child soldiers that they reinforce.

So far, the ad hoc tribunals have been geographically centered, focusing on individual conflicts, such as in Rwanda, Sierra Leone, and the former Yugoslavia. However, their scope has not been limited by state borders. For example, the tribunals have indicted and sought war criminals who took refuge outside the countries of their original jurisdiction. This provides the potential for a new mode in the use of ad hoc tribunals. One idea that merits exploration is the UN Security Council convening a new issue-centered tribunal, in this case one that would tackle the international child soldier problem. Such a tribunal would be structured in the same way as the previous courts. However, it would differ in its target, seeking out offenders regardless of the specific conflict in which the crime was committed. Admittedly, such a new direction for ad hoc tribunals would be highly controversial. It would likely meet only with approval if the crime was widely agreed upon and met with incontrovertible proof. International opprobrium against the use of child soldiers and the investigative evidence already gathered by the United Nations on the issue could provide such an opening.

The second avenue for building legal deterrents against the use of the child soldier doctrine would be through the more permanent structure of the International Criminal Court (ICC). Signed by 139 countries, the court seeks to establish a global system of punishment for those who violate the rules of war and are not punished by their own countries. In particular, the court has jurisdiction over the use of child soldiers in both international (article 8 [2] [b] [xxvi]) and noninternational armed conflicts (article 8 [2] [e] [vii]).

Unfortunately, the United States, along with its unlikely allies of Saddam Hussein's Iraq and China, decided to pull out of the treaty that set up the court. It has also worked diplomatically to undermine the court's authority. It has advocated against it with weaker, developing world allies and set up a series of bilateral agreements that exclude its own citizens from coverage; those that don't sign are threatened with being cut off from aid. The concern of some in the United States was that the international court would somehow run rampant over U.S. law and that American soldiers might be targeted for politicized prosecution for war crimes (as was once threatened under Belgian universal jurisdiction laws).

This concern has been greatly overblown and is more reflective of a general, unfounded suspicion of international institutions among a minority in the U.S. body politic. In short, international law is about capturing and punishing evil leaders who would otherwise get away, not about railroading soldiers doing their duties. The United States and its allies would play a key role in selecting both the ICC's judges and its prosecutors, giving them a way to guarantee the court's professionalism for themselves. In addition, there are a number of procedural standards in the court's bylaws that would make politically motivated prosecutions nearly impossible. Respect for domestic laws is at the basis of all the court's bylaws, such that as long as a nation followed its own laws in the investigation of suspected crimes (which the United States would hopefully do), the international court would have no means to intervene.

Thus, an American agenda to counter the prosecution of war crimes is a shortsighted policy. More importantly, it runs counter to the strategic goals that American foreign policy has held for much of the last century. The United States once sought to build international institutions as a means of extending global justice, peace, and stability.

More recently, it has sought to tear them down. Benjamin Ferencz, one of the last surviving American military prosecutors at the Nuremberg trials, is among those who worry about how the ideals that won World War II are being lost. Speaking at the opening of the ICC, he noted, "The current leadership of the United States seems to have forgotten the lessons that we tried to teach the rest of the world."[35]

Without U.S. support, however, the court will be hamstrung, as the absence of the world's leading power will weaken its influence. Given the benefits of establishing accountability and ending the impunity of war criminals, the United States would do well to reconsider its abandonment of international legal institutions. This will not only help ensure the punishment of those who abuse children, but also return the United States to its noble, decades-long tradition of leading international institutions, rather than undercutting them because of the overblown fears of a few conspiracy theorists.

The United States, as well as other members of the international community, should also support modifications to the ICC that will allow it to become a more effective tool in combating the use of child soldiers. For example, amendments might be made to the court's rules in order to allow children to testify before the court (so direct sufferers can bring the practice to the fore). Consideration should also be given to convening the tribunal in cases that do not respond directly to the aftermath of specific wars, but rather indicts and prosecutes those presently using child soldiers around the globe. If a war crime is ongoing, there is no rationale to wait for its termination. The leaders of twenty-three warring groups that have been found by the United Nations to be using child soldiers, as identified in the secretary general's report pursuant to Resolution 1460, would be an excellent starting point.

The purpose of this program of criminalization would be to affect the decision calculus behind the use of child soldiers. The use of children as a weapon of war would be made like the use of chemical or biological weapons—simply unacceptable to the entire world, under any circumstances. Those groups that consciously choose to transgress international law would then open themselves up to the risk of prosecutions, sanctions, and asset seizures. Such prosecution must be judicious enough to limit their focus to those who were in leadership positions, either politically or militarily, and not waste time and effort on followers. The idea behind criminalization and prosecution is not revenge but deterrence.

A difficult question in either the tribunals or the ICC is whether to prosecute children who committed mass atrocities while serving in a conflict. Besides the fact that they are children, many were abducted, abused, and often forcibly put under the influence of drugs. When determining punishment for criminal behavior, there is a general recognition that, as once expressed by Florida governor Jeb Bush (brother of the U.S. president), "There is a different standard for children. There should be some sensitivity that a 14-year-old is not a little adult."[36] Likewise, the U.S. Supreme Court has ruled that capital punishment is not an option for those under the age of sixteen, as they lack the proper judgment skills to be held accountable as adults.

This ruling should also be kept in mind as the United States seeks to determine what to do about underage detainees, such as those it is holding at Guantánamo Bay. They may have been found to be "illegal combatants" by the United States, but it would behoove the United States to follow the spirit of the laws in their treatment and punishment, even if it thinks it is not so required. For example, Secretary of Defense Donald Rumsfeld has stated that "these are not children," and thus can be treated in the same manner as adult detainees. However, both national and international law, as well as general public sentiment, find that he is simply wrong.[37]

Regardless of their crimes, those under eighteen are different from adults on a wide range of emotional, physical, social, political, and legal levels, and should be held in separate areas until the courts are able to determine their guilt and punishment. At the end of the day, though, what defines a child and how to hold them in prison is simply not a decision that the secretary of defense ought to be making. Likewise, while the U.S. military has bent over backwards to treat its young prisoners well (the juvenile detainees under age sixteen at Camp Iguana lived in a compound set on the beach, complete with a TV room to watch videos—*The Call of the Wild* and *Castaway* being reported favorites—and a playing area for volleyball, soccer, and bocce), the business of running a youth prison is not good for the U.S. military itself.[38] The most apt solution is to turn these children over to their home state governments, with arrangements set in place to ensure their rehabilitation and prevent re-recruitment.

> *The guilty can be prosecuted. They should be taken to court, and let them explain what happened. Thinking about the part I've played, I'm thinking I may be liable to appear in court.*
> —A., age fourteen[40]

The same considerations hold even when dealing with horrible war crimes. The goal of deterrence is secondary with child soldiers. The needed factors of intent and awareness of the consequences are not the same for child soldiers or for future recruits. International legal norms also find that criminal responsibility may be excluded in cases where there is duress by threat of bodily harm or death or where atrocities were committed under the influence of intoxication, both of which are often the case with child soldiers.[39]

The strategy recently adopted in Sierra Leone toward child soldier perpetrators seems the one best suited both to serve the interests of the victims and promote long-term stability and societal recovery. While the statute of the special court does allow for the prosecution of those between the ages of fifteen and eighteen, the prosecutor has not taken such action yet, instead focusing his efforts on the adult leaders. Children implicated in particularly heinous crimes are given hearings in special closed juvenile chambers (to keep their identity secret) as well as psychological counseling and other forms of assistance. They are not sentenced to prison with adult perpetrators, but placed in special custody, rehabilitation/demobilization programs, and foster care. This response seems to best recognize the unique war crime that is child soldiering, where the perpetrators are also the victims.

Taking Action, Indirectly but Effectively

Building a system of deterrence, including criminalization of the overall doctrine, also produces a greater menu of indirect but still tangible actions that can be taken against those who use child soldiers. Criminalization also allows activists to use domestic courts to press countries to adhere to their own legal standards and hold the UN's feet to the fire when it countenances agreements with known child soldier users.

First, criminalization would make less tenable the split policy toward children and war that many states now have. A number of states do not directly use child soldiers, but still serve as primary suppliers of aid and weapons to those groups and states that do. These include many signatories to the treaties banning child soldiers. One example is the military and economic support given by China, Malaysia, India, and several western European states to Sudan. Another is the military training and assistance given to endemic child soldier users such as the RCD group next door in the DRC by Rwanda and Uganda (which in turn receive millions of dollars of aid from U.S. and British taxpayers).[41]

Establishing the doctrine itself as a war crime would make such policies more difficult to support, as states would be less willing to associate themselves with indicted war criminals, either directly or indirectly. It would also provide new means for external actors to seek to pressure these governments to stop. The removal of these support structures could provide a valuable mechanism to convincing groups and governments that it is no longer to their advantage to utilize children in combat.

Criminalization would also provide a new impetus to the priority of limiting the small arms trade to non-state actors. The easy availability of weapons and their low cost make the entire child soldier doctrine possible. In many cases, this will involve the simple targeting and seizure of illicit arms dealers, who are often well known to authorities, as well as their assets.[42] Other priorities that can be connected to helping with enforcement include the destruction of surplus small arms and better stockpile management.

Of particular note is that the United States is both a signatory to the various legal regimes against child soldiers and has often given aid to victims of war, including children (for example, the United States provides millions of dollars in aid to displaced children and war victims in places like Afghanistan, Angola, Croatia, DRC, Mozambique, and

Uganda). Since 1995 it has also spent $230 million to fight international child labor practices. However, at the same time, it has often turned a blind eye toward the use of child soldiers by its military trading partners. Over the 1990s it averaged an annual transfer of a quarter of a billion dollars of military weapons and training to state armed forces that used children sixteen and under and another quarter of a billion dollars in foreign and commercial military sales. These erring partners ranged from Colombia to Rwanda.[43] With the expansion in military aid as a result of the war on terrorism, these figures are expected to grow.

In the United States, activists already have legal means available. To remain in accordance with the Leahy amendment, American military training is forbidden to foreign units found to be human rights abusers. A focus should be made to ensure that the use of child soldiers is included in this screening.

The use of fair labor laws may be another avenue for an indirect means to enter the decision cycle of child soldier groups and alter their calculations. The International Labor Organization (ILO) has long defined child soldiering as one of the worst forms of child labor, and even lists it as a form of effectual slavery over abducted children. In 1973, in the ILO Convention 138, it determined that eighteen was the minimum allowable age for participation in hazardous labor—and if serving as a soldier is not hazardous, then nothing is. It elucidated on this in 1999, with ILO Convention 182, determining that forced or compulsory recruitment of anyone under the age of eighteen is not permissible under international labor law.

Those groups that use child soldiers should be treated in the same manner as other international actors that violate these most basic labor standards. Activists would do well to move from pressing the formation of new international agreements to seeking to exact real costs on violators based on existing ones. The strategies of stigmatization, boycott, and lawsuit are worth exploring. These have been used fairly successfully in the anti-apartheid and anti–child labor movements. Mere threat of their imposition has also helped convince multinational clothing, chocolate, and mining firms to adhere to greater human rights–monitoring standards.

A particular tactic would be to target the trading partners of states and groups that follow such practices. Indeed, the problem of child soldiers is most acute in countries that are rich in natural resources and often driven by groups that seek to gain riches by dominating trade in these resources with the international system. Examples include Charles Taylor's takeover of the timber and rubber trade in Liberia and the RUF's attempts to control the Sierra Leone diamond trade during the West African wars. During this period a lucrative trade was conducted by a series of French, Belgian, Chinese, Taiwanese, and Turkish businesses, whose funds fueled both the fighting and the use of child soldiers. A significant portion of this trade eventually ended up in U.S. markets.[44] Similarly, some eighty-five Western corporations are thought to have been involved in the illegal trades connected to the war in the Congo, where child soldiers are present.[45]

Given that the leaders of child soldier groups are unconcerned with morality and are often beyond legal controls, the ethical appeals made to them may be aimed at the wrong ears. Instead, their trading partners, upon whom such leaders depend for their riches, may be the weak link upon which to focus. In these zones, external economic actors such as multinational corporations often have dominant influence with both the state and local armed factions. They are also often complicit in paying for protection from groups with child soldiers.[46] As the quickly revised practices of such corporate giants as Coke, the Gap, and Nike illustrate from the child labor and apartheid boycotts, businesses might be more vulnerable to outside pressure than governments. They are often more concerned with negative public exposure and the underlying threat of lawsuits and global boycott. Their potential greater sway on local actors should thus be leveraged.

One potential mechanism that deserves greater attention is the filing of lawsuits under the Alien Tort Claims Act. This law, passed back in 1789, allows corporations to be sued by citizens of countries lacking legal protections against human rights violations, of which child soldiering could be easily included. While the law's standing is in deep dispute (big business groups have sought to nullify it), the threat of such lawsuits has been very effective in pressuring such corporations as Occidental and Unocal to revise and upgrade their human rights practices outside the United States.

In all of this effort to proscribe the practice of arming children, an underlying realization must be that non-state groups are less amenable to such external or legal pressures than are government-sponsored armies. Even such organizations, however, are vulnerable to certain measures that can change their calculations of the costs and benefits of using children. Under international law, all non-state groups must respect the prevailing codes of warfare, including the prohibition on recruiting and utilizing child soldiers, regardless of whether they signed the initial agreements or not. Their leaders are, therefore, liable to the same measures of legal prosecution and stigmatization as state leaders. These include not only their indictment as war criminals but also the use of targeted sanctions against them and their business associates.[47] These might encompass freezing bank accounts and visa restrictions. Given the profit motivations, the prevention of trade is a key step. This should proscribe not just weapons transfers, as happens in most UN embargoes, but also the secondary and often illicit trade in valuable areas like lumber or cigarettes that are then used to pay for illegal arms.

Given that they are violating one of the most basic tenets of international law, those armed groups that refuse to acknowledge and follow through on the prohibition of child soldiers should be denied recognition and legitimacy within the international community. This sense of legitimacy and respect is something that is surprisingly craved by many such warlords. Besides the boost to the leaders' egos, international connection offers a means to distinguish themselves from their peers and deter subordinates and would-be competitors.[48]

In the 1990s, the U.N., multiple state governments, an assortment of corporations, such as Unocal, and even a range of NGO leaders, such as Pat Roberston, sought to profit by engaging with warlords like Charles Taylor, Mullah Omar, and Laurent Kabila as if they were reputable and sovereign leaders. Besides being known despots, these same leaders were endemic child soldier users.[49] Such shameful acts should not occur again. Likewise, the urge to rehabilitate such former "rogue states" as Libya must take into account their role in supporting child soldier users elsewhere (such as Libya's support to the RUF in Sierra Leone and Charles Taylor in Liberia), in full violation of international law. Finally, the rewards given to child soldier groups that make only token demobilizations, such as the elevation of warlords in the eastern Congo to statesmen, must be ended. Instead, the burden of proof must fall on these child soldier users and abettors to prove they are compliant with international law before they are allowed to take on the role of legitimate players in the international arena.

NGOs and interested state governments should lobby and pressure the international community to withhold recognition and all the benefits that accrue (ranging from seats at the United Nations to international aid and trade) to any groups that seize power through the use of child soldiers or to those that aid them. This would send an effective message to other groups that they will not be able to achieve their aims if they adhere to the child soldier doctrine. As long as they do, humanitarian organizations should also hold them at a distance the same way they would those who are actively engaged in ethnic cleansing or genocide. They should also pressure other groups and states to do so as well. As a means of providing further incentive on the positive side, NGOs and interested states might want to connect such efforts with proposals to broker agreements that connect the flow of aid to the ending of child recruitment.

Even here these efforts may admittedly prove insufficient, as the decision calculus of some child soldier groups is not driven by political rationales. These groups will require other action to sway them. The payoffs of using children by predator groups and warlords should be limited by proscribing trade with such groups, as outlined in targeting corporate bodies and other trading links. Research has shown that the majority of "war economies" that act to reward local warlords are linked to the global economy.[51] The current international campaign against the market for "blood diamonds" from Sierra Leone and Angola provides a blueprint to target these profits.

Another potential avenue is to target these groups' external support structures. Many such conflict groups rely on donations and backing from support groups. For example, the LTTE has supporters in the Tamil communities of Australia, Canada, France, India, Norway, and the United Kingdom, who provide critical monetary and logistical backing.[51] Any external support groups should be targeted for lobbying and stigmatization efforts.

Finally, while they may be non-state actors, at the end of the day, many non-state groups are dependent on the backing of certain states. An example is the LRA's use of southern Sudan as a training refuge or the RUF's basing in Liberia. This is the equivalent of hiding a criminal in one's garage. The support or presence of such groups that use child soldiers should also put host states in violation of international law. This then opens the host state up to outside pressure, including sanctions and asset seizures, which may indirectly affect the practice of its child soldier–using protégés.

Conclusions

While certainly well intentioned, the present strategy of raising awareness and shaming child soldier users will go only so far. For the practice to end, an additive of deterrence is required. Groups seeking to end the use of child soldiers need a new strategy. They no longer need to convince the international community that using child soldiers is ethically wrong. Instead, they must change another belief, the common thinking by conflict group leaders that the benefits of using child soldiers outweigh the costs. By directly responding to the doctrine itself and its underlying political and economic rationales, groups seeking to end the use of child soldiers stand a far better chance of affecting the calculus of would-be child soldier groups.

At the end of the day, though, governments and activists must also acknowledge that these new programs may not be able to fully end the practice of using children as soldiers, certainly not in the short term. Even if successful, they will take time to mature to effectiveness. Moreover, the threat will likely remain, much as with chemical or biological weapons. Even when their use has been proscribed, there will remain the potential for groups to reassess the matter and use the child soldier doctrine in the future. Therefore, militaries must still steel themselves for the hard choices that result from facing children in battle.

CHAPTER 9

Fighting Children

Therefore, I say: Know your enemy and know yourself; in a hundred battles, you will never be defeated. When you are ignorant of the enemy but know yourself, your chances of winning or losing are equal. If ignorant both of your enemy and of yourself, you are sure to be defeated in every battle.
> —SUN-TZU, ancient Chinese military theoretician

Do you shoot a child that looks like he could be your son, even if it looks like they are going to shoot you?
> —UN peacekeeper in the DRC

At the same time as this effort to criminalize and deter the use of child soldiers grows, militaries around the world must recognize that children are a new feature of the modern battlefield. They are present in nearly every ongoing conflict. The hard reality is that our soldiers must be trained and prepared for what to do in the certain eventualities in which they will come face-to-face with child soldiers.

Indeed, not only have many developing world militaries fought against these units, but Western military forces and child soldiers have also come face-to-face in a growing number of occurrences. The situations in Afghanistan and Iraq have already been mentioned, but are far from the only ones. For instance, when U.S. Special Forces found themselves engaged in the battle of Mogadishu in 1993, among the forces surrounding and firing upon them were multiple Somali boys, some as young as ten, armed with AK-47s.[1] Likewise, when NATO forces were deployed to Kosovo in 1999, a series of grenade attacks occurred, targeting Serb civilians and threatening to disrupt the fragile peace. When the perpetrators were caught, 75 percent turned out to be children, including two fifteen-year-old girls. Reportedly, they carried their weapons in handbags or gave them to even younger children to transport, aware that NATO soldiers would not search them.[2]

Similarly, British paratroopers deployed to Sierra Leone in early 2000 had a series of skirmishes and violent encounters with youngsters from the RUF. Later in the operation, a full squad of military trainers from the Royal Irish Regiment was held hostage for two weeks by another armed group made up almost entirely of child soldiers, a rogue militia known as the West Side Boys (WSB). The soldiers had been on patrol and were surrounded and then captured by the boys when their squad commander was unwilling to fire on what he termed "children armed with AKs."[3]

The British then launched Operation Barras, designed to rescue the soldiers and break the power of the WSB. It entailed the suppression by helicopter fire of the WSB's main camp, to knock the opposition off balance, quickly followed by a helicopter assault carried out by 150 British SAS special forces and paratroopers. The fighting was reportedly "brutal."[4] Estimates of enemy dead ranged from 25 to 150, with one SAS trooper killed and almost 70 wounded.[5]

In the end, though, Operation Barras was fairly successful. All hostages were rescued. Almost the entire WSB force fled into the bush and another two hundred child soldiers surrendered in the following forty-eight hours. However, there were no follow-through operations and a core group of leaders escaped into the jungle to regroup.

The rescue in Operation Barras may have involved relatively small numbers, but it brings to the fore the difficulties of this new feature of global violence. The general presence of child soldiers is part of the harsh reality of contemporary conflict for which Western militaries, including the U.S. military, are often ill prepared. For example, when U.S. Marines were deployed off Liberia, the epicenter of child soldiers, in

August 2003, they had little intelligence on child soldiers and no instructions on how to respond if they came into contact with them (among other information, offiecers were then provided early drafts of this book).[6] This absence of planning and training for dealing with child soldiers not only presents added dangers to the soldiers in the field, but also added challenges at the strategic level. For example, Germany has been at the forefront of developing an independent military capability for the European Union (as opposed to one dependent on the United States and NATO). However, in summer 2003 its policies came to the test when it was asked to send combat troops to the DRC as part of the refugee protection program in Operation Artemis. Because of the child soldier issue, though, it balked. It chose not to send any troops, so as to avoid German soldiers having to face child soldiers.[7] Given the global presence of the doctrine, being unwilling or unable to operate in child soldier zones is a recipe for strategic inaction.

Importantly, Barras also illustrates the differences between encounters with child soldier units and other regular armed forces. In many ways, these result in certain weaknesses that can be exploited, but only if the professional force makes the proper adjustments. For example, American military doctrine traditionally has focused around attrition, large amounts of firepower, and the total destruction of the enemy.[8] As a counter to an opponent using the child soldier doctrine, however, adherence to these principles may be worse than useless, perhaps even counterproductive.

Prepare Thyself

Not only must official policies and effective solutions be developed to counter the dilemmas that the spread of the child soldier doctrine raises, but militaries must also begin to prepare for its eventualities.

While some U.S. military commanders worry that we shouldn't "dwell on this issue too much," for fear of dulling a force's combat edge, training is actually quite necessary in two key ways.[9] It affects both the ways that soldiers perceive dangers and their own effectiveness in dealing with them, as well as prescribes and proscribes actions for specific situations. As such, preparation for the dilemmas, including the drafting of rules of engagement and preparation for child rights issues, should occur prior to deployment into zones where child soldiers are present. Ideally, it should also be harmonized across the advanced training programs in the U.S. military services, the training provided to our foreign military allies, and even within the UN peacekeeping training center system. For example, the Joint Readiness Training Center (JRTC) at Fort Polk in Louisiana is where the U.S. Army prepares itself for likely scenarios of war. In recent years it has updated its programs to include urban combat and the presence of NGOs. Given the continued challenge of child soldiers for U.S. forces, child soldier scenarios should routinely be included in future JRTC rotations.

At the same time, intelligence systems must become aware of and attuned to the threat and ramifications of the child soldier. Intelligence agencies should be sure to include the use of child soldiers in their collection and analysis activities. This is important in forecasting broad political and military events upon which child soldiers now impinge, as discussed in Chapter 6. It also ensures that soldiers in the field are not taken by surprise at the presence of child soldiers. This kind of shock can be deadly. If soldiers have to formulate their response on the fly, it causes the sort of micro-second hesitations or delays that can be the difference between life and death.[10]

Additionally, knowledge of the makeup of the adversary is a critical factor in determining the best tactical response. Intelligence should be sensitive to what method of recruitment and training the opposition utilizes, as well as the average child soldier's period of service. Those groups using impressment tactics, with minimal training, or with recent cadres will be more likely to dissolve under shock than those with voluntary recruits, thought-out training programs, or children in service for more than a year. Prior knowledge and understanding of the presence of children will also allow mission planners to include personnel with special expertise in this doctrinal area.

Unfortunately, the U.S. military intelligence community remains unprepared for the child soldier issue. It is presently far too orientated toward signals intercepts and imagery analysis of heavy weapons (i.e., missile and tank counting), its modus operendi during the Cold War.

The result is that the U.S. military often does not have a good order of battle knowledge on the primary actors in most global violence, non-state actors and rebel groups.[11] We see this darkly illustrated in Iraq.

Presently, the only broad preparation for child soldier issues in the U.S. force occurs for marines, through a limited set of cultural intelligence seminars. These one- or two-day seminars are designed for units set to deploy to the field and cover an entire region's culture and politics. Obviously, there is limited time to cover any issue in sufficient depth in this context or to connect them with the tools or training they will need to respond. Through the efforts of the Marine Corps Warfighting Lab, the force is slowly beginning to expand these offerings to its officers, such as adding child soldier issues to the curriculum at the Marine Corps University and including the issue in a few war game scenarios. But the issue remains an undercovered one for the marines and an ignored one for the rest of the services.

The result is that American forces, when facing child soldier groups, may therefore suffer from a rare case of information inferiority. For example, when deploying into Iraq, American units in the field had little to no warning of the possibility of child soldiers, let alone the Fedayeen paramilitaries that they ended up fighting. The same held true for deployments to Afghanistan, Colombia, the Philippines, and so on. Each of these locales saw U.S. forces face child soldier groups.

The Hard Choices

The new presence of children in the realm of war means that professional military forces must also steel themselves for hard choices. The sentiments of the British officer captured before Operation Barras, who was unwilling to fire on "children armed with AKs," were both understandable and laudable. However, his tactical choices, and the fact that he was put into a situation where he had to develop an ad lib response, not only threatened the overall mission, but also might have led to more deaths in the end.

The core dilemma child soldiers present for professional militaries is as thorny as they come. Troops now face real and serious threats from opponents whom they generally would prefer not to harm.

Every time I look at them, I think of my son. They are so small.
Sometimes, when I am here, I put myself in God's hand.
     —UN peacekeeper deployed in the DRC[12]

On one side, a bullet from a fourteen-year-old's gun can kill just as well as one from a forty-year-old's. Therefore, when forces deploy into an area known to have child soldiers present, they must take added cautions to counter and keep the threat at a distance. All children are not threats and certainly should not be targeted as such, but force protection measures must include the possibility—even likelihood—of child soldiers. This includes changing practices of letting children mingle around checkpoints and roadblocks, and putting them through the same inspection and scrutiny as adults. Soldiers should also be prepared for innovative and novel attempts to either target or pass through these checkpoints. For example, in 2002, the FARC in Colombia had two young children lead a horse loaded with explosives toward an army checkpoint. The charge exploded prematurely, killing one of the children. In a separate incident later that year, the group booby-trapped the corpse of a fourteen-year-old boy to try to pass it close to an army barracks.[13]

The presence of girl soldiers creates a special complication to forces with this task. It may require a deliberate policy of employing female soldiers at checkpoints, who can better address the special privacy needs of women and girls during body searches.[14] At present, the distribution of women across U.S. military units is ad hoc, depending on the specific service and unit. In turn, women are absent from most other armies. Ghana, for example, was the only force to have women deployed in ECOMOG operations in West Africa. If this employment policy is not possible, alternative, culturally sensitive responses must be designed.

The rationale for these steps is that child soldier forces are often well armed and can cause great damage to an unprepared force. Tactical leaders must be aware that just because they are children, the opponent can still launch sophisticated ambushes, surprise attacks, or even large-scale wave attacks. At times, these will include preparatory fire by mortars, rocket-propelled grenades, or machine guns.

Moreover, child soldiers tend to operate with terrifying audacity, often taking risks that regular soldiers might not anticipate. When infused with religious fervor, overtaken by the influence of narcotics, or simply excited by the encounter, many child soldiers fight with an absolute disregard for their own death. In describing the shooting of a medic in his unit by a fifteen-year-old al Qaeda fighter, one U.S. Green Beret soldier commented: "That wasn't a panicky teenager we encountered that day. That was a trained al Qaeda, who wanted to make his last act on earth the killing of an American."[15]

In particular, American soldiers should also be prepared for the fact that while their foes may be children, they have the capacity to fight with a terrible ferocity and commit horrifying acts of violence. Their life experiences were not the Generation X milieu in which most American GIs grew up, but instead a life of constant danger and hunger. Indeed, one military expert warned bluntly that any American forces facing child soldiers in Africa should expect the worst, describing what happened to several ECOMOG soldiers in Liberia: "They will capture you, strip you naked, run you through the streets, cut off your testicles and fry them in a pan in front of you, fillet you from head to toe and then cut off your head to put on a stake."[16]

Where child soldiers are present, respect for the traditional rules of war will not be likely. Instead, soldiers should expect false surrenders, hiding among civilians, and POW executions—much as U.S. forces were "shocked" to find out in Iraq. As one young child soldier explained of his compatriots, "These warriors don't play by the rules."[17]

> I killed people, but when you are fighting in the jungle, you never know how many. It is difficult to verify. It wasn't so much—a lot of children fought a lot more than me.
> —R., age fourteen (fighting since age nine)[18]

An added challenge is that these young soldiers will often come to the battlefield with a great deal of combat experience and individual military skills. Child soldiers across a number of conflicts literally grew up fighting. Many child rebels in Liberia, for instance, were veterans with seven to ten years of combat experience. The more experienced will often have fought in multiple wars, perhaps even in multiple armies.[19] The result is that they may be even more effective combatants than their adult counterparts.

> *My training was four and a half months. I learned how to use a compass, how to attack a police post, how to carry out an ambush, and the handling of weapons, By the end I was using an AK-47, a Galil, an R-15, mortars, pineapple grenades, M-26 grenades, and taucos [multiple grenade launcher].*
>
> —R., age fifteen[20]

At the same time, though, the quandary of facing child soldiers is that one's opponents are traditionally considered illegitimate targets. Rather than hated enemies, they are instead foes with whom professionals can expect to feel a great deal of empathy. The interesting aspect is that the presence of children on the battlefield, in a sense, reverses a usual aim of combat engagement—to destroy the enemy's ability to fight. The traditional measure for this mission is casualties inflicted upon one's enemy. However, the unwillingness to slaughter enemy combatants is not unique to child soldiers. For example, the 1991 Persian Gulf War ended—many would argue prematurely—primarily over concern of the images of inflicting too many enemy casualties on the "Highway of Death," a road from Kuwait leading into southern Iraq.[21]

The essential matter, though, is that it is especially demoralizing for professional militaries to be forced to fight and kill children.[22] One Colombian army officer tells of the profound effect: "I had to kill a little girl today. But what could I do? She was shooting at me."[23]

While hatred of an enemy can act as a motivating factor for combat troops, pity has the opposite effect. It acts as a force that leads soldiers to question their roles.[24] For example, there was little dilemma or controversy over actions against the Hitler Jugend troops in 1945. The youths were fighting to defend an absolutely evil regime which there was general agreement had to be defeated completely. Yet, the experience was so unsettling to U.S. Army forces that had to fight these units that troop morale was brought to its lowest point, despite the fact that the end of the war was in sight.[25] Not only did no soldier want to be put in a position to have to shoot and kill a child, but no soldier wanted to be shot by a child, who shouldn't be there in the first place and has been tricked into fighting for a lost cause. A more contemporary reaction was that of one U.S. soldier in Iraq who fought child soldiers in the fighting for Karbala:

> Anybody that can shoot a little kid and not have a problem with it, there is something wrong with them. Of course I had a problem with it. After being shot [at] all day, it didn't matter if you were a soldier or a kid, these RPGs [rocket-propelled grenades which the children were attempting to deploy against his unit] are meant to hurt us. . . . I did what I had to do.[26]

This demoralizing effect is potentially heightened in intervention or peacekeeping missions, where the rationale for becoming involved is more complex and the duration often open-ended. For example, during its peace intervention into Sri Lanka in the early 1980s, the Indian army was so worn down by its experience against the child cadres of the LTTE that it became a concern for the health of the larger organization. The military leadership pressured the political leaders into terminating the mission. Likewise, British forces operating in West Africa in 2001 faced deep problems of clinical depression and post-traumatic stress disorder (PTSD) among individual soldiers who had faced child soldiers.[27]

This last point underscores the general proviso that force should be used only when and where the objectives warrant it. The eventuality of engaging child soldiers will be a terrible tragedy regardless of the mission rationale. At the same time, images of children killed by American forces will have a terrible resonance on TV screens back home and around the world, no matter the context. One can only imagine the impact that pictures of tiny bodies would have on CNN, even if the soldiers were carrying out a moral and popular mission and facing a direct threat to their lives. A primary worry for militaries is that a traditional measure of success in defeating their opponent may end up undermining their domestic support. How these images play out on foreign public opinion might complicate our diplomacy as well. Being forced to kill child soldiers would obviously hamper U.S. public information efforts to demonstrate the rightness of a cause.

Thus, the use of child soldiers by an opponent might raise certain added pressures on policymakers. If child soldier incidents take the fore, commanders could then expect pressure from the political side to speed the pace of operations, in order to get the issue off the world's TV screens. However, in certain situations, this might prove counter to the best military advice.

The Lessons from Fighting Children

Therefore, forces must seek new strategies and means to solve the quandary child soldiers present. The rationale for responding extends beyond just the moral quandary, however. Child soldier units are recruited differently than regular military units and operate in different manners, also adding to the need for change. The key is to recognize the duality that is at the very nature of the problem: real threats offered by children operating in a place they should not be, the realm of war.

To begin, forces must make tactical adjustments in order to mitigate the threat and develop a more effective response to the child soldier danger. For example, most developing world military forces that have faced child soldier forces have suffered greater losses because they have been unable to hold the threat off at a distance. A large part of this is simply the result of poor training programs, often instigated by outside military advisors. As an example, marksmanship and simple defensive doctrine are not stressed enough. Too often, the local troops tend to think that 100 meters (328 feet) is the maximum range on their weapons. The result is that, when under threat, in the words of one military advisor, "They simply turn [their rifles] onto auto [automatic fire] and waste ammo and then die . . . They [the children] generally overrun the objective with some ease, as the defenders are simply not much better."[28] Instead, a force that is able to dig in under protection, use trenches and wire to shape the battlefield, and stretch the opponent engagement zone (to the 300 meter [984 feet] and beyond distance) may be able to do far better with far fewer losses.

While these simple lessons are arguably good military practice in general, for child soldier forces, more specific changes will be in order. A counter to the doctrine of child soldiers must take into account the unique challenges child soldiers present.

This is obviously far more complex. A crucial aspect is an appreciation of the fact that the opposition is, in the end, often made up of soldiers who are looking for a way out. The center of gravity for child soldier groups is the hold that leaders have on their troops; thus, a primary task for defeating them is the breaking of that chain. This is particularly the case with units where the children have been recruited through involuntary means or where they have been in roughly less than a year. Ex–child soldiers reveal that they were often just waiting until fighting broke out to steal away in the confusion, but only if it was possible. Thus, units should prioritize the targeting and elimination of the adult leaders whenever possible. If the adult leader is killed or forced to take cover, the whole organization can break down rapidly. Some children simply drop their weapons, while others flee into the bush. For example, LRA escapees tell of how, if this link were broken, their entire unit would disappear within seconds.[29]

While it is preferable to target adult leaders, both for moral reasons and efficiency, this is obviously not always a possibility in the chaos of modern warfare. Thus, alternative means may have to be utilized to break that hold. Specifically, traditional targeting and set-piece movement will be less effectual than the imposition of shock and the deliberate creation of avenues and openings to shape the enemy's response.[30]

Even for professional, well-trained adult units, the experience of being attacked by a distant, unseen foe is consistently described as among the most difficult to endure. The lack of opportunity to take action combines with the intrinsic danger of the experience to create an extremely frustrating, demoralizing, and overwhelming event that can cause breakdowns in units.[31] This effect is magnified among child soldier units. Not only are children inherently more frightened of the unknown, but these units will usually have lesser internal bonds and training.

Therefore, in facing off against child soldier units, chaos and confusion are more valued than pure destruction. In many ways, this is the low-intensity warfare equivalent of the high-tech "effects-based warfare" that has garnered so much recent support among Pentagon thinkers. (One is also reminded of the axiom that in bush skirmishes, "he who makes the biggest noise wins.")[32] As such, the heavy use of smoke and demonstrative air, armor, and artillery fires will often be enough to break down a force based on child soldiers.[33] The use of rolling barrages (which move slowly from one side of the battlefield to the other and thus create a seeming direction to the flow of danger) and mortars for immediate suppressive fire have also proven highly effective in tending to cause child soldier units to break and run.

Helicopter gunships, in particular, have been found to be especially intimidating and thus most effective. As one expert on West African warfare describes, "The helicopter is feared as it is unknown, it comes out of nowhere, [a] big psycho thing, spitting death. It attacks low to the ground on the treetops. It is very noisy."[34] Indeed, many describe the one gunship that the Sierra Leone government contracted from a private military firm to have been more valuable in stopping the child-based RUF than the entire UN peacekeeping force and Sierra Leone army combined.[35]

Importantly, a counterdoctrine of shock will also likely cost fewer lives for both sides, answering the other part of the dilemma. The possibility of these engagements also presents an ideal rationale to explore the integration of new non-lethal technologies. While non-lethal weapons (NLWs) are still in development, it appears that they will offer new, more efficient means to hold threats off to a distance, shape the battlefield, or dissolve attacking forces before they are able to present real harm. At the same time, they avoid the unique concern over inflicting too much deadly harm on opponents.

NLWs seek to temporarily disable one's senses or cause some sort of incapacity without permanent harm. Some examples of the possibilities presently being researched include acoustic weapons that use very low frequency waves to disorient and frighten, microwave beam weapons that excite one's nerves into thinking that the skin is burning, neural inhibitors that temporarily incapacitate a target, calmative agents that induce a slumber state, malodorous chemicals that provoke intense nausea and vomiting, and adhesives or "slimes" that immobilize targets in either a sticky or slippery foam.[36]

All offer a broader range of choices for the local commander, which is generally a good thing, as long as doctrine is developed to guide their use. As one Marine Corps expert notes, "The whole idea of joint non-lethal force is to provide a field commander with more options for controlling crowds or locations without resorting to lethal force."[37]

For example, a plausible scenario is that a tactical commander could face the massing of child soldier units outside his lines. Presently, this officer would have only the moral and tactical quandary of either calling in artillery fire upon unsuspecting children or forcing their soldiers to wait until the children attack and then battle them at close range. NLWs offer the alternative of breaking up the attack beforehand without the incumbent harms of the other two options, while still leaving these choices available. Indeed, in many of the situations where U.S. forces faced child soldiers in both Somalia and Iraq, NLWs might have helped mitigate the terrible dilemmas that U.S. soldiers faced. Instead, they could only fire warning shots and then shoot to kill, just as they were trained.

A crucial aspect is that all of these technologies have temporary and reversible effects, but can still allow forces to accomplish their goals, in some cases more effectively than with conventional weapons. Unfortunately, the current U.S. Joint Non-Lethal Weapons doctrine (established in 1997) does not even mention child soldiers and no training curricula apply.[38] Likewise, there are only sixty-eight non-lethal capabilities sets in the entire U.S. military (other militaries, including those that frequently participate in UN peacekeeping, have none), of which only six were deployed to Iraq.[39]

Therefore, it is in professional militaries' interest to continue NLW research and begin doctrinal development and deployment of NLWs as they apply to children. A key issue will be matching the use of NLWs to account for children's smaller size. For example, some types of NLWs, such as kinetic weapons (using plastic or rubber bullets), could cause permanent damage to children, as they were originally designed for adults. Militaries should also coordinate with NGOs and international law groups in a frank discussion of the use of NLWs as a lifesaving tool for both soldiers and children.

However, while these NLW technologies may ultimately offer a means to replace more lethal alternatives, at this time they should be utilized only as complements. An underlying reality is that forces deployed into such high-threat environments still face real threats and require the capability to ensure their own safety.

The irony is that such needs often run contrary to the direction many militaries have taken toward lighter and more sophisticated forces. As an observer of Operation Barras noted, "You cannot resolve a situation like this with a laser-guided bomb from 30,000 ft."[40] Peacekeeping operations, which are among the most likely situations for Western forces to come into contact with child soldier–based forces, may be the most ill equipped of all to respond. They are often lightly armed, lacking in the type of heavy weapons that can "shock" or quickly overwhelm foes. In each situation where peacekeeping forces have run into the most difficulty with child soldiers, they were small arms–based, light infantry forces, lacking in heavy weapons support or new alternatives.[41]

Militaries currently reconfiguring their forces for intervention, such as the restructuring ongoing in the United States and Europe, would do well to remember the continuing importance of having firepower available for deterrence, demonstrations, and, if necessary, use as backup, even in peacekeeping operations. These forces should make certain to deploy with the equipment packages necessary to accomplish this task. If not, the result may be the outcomes similar to what happened during the UN's deployment to the DRC in 2003. In Bunia province, "child soldiers taunted the blue helmets, first with insults, then mortars, then by tossing a body over the fence into the United Nations compound."[42]

While units based on child soldiers are vulnerable to shock tactics, they must still be viewed as very real threats. In particular, no single weapon or tactic is the end-all panacea when facing well-trained forces, even those comprised of children. Much like regular adult forces, child soldier units have been known to endure heavy fire and develop innovative and effective counters. The key variables seem to be the amount of training and the level of control that the organization has over the units. For example, the lightly trained and often abducted child fighters of the RUF would break and run at the first sight of a helicopter gunship. In comparison, the hardened SPLA cadres would lay a fairly expert ambush for the helicopters, such that the Sudanese air force now primarily operates them from higher, and less effective, ranges.[43]

Think Strategically

Changes in tactics for mitigating the child soldier threat must also be matched by efforts to take a more strategic approach. Even a successful first encounter with child soldiers, which dissolves an adversary force, is a battle half won if it does not prevent the adult leaders from regrouping. For example, a constant flaw in operations in Sierra Leone was that there was limited follow-through and a core group of RUF leaders escaped, allowing them to re-form and regroup later. This means that while fairly passive defense is best suited for the first stage, after contact, active measures must be taken to search out and run down the leadership. Such actions will require both patience and the use of small units of dedicated counterinsurgency specialists.

Another key recognition is that the recruiting pipeline is a key sustaining factor for forces that use children. It will even direct the course of their operations. The LTTE, for example, developed computerized databases that kept track of the juvenile population pool under its rule. When it appeared that the group was facing a recruiting shortfall in the mid-1990s, it not only established controls to regulate the travel—and feared exodus—of youths in its areas, but also launched a series of offensives to widen its territorial control for recruitment purposes.[44]

This points to a potential vulnerability of which opponents should take advantage. A child soldier force can be defeated not just by direct attempts to dissolve it under shock, but also indirectly, by taking away its primary recruiting zones. Militaries facing such movements should keep this in mind as they plan their broader operations. At the same time, they must understand that defending high-density target zones (i.e., places where there are large groups of vulnerable children such as refugee camps) is not only the principled thing to do, it is also a means of preventing their opponents from regrouping. For groups sustained by children, these sites are strategic locations, much like key bridges or crossroads.[45] In Sierra Leone, for example, the initial UN peacekeeping forces did not provide any defense for the camps where former child soldiers were going through rehabilitation. When the war flared back up, RUF leaders simply showed up at the camps and rebuilt their cadres.

The aspect of recruiting zones also indicates the potential utility of psychological operations as a supplement to traditional military operations. Dating back to Sun-tzu's teachings, such operations, which include everything from leaflet campaigns and loudspeakers to TV and radio broadcasts, have been designed to achieve almost costless advantages over one's adversaries. In particular, they aim at subverting the will of the populace and soldiers in the field, in addition to damaging the authority of those in command. Related to child soldiers, their aim should be to convince child soldiers to think of their families, stop fighting, leave their units, and begin the process of rehabilitation and reintegration into society. Efforts should also be made to deter adult leaders from employing child soldiers by reminding them that, just as with weapons of mass destruction, sending children to fight is a war crime that will bring about their prosecution, even after the war is over.

Now that I am back, I hate even looking at a Kalashnikov. I think young boys should not go to war since it is very dangerous. You have to face hunger, the enemy and a very rugged terrain. I used to really miss my mother and sisters during my stay at the frontline. I was sad there, it was a hard and tough time and now that I recall those times, I get extremely terrified.

—M., age seventeen[46]

Such operations can also seek to drive wedges between the local populace and groups that use children, as well as between child soldiers and their adult handlers. Areas to cite include the breaking of cultural norms, the undue casualties children tend to suffer, and the hypocrisy of adult leaders sending other people's children to fight for their gain.

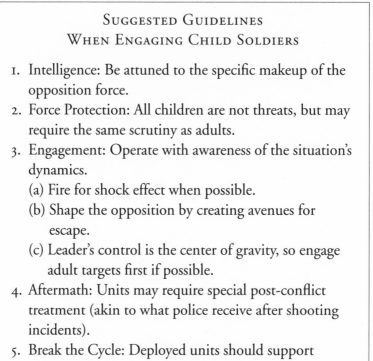

SUGGESTED GUIDELINES
WHEN ENGAGING CHILD SOLDIERS

1. Intelligence: Be attuned to the specific makeup of the opposition force.
2. Force Protection: All children are not threats, but may require the same scrutiny as adults.
3. Engagement: Operate with awareness of the situation's dynamics.
   (a) Fire for shock effect when possible.
   (b) Shape the opposition by creating avenues for escape.
   (c) Leader's control is the center of gravity, so engage adult targets first if possible.
4. Aftermath: Units may require special post-conflict treatment (akin to what police receive after shooting incidents).
5. Break the Cycle: Deployed units should support demobilization and rehabilitation efforts.

Aftermath

The defeat of a child soldier–based opposition does not just take place on the battlefield, no matter how successful. A force must also take measures quickly to welcome child escapees and POWs so as to induce others to lay down their arms. To help break the system of control that brought them into warfare, children should be kept separate from adult POWs (for example, in the 2003 Iraq war, they were not separated). Once the force has ensured that the child does not present a threat, any immediate needs of food, clothing, and/or shelter should be provided for. Invariably, the child will have previously depended on his or her armed group for these things, so the surrogate void must be filled. Then, as soon as possible, the child should be turned over to health care or NGO professionals. The Philippine army, for instance, has guidelines that mandate the turnover of child POWs to social workers within twenty-four hours.

Given the scandal over abuses against Iraqi prisoners held at Abu Ghraib prison, it has to be underscored that all detainees, particularly child soldiers, must be afforded the full protections of the Geneva Conventions. To do otherwise not only violates the very laws of war, but also backfires on those troops in the field who are fighting to win the war. Torture rarely reaps usable information, but more importantly turns the opposition's darkest propaganda into truth and becomes a powerful recruiting tool for the other side. Unfortunately at Abu Ghraib, longstanding codes of behavior against torture and abuse were broken and a tragedy that will haunt the reputation of the United States for years to come ensued. The abuses that the U.S. army investigators determined were carried out against juveniles included keeping young detainees naked in their cells, the use of dogs to frighten juvenile detainees—to the extent of urinating on themselves, and an alleged rape of a male juvenile detainee.[47] One disgusted military officer said, "People know that in war, you know, you have to break eggs. But this crosses the line."[48]

The causes of this breakdown will be debated in the history books for years to come, but it is clear that they include a series of problems that fed off of one another: collapse in the local unit's leadership and professionalism; confusion over the chain of command; self-destructive choices by U.S. political leaders to set aside long-standing doctrines against torture; and a significant and inappropriate placement of private military contractors, who were involved in 36 percent of the proven abuse incidents at Abu Ghraib, into what should have been public military roles and responsibilities (100 percent of the interpreters on site were private employees from the Titan company. As many as half of the interrogators were private employees of the CACI company. Interestingly, U.S. Army investigators found that "approximately 35 percent of the contract interrogators [from CACI] lacked formal military training as interrogators").[49]

Beyond the initial reception, though, military forces in these areas must take steps to assist in the long-term processes of child demilitarization and demobilization. These are discussed further in Chapter 10. Tasks for military units in these roles include coordinating with local aid groups and providing support to civil society activities that seek to pull children away from warfare. Some of the more successful activities taken by prior military operations include providing clinics and emergency medical services to civilians in their area of operations; helping to repair or construct schools, orphanages, and hospitals; organizing safe transportation networks for women and children; building identified reception centers/safe havens that offer shelter and protection to child soldier escapees; and providing civil affairs outreach, such as the organization of education and recreation activities.[50]

Given the atrocities they may have committed against the local population, child soldier rehabilitation centers may also have to be protected from revenge attacks. In October 2001, for example, a camp for former LTTE child fighters was surrounded by a mob of local citizens. The angry crowd then overran the camp and beat twenty-six of the children to death. The children were being provided vocational training and psychological counseling by the Sri Lankan government so that they would not return to being child soldiers.[51] Incidents like this are not only tragic, but also risk deterring other child soldiers from demobilizing, possibly unraveling the peace.

There is also an opposite side to the aftermath of encounters with child soldiers, a legacy effect on the troops involved. Despite all the attempts to create new, more effective means to counter the child soldier doctrine, for the near term at least, troops will likely still be placed in the difficult position of having to fire on a child for their own protection. Military leaders must anticipate this terrible dilemma and prepare their soldiers with strict guidelines on when to make this decision. They must also be ready to deal with its repercussions, for this is an added way that the use of child soldiers puts professional forces at a disadvantage.

Troops may require special post-conflict treatment, akin to what many police organizations offer after shooting incidents. Otherwise, the consequence of being forced to kill children may ultimately undermine unit cohesion and combat effectiveness. As one British Royal Marine officer noted of his experience in Sierra Leone, "The impact of being fired on by a child is a terrible shock, but the soldiers will do their job. But if you don't care for them when they come home, it might destroy them."[52] When deploying into child soldier zones, military field hospitals should therefore include Combat Stress Contingents that include trained professionals to debrief and counsel forces when necessary, as part of their overall task of keeping soldiers healthy.

Engagement against child soldiers also has an important public affairs side. Images of children killed by American or allied forces will certainly be heartrending to the public. The added misfortune would be if these media images were to undermine domestic or international support. If not carefully managed, this aspect of the information war will be an easily lost one. The Israeli military's public travails in facing off with child fighters in the intifada are a clear illustration.

Public affairs specialists must also be prepared for the repercussions of such engagements. In explaining the events and how children ended up being killed, they should stress the context under which they occurred and the overall mission's importance. The public should be informed that everything possible is being done to avoid and limit child soldiers from becoming casualties (use of non-lethal weapons, psychological operations, firing for shock effect, etc.). At the same time, the public should be made aware that child soldiers, although they are children, are just as lethal behind an assault rifle as adults. Most importantly, spokespersons must seek to turn blame on where it should properly fall—on those foes who send children out to do their dirty work.

At a broader level, if the decision is made to go to war against a force known to have child soldiers, then the U.S. government and its coalition allies must begin to sensitize the public and the wider international community to the issue. The United States should set the stage for this effort by mobilizing the United Nations, regional political leaders, and relevant religious experts to condemn the practice for what it is—a clear violation of both international and religious law. They should stress how the local party has intentionally created this system of child soldiers, knowing that it would lead to the deaths of children.

An additional avenue is to seek prior indictment of local leaders for violation of the myriad of international laws proscribing the recruitment of children into armed forces, so that their later use might be interpreted in the context of a continuing war crime. These efforts could then be integrated into broader psychological operations, including warning field commanders of their possible punishment for the practice.

In sum, professional military forces, and their frequent critics in the humanitarian world, may not want to deal with the real battlefield dilemmas that child soldiers present, but that is beside the point. Child soldier incidents will continue to occur over the next few years, perhaps in even greater numbers. The only question is whether our troops will be prepared.

CHAPTER 10

Turning a Soldier Back into a Child

The nights are the worst. Sometimes I am too afraid to sleep. For when I sleep, I am dead. . . . I see someone take a gun and then they shoot me—not just once but three times. . . . Is that called a dream or a nightmare? —V., age sixteen[1]

The final task in responding to the doctrine of child soldiers is to deal with its aftermath. It has a particularly pernicious potential to ruin the lives of children and, in doing so, lay the groundwork for future conflicts that harm society writ large.

The challenge we face is therefore how to reverse the effects of the doctrine, and, in doing so, restore children's future. The healing is not one step but is a process. It involves disarming and demobilizing the children, conducting an arduous process of rehabilitation, and then capping the transition back to childhood through reintegration with families and communities.

Don't Forget the Children

Unfortunately, there are typically few mechanisms in place after conflicts end to deal with the issues unique to child combatants. In most peace settlements and post-conflict recovery programs, child soldiers are either forgotten or lumped together under the general grouping of "ex-combatants." The result is that children usually get shortchanged in the support they need, not only to their detriment but also to the detriment of broader peace prospects. For example, in its first Sierra Leone operation in the mid-1990s, the United Nations earmarked $34 million to disarm, demobilize, and reintegrate ex-combatants. However, only $965,000 of this already small amount was directed toward the tens of thousands of child soldiers in Sierra Leone, despite the fact that they made up the bulk of the fighters in the war.[2] As a result of the failures of the peace process, the original settlement never fully stuck and the fighting began again, with most of the ex–child combatants simply rejoining the warring groups.

Such a dangerous lack of attention to the child soldier doctrine in peace processes and postwar planning continues today. In East Timor, for example, the under-eighteen members of the rebel FALINTIL group were simply sent back to their home villages. The United Nations had few specialists to assist them, and the youths were not provided any of the added support that normally occurs with formal demobilization programs. To gain access to these programs, some of these child soldiers even resorted to taking on the false identity of killed adult soldiers. Similar circumstances have occurred in Liberia, where only 11 percent of the child soldiers were assisted in the first war's demobilization programs, as well as in Afghanistan, Kosovo, and so on.[3]

In fact, it was not until the UN's second try in Sierra Leone, the 1999 Lomé Accords, that any peace treaty even recognized the very existence of child soldiers or made any specific provisions for their rehabilitation and reintegration into society. As such, the agreement was groundbreaking. It stated that "the Government shall accord particular attention to the issue of child soldiers. It shall accordingly mobilise resources, both within the country and from the International Community, and especially through the Office of the UN Special Representative for Children and Armed Conflict, UNICEF and other agencies, to address the special needs of these children in the existing disarmament, demobilisation and reintegration process."

A key impediment to the inclusion of child soldiers into postwar planning and peace settlements is often the denial by the local parties, in the face of obvious evidence, that child soldiers are even part of their forces. For example, in Mozambique, despite the fact that more than a quarter of the total troops in the war were child soldiers, neither party admitted it. Unfortunately, the United Nations acquiesced to this façade. Thus, the formal demobilization programs did not include child soldiers and the mass of kids returned to civilian life with no help or support. The outcome had long-lasting societal repercussions, including extremely high levels of banditry that plagued Mozambique for the following decade.[4] Similarly, in Angola, the government's demobilization program was designed to avoid the financial costs of providing benefits to nearly seven thousand former child soldiers. The government never admitted their presence in its forces and the children have been essentially abandoned to their own devices.[5]

A particularly egregious subset of these denials is the frequent attempt by groups to retain girl soldiers even after the fighting has ended. They do so because the adult leaders often want to retain the girls' added value as "wives" or servants. For instance, in Sierra Leone, the RUF returns of abducted children included only a small percentages of girls. In one case, when 591 abducted children were released, only ten were girls. This was obviously not in line with their much larger numbers within the force.[6] Similarly, in Mozambique, visits by international observers to RENAMO camps during the war found that around 40 percent of its child soldiers were girls. After the war ended, though, nowhere near this figure were repatriated.[7]

An additional group typically forgotten by peace settlements and postwar assistance is former child soldiers who have grown up over the course of the war. Many conflicts last so long that children brought into the fighting before the age of eighteen may become adults. However, growing up within war means that they likely will have problems far more extensive than those who joined the fighting as adults. Even though they are now adults, they may also require specialized support to deal with the aftereffects of child soldiering. These include psychological harms, as well as the loss of educational prospects. Unfortunately, these former child soldiers are generally ignored in post-conflict processes as well.[8]

These sorts of failings and omissions are not just tragic but dangerous. Unless the needs of children are explicitly incorporated into peace and reconstruction plans, they will not be given the priority status that they merit. As a result, just as forces in the field must now deal with the younger makeup of their likely adversaries, so, too, must post-conflict operations plan for the younger ex-combatants they must now work with. Too often, peacekeeping operations are ill prepared for the reality they will face on the ground. As a result, many former child soldiers do not have access to educational programs, vocational training, family reunification, or even food or shelter, all of which they need to successfully rejoin civilian society. In Sierra Leone, for example, the sheer number of former soldiers (both adult and child) overwhelmed the limited relief efforts. Half a year into the operation, only 30 percent of the child soldiers in the RUF had even been demobilized and disarmed. The amount of rehabilitation that many former child combatants received was often no more than one week, hardly sufficient.[9]

In general, funding to support these programs is also far from sufficient. For example, UNICEF's child soldier demobilization programs in the DRC needed $15 million in 2001; they received $4 million.[10] The result of these gaps is that programs often run well beyond capacity. The Colombian government, for example, has two well-regarded rehabilitation programs, the Family Welfare Institute and the Reinsertion Program. Both, however, are often so full that children sleep in bunks placed in the hallways. In turn, World Vision's child soldier rehabilitation centers in northern Uganda often run at six times their capacity.

Thus, a great number of these child soldiers end up on the street, become involved in crime, or are drawn back into armed conflict. This starts the trend of child soldier recruitment all over again. As Neil Boothby, a child psychologist and former senior coordinator for refugee children with the United Nations, states, "I think it's safe to say unless we're able to break the cycle of violence, unless we're able to focus on this teenage population specifically . . . it'll be the teenager who picks up the gun and starts the next cycle."[11]

Thus, negotiators and other signatories should refuse to acquiesce to any warring party's unwillingness to acknowledge the presence of child soldiers in its forces. It is critical that when child soldiers are present in a conflict, peace agreements and post-conflict planning clearly incorporate provisions for their rehabilitation. Without proper recognition given to the makeup of the warring parties, there is no reason to suggest that the conflict will be properly settled and not occur again. This need cuts across the agendas of peace processes, peacekeeping strategy, and reconstruction planning.

The United Nations and other diplomatic agencies that run and advise such processes should include special planning for children's needs. Some of these additional aspects may include adding language in the tone of the Lomé Accords to treaties which gives a mandate to such efforts, ensuring that child-centered funding for post-conflict recovery is sufficient, and planning and coordinating civil-military cooperation (CIMIC) operations in peacekeeping forces that are best suited for aiding child soldiers. As organizations prepare to deploy into the field to support peace agreements, they should have the proper number of child protection advisors and human rights experts within their personnel staffing, commensurate with children's overall makeup of the local warring forces. Another aspect is that, as experience in West Africa shows, peacekeeping operational planners should consider the potential need to include contingents of female soldiers, who may be better prepared to deal with the special needs of girl soldiers.[12]

Likewise, outside governments and agencies can do a better job in preparing to support the changing requirements from the increased presence of children in war. For example, within the U.S. government, the responsibilities for backing disarmament and demobilization efforts are disjointed, spread out over a number of federal agencies, and often have little programmatic expertise on how to respond to the growing use of child soldiers. Therefore, a key need is the establishment of a bureaucratic focal point which could better coordinate the U.S. government response and deal more effectively with the issue from a multi-dimensional standpoint. One proposal that merits further consideration is the creation of an Office of Disarmament, Demobilization, and Reintegration (DDR). It could be placed within USAID (U.S. Agency for International Development), but include seconded staff from other relevant agencies, such as the Pentagon, the Department of Health and Human Services, and even the Department of Education. Such reorganization would help produce an overall strategy for how the world's superpower will react to the issue and better coordinate its planning and responses.[13]

Disarmament and Demobilization

While the child soldier doctrine is still relatively young, its explosive spread has meant that the United Nations, local governments, and humanitarian groups have had to wrestle with the aftereffects of children serving as soldiers. Unfortunately, it has been a gradual learning process for all involved, such that none of the operations that dealt with this issue can be described as a full success. They have, though, begun to form the basis of a set of hard-won general lessons learned.

The predominant belief in the field is that the process of turning a child soldier back into a child must take place in three essential phases: (1) disarmament and demobilization; (2) rehabilitation in both the physical and psychological realms; and (3) reintegration with families and the community, which must include sustained follow-up support, including self-capacity building and extended counseling.[14] The requisite time for each phase varies, but the general consensus is that the overall process must be measured in terms of months rather than the weeks or days that too often happen because of a lack of resources or improper attention to needs. Likewise, the course is not a clean, separated process into three distinct parts, but rather must be part of an overall strategy that flows toward a unified direction and goal, restoring the freedoms and opportunities of a lost childhood.

Once the fighting is ended, one of the most urgent priorities is to mandate the immediate removal of all soldiers under eighteen from the local armed forces and support their disarmament and demobilization. This should involve programs to end individual possession of weapons by children. The best programs bring the weapons under the control of outside organizations, such as an internationally monitored weapons cantonment. There may also be an opportunity to link this need with other priorities. For example, the United Nations Development Program's "weapons in exchange for development" program has sought to link disarmament with projects designed to help create alternative (i.e., legal and productive) livelihoods for combatants.[15] However, some programs have made the mistake of requiring weapons turn-in as the price of admission into demobilization and rehabilitation programs. In Sierra Leone, for instance, the handover of an automatic rifle was sometimes required to receive ex-combatant benefits. Such policies exclude child soldiers who escaped without their weapons or served as spies, porters, or "wives."

Given the different concerns and dynamics at play with child soldiers, their process of disarmament and then demobilization should be kept distinct and separate from those of adult soldiers. This also would have the positive side effect of breaking leaders' direct controls over the children. Added attention should be given to dismantling command and control structures within child soldier units, such as ending any hierarchy or organization that rewards the most zealous or vicious child soldiers with added powers over their compatriots.

I started fighting at the age of six. I decided to turn in my gun because I want to go back to school.
　　　　　　　　　　　　　　　　　　　　　　　—R., age thirteen[16]

After disarmament comes the process of demobilization. This usually involves the movement of ex-combatants into some type of formal housing situation, such as camps, where the children are prepared for a return to civilian life. A number of key lessons have emerged from the international community's experience with this process over the last decades. Two critical requirements are that, first, any assembly areas should be located sufficiently far from the conflict zones. This is to ensure security and impede re-recruitment. Secondly, no weapons should be permitted into these camps. This is necessary both to achieve the clear break from the child soldiers' former life (as demobilization is the first step in their social reintegration) and to prevent the risks that intractable combatants might act as spoilers for the entire peace process.

Disarmament and demobilization programs of children are generally successful only outside crisis situations. In cases where it was tried while the situation was unstable or the fighting still went on, such as in the DRC by UNICEF, the programs were often in vain. As one Congolese NGO noted, "Demobilization in the middle of war is neither possible nor permanent."[17]

The idea of disarming can be a daunting one, particularly in the uncertain political environment that surrounds this process. This means that the number of groups and individual soldiers who willingly participate is greatly reduced if the fighting is ongoing or the situation otherwise unsettled. One problem is re-recruitment by either recalcitrant parties or even the opposing force (such as former child soldiers on the rebel side, now being drafted by the government). For child soldier groups, there is the fear that they will be taken advantage of and that their opponents will sweep up "their" children. As one commander in the DRC noted, "You can't demobilize [our] child soldiers, because others will enroll them."[18] For children, there is also often a great fear of retribution, as well as an underlying uncertainty about their future place in society.

Therefore, all measures must be taken to convince the important actors in the process (both the conflict group leaders and the individual soldiers) of the need and benefits of demobilization. Programs must be set in place that offer incentives to groups and individual soldiers to demobilize. Examples range from group leaders gaining greater political roles in the postwar governing structure if they act appropriately to combatants receiving education and job training that will aid them later in gainful employment. In general, though, direct cash payments to demobilized soldiers have not been successful and should be avoided.[19]

Security guarantees (often protective deployments from local security or peacekeeping forces) must also be provided to offer assurances that no one will be taken advantage of in his or her new position of greater vulnerability, and that re-recruitment does not occur. Another novel way to think about child soldier demobilization is its potential as a confidence-building measure between the warring parties. In negotiations, groups often are looking for proof of the other side's good intentions. The demobilization of children by both sides can thus be a first step for them to ramp down their conflict, which would carry important positive externalities for the children as well.

Throughout the demobilization process, child soldiers should be afforded added levels of care and protection to ease their transition. All efforts must be made to provide them with a sense of security and familiarity. The children should be afforded structure and routine in their daily activities. Thus, the staff that deals with them should remain as consistent as possible, to reinforce familiarity (this is often difficult, though, given the high stress of working with former child soldiers and resulting high rates of staff turnover). Another priority is that, wherever possible, the aid workers and counselors should be made up of those from the local culture or at least those who are familiar with the local culture's rites, practices, and values. If possible, many believe that it is better to house the children in smaller living units rather than large, impersonal barracks. For example, programs in the DRC even have the children help build and maintain their houses and cook their own food, to add to the sense of togetherness and self-reliance.[20]

Now after disarming I'm going back to my family to begin a new life and to beg my neighbors, the people in my community, for forgiveness. —M., age fourteen[21]

Special consideration must also be given to issues of protection and confidentiality. At the onset of the program, this may include providing a separation between living quarters of any children from opposing forces. Girl soldiers may also need to be treated as a special group during demobilization, as they may require added protective measures, sensitive to the local culture.

An initial interview with each demobilized child soldier is usually mandated upon the child's entry into a demobilization camp. This should be conducted on an individual basis and certainly not in the presence of former superiors. Separation during the interview process allows more freedom of discussion away from any fear of punishment, adds to the sense of change, and aids the recovery of the child's individual, as opposed to group, identity. At this initial interview, hypersensitive matters like personal losses or specific actions that the child committed during the fighting are not yet appropriate for exploration. Rather, this initial stage should limit itself to informing the child of the reasons behind the upcoming process and what he or she can expect. Assessments of the individual's physical and preliminary psychological needs should also be made.

Programs must then immediately focus on providing children's basic needs: food, health, shelter, and safety. At the same time, though, they must also begin the important work of locating the child's immediate or extended family. Given the long delays and hardships in locating and then bringing families back together, getting a jump start is important to the reunification of families at a later time, when children are prepared. This ultimate goal is important not just because of the inherent appeal of reuniting broken family structures, but also because of the positive long-term effect on the children themselves. Studies show that children are less likely to suffer from negative psychological aftereffects of trauma, such as post-traumatic stress disorder, if they are placed with members of their family.[22]

Because of the importance of the task, organizations should seek to establish a family-tracing program as soon as possible. This entails creating a shared network of contacts and resource centers, where families and aid workers can place needed contact information. Ideally, the program would involve the creation of a shared computerized database. Such a resource could be accessed at multiple sites, not just within the country at conflict, but also in resource centers in neighboring states and other likely refugee zones. One example of this is the Child Connect program, which provides an interoperable database that can help track down children, as well as share information across agencies.[23]

A key lesson is that tracing activities must involve the local government, the varied warring parties, and humanitarian groups to be fully effective. No communication tool should be ignored either. For example, in Sierra Leone, UNICEF-supported tracing agencies established registration points across the country and used radio publicity to help families find missing children. A tracing network should also be kept in place after the reunification of children with families, to allow groups to monitor the status of children and provide any follow-up assistance. Former child soldiers should also be provided with some sort of documentation at this stage, which will help ensure that they have access to these programs and are not excluded from any governmental benefits.

Rehabilitation

Disarmament and demobilization, which make up the disengagement of children from military life and control, are the essential first steps. However, many believe that the hardest work comes next, in trying to rehabilitate and reintegrate the former child soldiers into society. The challenge of rehabilitation for a child soldier is a quintessentially difficult process, primarily due to the added psychological and physical scars that former child soldiers carry.

It should be noted that all programs must have a long-term perspective in that they will have to be sustainable well after the conflict. Ideally, they will involve the participation of not just international aid workers, as is too often the norm, but also local community members and spiritual leaders. Giving the appearance of a welcoming and stable local social environment provides a crucial context for the rehabilitation. Additionally, the intent of external intervention must be to support, rather than replace, local society's coping strategies. This means that there is no one standardized approach to rehabilitation.

The beginning of any rehabilitation process involves building an understanding of the situation children have been placed in (in a sense, gaining a better idea of the "clients" of the process), and learning how the local society has dealt with trauma, suffering, and healing in the past.[24] An example of this is to integrate traditional spiritual cleansing activities into rehabilitation programs.[25] As will be discussed later, such programs also ease the reintegration of children back into local society.

Physically, child soldiers often enter the demobilization camps with many severe health problems. They will frequently be sickly or malnourished. With little concern for public health or cleanliness among child soldier groups in the field, they will also often suffer from high levels of disease, ranging from measles and diarrheal diseases to higher levels of sexual transmitted diseases (STDs) (as discussed in Chapter 6). Children are more likely to enter demobilization programs with debilitating or disabling wounds from the fighting. Many of the girl soldiers may also be pregnant or suffer from sexual abuse traumas, which carry added health and disease risks.

The psychological effects of serving as a child soldier are even more varied. Typically, ex–child soldiers will have undergone and/or carried out shocking and disturbing events of terrible violence. In that they are young, the effect on their psyche is magnified, as the violence takes place during the period when personalities are being developed. In the near term, the resultant trauma can manifest itself in reactions like constant weeping, mutism, repeated nightmares, and depression. For example, one survey of former child soldiers in Africa found that 50 percent had severe nightmares on a regular basis, 25 percent suffered some form of mutism, and 28 percent experienced some form of paranoia.[26] If not reversed, these psychological harms can have more lasting consequences.

Trauma is an external event that is so intense that it overwhelms the person's capacity to cope or master it. In psychological terms, "traumatic stressors" are those events that are "outside the range of human experience and must be of sufficient intensity to invoke symptoms of distress in most people."[27] The range of terrible shocks and activities involved in the child soldier doctrine certainly fits these definitions.

Because of children's vulnerabilities or lack of coping mechanisms, the experience of child soldiering often results in post-traumatic stress disorder (PTSD). One study found that as many as 97 percent of child soldiers may suffer from PTSD, regardless of the time they spent in violence.[28] This is a psychiatric disorder that was first associated with battle fatigue among regular soldiers during World Wars I and II, but that can affect anyone. It comes from witnessing traumatic or life-threatening events. These can range from extended stays in war zones and living through natural disasters to very specific or personalized suffering, such as being assaulted or raped. PTSD can result in both physical and mental symptoms, such as weight loss, depression, nightmares and flashbacks, and memory and cognition issues. Thus the disorder impairs a person's ability to function in day-to-day living.[29]

Most times I dream, I have a gun, I'm firing, I'm killing, cutting, amputating. I feel afraid, thinking perhaps that these things will happen to me again. Sometimes I cry. . . . When I see a woman I'm afraid of her. I've been bad with women; now I fear that if I go near one she'll hit me. Perhaps she will kill me.

—Z., age fourteen[30]

Ex–child soldiers frequently demonstrate some or all of these symptoms, which most health professionals believe are triggered by a combination of their dislocation from family and society, sense of uncertainty about the future, and memories of extreme violence and loss. Depression, anxiety, higher levels of aggression or introversion, extreme pessimism, limited capacity to accept frustration, and a lack of adequate personal mechanisms to resolve conflict are all common among former child soldiers going through rehabilitation. PTSD also results in secondary effects that trouble the youth's ability to rejoin society. These include learning difficulties, lowered ability to concentrate, changes in memory, and greater intellectual inflexibility. Physical manifestations include sleep disorders, severe headaches, and stomach pain, which are all common psychosomatic disturbances. As one aid worker in Uganda describes, "Some of the children sit rocking; it's like they are not there. They're a shell. . . . Some children sit and look at running water and just see blood."[31]

The severity of these reactions varies from mild manifestations to the extreme and often debilitating forms. Some of the determinants of the degree of acuteness include the duration of the traumatic experience, extent of involvement in violence as perpetrator or subject, cultural norms and expectations, age, and gender.[32] For example, victims of sexual abuse frequently experience heightened levels of acute PTSD. For them, the experience often becomes tied in with a sense of personal shame and/or suppression of connected emotions. A particularly worrisome statistic is that former girl child soldiers are 52 percent more likely to commit suicide than their boy child soldier equivalents.[33]

As a result, the long-term psychological costs from the use of the child soldier doctrine may be dire. PTSD, for instance, can last from months to years. Surveys in Uganda, for example, have found the symptoms caused by LRA captivity to persist more than five years.[34] Psychologists think that it can be as much as fifteen to twenty years before the full extent of trauma's damage on one's psyche can be determined. Indeed, psychological surveys of former adult combatants show that the impact of war-related stressors can last for a lifetime.

Given the relative newness of the child soldier doctrine, extended-year studies have not yet been carried out for ex–child combatants, indicating a clear research need in the future. One postulated worry, though, is that the effects may be magnified on children in the long term, or that children will suffer from what is known as the "exhaustion model." This is where even those who develop coping mechanisms to deal with trauma in the near term eventually run out of the energy needed to cope with the stress over the long term. Thus, even if the psychological harms are not evident at the start, their effects might magnify later.[35]

However, it is both premature and without scientific justification to assume that former child soldiers are forever "damaged goods" or simply beyond rehabilitation.[36] Thus, the need to support rehabilitation is imperative. While tailored to the individual conflict and even to individuals, the underlying strategy must approach the rehabilitation task from a holistic standpoint. A child's need for physical and mental health treatment, counseling, and placement within a broader security environment are all integral and interrelated.

The physical treatment side is fairly self-evident. Whatever malady troubles the youth should be aggressively and effectively eliminated as soon as possible. This will require that post-conflict assistance help to restore broken local health networks. Operational planning should therefore include much larger external assistance for hospitals and treatment clinics, which may have to be located in demobilization camps. Rehabilitation operations should also come prepared to aid in the full range of health problems. Health care workers working with child soldiers will find themselves doing everything from treating anemia, skin disorders, worms, and STDs to administering tranquilizers to help children sleep.[37]

> It was hard when I got back to Freetown [Sierra Leone]. There was
> no more marijuana or gunpowder, so I smoked cigarettes.
> —I., age twelve[38]

Aid agencies must also be prepared to help children with more lasting ailments, including those with incurable diseases, damaged or lost limbs, or other handicaps. Too often, the resources for such operations are insufficient. One sad example is the frequent lack of good prostheses for children in need. Consideration in post-conflict planning should therefore be given to how the local construction of such devices can be encouraged. This has the side benefit of spurring positive economic activity, as well as long-term sustainability.[39]

The special situation of children who have been "branded" by their organizations or otherwise physically scarred by the war should also be considered of importance, rather than treated as just a cosmetic matter. These wounds not only harm the psyche of their victims, but also impede their reintegration into the local society. As such, sometimes, children will go to great lengths to hide the marks.

One positive pilot program in Sierra Leone illustrates a potential ray of hope toward reversing this damage. It is run by the International Medical Corps, based in Los Angeles. In an innovative and rewarding program, IMC has enlisted plastic surgeons to perform skin grafts and other reconstructive surgeries on former RUF members who have such scars, which threatened to make them outcasts within their communities. This program was funded by USAID and administered by UNICEF.[40] Sadly, the program was able to help just 120 ex–child soldiers in Sierra Leone. It does, however, provide a model that can be built upon by other aid agencies, both in West Africa and elsewhere. As part of a program to stimulate effective action on the ground, a unified effort might be taken up by the advocacy community to link up with the American Society of Plastic Surgeons, in order to build a pool of willing surgeons for such important and rewarding efforts.

Special attention to the psychological adjustment of children must be at the core of any rehabilitation program. Projects should support healing processes and seek to reestablish a sense of normalcy. These can be accomplished through the institution of safe daily routines and community care networks. Almost all rehabilitation camp activities can be integrated with psychosocial programs that aid healing and adjustment.[41] These should also encourage self-expression, as articulation often provides an important role in psychosocial recovery. Some of the most effective include:

- "Normalization" activities that involve children in the positive responsibilities and routines of camp living, such as gathering wood, getting water, and washing clothes.
- Basic schooling, which, besides building standards of literacy and mathematics, can emphasize communication skills, civics, and cultural or peace studies.
- Recreational programs that release energy and encourage normal interaction, including games, story-making, individual and collective art therapy, interactive plays, and other creative educational workshops designed for children in need (one prominent example being the Playing to Grow program).[42]

There is also usually a requirement of some form of counseling for ex–child soldiers. These may involve one-on-one or small group therapy sessions. One of the most effective and important strategies for dealing with PTSD and aiding rehabilitation is known as cognitive-behavioral therapy (CBT). CBT for children generally includes gradual counseling that provides the child with anxiety management techniques, such as relaxation and assertiveness training, and correcting inaccurate or distorted trauma-related thoughts. The process then builds toward allowing the children to relieve negative memories and anxieties by being able to discuss the traumatic experience and learn that they no longer have to be afraid, even of their own memories.[43]

After crossing that line [killing], I was not a normal kid. I was a traumatized kid. I became completely unaware of the dangerous and crooked road that my life took. In fact, most of the horrible events that I went through didn't affect me until after I was taken out of the army and put in a psycho-social therapy home years later.

At the psycho-social therapy, I began to experience my trauma. I had sleepless nights. Every night I recalled the last day that my childhood was stripped away from me. I felt I had no reason for staying alive since I was the only one left in my family. I had no peace. My soul felt corrupted and I was lost in my own thoughts, blaming myself for what happened to me. The only time that I

found peace with myself was when I began writing songs about the
good times before the war. Through these writings, as well as the
help of the staff in my psycho-social therapy home, I was able to
successfully overcome my trauma. I once again found my child-
hood that was almost lost. I realized that I had a great determina-
tion to survive.   —I., age fourteen[44]

Unfortunately, the need for counseling and other rehabilitation activities is too often ignored in post-conflict programs. For example, in the first Sierra Leone operation, the United Nations made provisions for only one trained child psychologist to address the special needs of the tens of thousands of child soldiers.[45] Likewise, in a recent survey of child soldiers in East Asia, only one interview location had counseling available.[46] This is not just because of poor preparation on the part of the operational planners, but also broader resourcing issues. There are simply too few specialists skilled in children's psychology issues available to meet the growing needs of international relief and aid agencies. As in the issue of branding, a unified effort should be taken up by the advocacy community to build the pool of willing and ready child psychiatrists, psychologists, counselors, and social workers. This may involve formalized cooperation with relevant international occupational organizations, such as the International Council of Psychologists or the World Psychiatric Association. They must also work with mission planners to ensure that these specialists are then actually deployed in the operations in sufficient numbers.

In the end, time and stability appear to be what is most required for healing. If the child soldier had been within the military group for any extended period (a year or more), social workers tend to judge that programs in the range of six months are needed to achieve a safe and successful return to society (several times longer than what often happens in the field).[47] However, there is no exact determining point as to when a former child soldier is prepared to reintegrate back into society successfully. Here, one should defer to the experts for deciding when a child is ready, rather than any political schemata or prescribed timeline. Some of the indicators to help judge include whether the program has provided the child with effective coping tools, whether the child has overcome dispositions toward distrust and aggression, whether he or she demonstrates a sense of remorse for any violent actions, and whether the child is now able to operate on a personal level, guided by a traditional sense of right and wrong.

Reintegration

The final stage in the process of attempting to return childhood to young soldiers is reintegration. This step involves introducing the children back into their home or community, so that they can rejoin society on positive terms. As discussed in prior sections, the ideal outcome is to return them to their own family. This helps both the children and society regain a sense of normalcy. Placing them within their family is also thought to help speed recovery from PTSD.

Unfortunately, family reunification often faces an additional challenge of acceptance and willingness, beyond the already hard task of tracing and relocation. Even after a successful tracing, the families or children themselves may balk at reunification, often for very good reasons. For example, one survey in Africa found that 82 percent of parents considered former child soldiers to represent a potential danger to the population.[48] This may be because of fear of the child's actions, fears of retribution, or fear that the child or family still either identifies with or fears the group that once held the child. There may also be lingering displaced anger. As one rehabilitation worker in Uganda noted of many child soldiers who had been with the LRA, "They become very bitter and angry . . . They feel their parents have let them down, didn't do enough to prevent their capture."[49] As such, aid workers should ensure to prepare both children and parents for the challenges ahead. An emphasis on the importance of reconciliation and healing is often an effective theme behind such preparations.

Another sad outcome, though, is that sometimes children will have lost all family in the fighting or not be able to locate them. Arrangements should then begin to be developed for how the authorities plan on responding to these harder cases of ex–child soldier orphans. In several countries, including Colombia and Afghanistan, "youth houses," akin to halfway houses, have been organized for such children. Children in these programs live together under the supervision of a mentor and participate in educational and vocational training programs designed to allow their insertion back into the community.

If the local community is unwilling or unable to host them, experience in West Africa tends to show that children who are unable to return should be placed in localities outside the areas where they served as soldiers. This will ease their absorption into society and limit the dangers of retribution. Such orphan cases will also require additional support programs to reintegrate them into the community in a positive way. The underlying intent must be to create some form of positive self-sufficiency in the children. This will place them in a position to resist the lures of reenlistment or criminal activity.

Ultimately, a successful reintegration is as much about whether the families and communities are prepared for acceptance as about whether the children have been properly rehabilitated. For instance, in one survey in Africa, 80 percent of adults did not want their children to mix with children who had once served as child soldiers.[50] A significant program of sensitization should therefore be put in place to prepare the local society for the challenges and difficulties of reincorporating ex–child soldiers.[51] It is particularly difficult in places where the children may have committed heinous crimes against local civilians.

Efforts must be made to overcome the stigma and stereotypes that surround ex–child soldiers and describe them as perpetrators. Rather, they should seek to reinforce the acknowledgment by society that the children were also victims in the process. Truth and reconciliation programs have been run to some good effect in places like South Africa, but programs more specific to child soldiers are needed. In Sierra Leone, for example, UNICEF set up an agreement with local media to promote reintegration and reconciliation, including even producing radio spots that sought to educate the local populace and keep them informed of related activities.[52] More recently, Voice of the Children, a UN-sponsored radio station dedicated to children's issues, was launched. Another example is that children in Uganda are given a public presidential pardon for any activities they carried out while in captivity, providing an official sanction to societal forgiveness and reconciliation.[53]

I'm living with my parents now. I told them I'd been a fighter. At first, when I told them, they were afraid of me. They were thinking I'd do the same thing to them. But I told them I had been forced to fight. I wouldn't do these things again. I've been thinking about what I did. I will never forget it. I feel sorrowful now. I keep on telling people that I will not do this again.

—L., age twelve[54]

Child protection agencies can also act to reinforce reintegration. Some possibilities include running meetings and workshops with local families and communal leaders, as well as providing training on child soldier issues to local civil society groups. Incorporating civil society leaders, such as educators, religious figures, or tribal chiefs, is an important avenue for ensuring that the local community is prepared and willing to accept child soldiers back into the fold. Such individuals merit special meetings to lobby them to play a positive role and underscore the importance of their leadership in restoring the communal fabric. Freida Draisma, head of social welfare programs for the Red Cross in Maputo, describes some of the important roles that these figures played in Mozambique:

A community-based approach was therefore adopted, involving village and church leaders, teachers, traditional healers and Red Cross activists. Healers played a key role in the rehabilitation process. Believed to be a link between communities and their guardian spirit ancestors, they held purification ceremonies to cleanse the children of their past. These ceremonies were an essential step towards accepting the child back into the community. Rural families would normally make sure their returning children would take part in rituals, which included taking medicine, bathing in water treated with special herbs, inhaling smoke from burning roots, and periods of isolation. Church leaders, too, played a role by making children talk about their experiences in front of the congregation, or to a group of church elders, as a way of re-establishing contact with their community through confession.[55]

In traditional communities, healing and cleansing ceremonies may prove to be an effective mechanism to aid individual and communal reconciliation. These rituals, which are often witnessed by family members and the community, seek to purge and purify the children of the contamination of war, death, and the sense of guilt and sin that can surround them and of the avenging spirits of those who may have been killed by the children. These may vary by community and ethnic group. Examples include the symbolic burning of one's clothes (Mozambique) to the children washing themselves in a river at dawn and walking away without looking back (Angola).[56] Outside organizations should be sensitive to such traditions and seek to assist them, putting their own doubts aside.

Another way to support the acceptance and well-being of ex–child soldiers is to involve them in helping to solve their own communal problems. Examples include programs that help children to repair damaged community infrastructure, such as schools or wells, and to participate in weapons and land-mine location and disposal. These programs work best if structured into group activities, designed to decrease the stigma placed on the children and promote their sense of self-esteem and accomplishment. Such programs can have a powerful redemptive effect for both the child and the community. There may also be an avenue for the participation of elders in the community, who are often vulnerable in post-conflict situations as well. Programs can be designed that encourage and reward the passing on of skills and cultural heritage from elders to children.[57]

Ensuring that local security forces, which might have been on the opposing side, do not harass or attempt to re-recruit ex–child soldiers is another priority for reintegration efforts. This may require incorporating sessions on child protection into training programs and linking this concern to the duties of any relevant military observer or peacekeeping forces. Children should also be informed of the laws against their recruitment, so that they understand that the practice is not allowed and that they do have a choice in the matter. Some analysts even support the participation of ex–child soldiers in local recruitment prevention initiatives.[58]

The ultimate goal should be to create a community support network designed to reintegrate ex–child soldiers in a positive manner. Like other aspects of the overall process, the network should be as self-sufficient as possible. This means that outside agencies and experts should focus on aiding and training local actors rather than seeking to run such programs themselves.

Beyond the specific training and adjustment for families, civil society, and relevant government agencies to the reintegration process, a shift in the education system may be needed. Teachers will have to be prepared for the new challenges of instructing ex–child soldiers (who will often present greater psychological needs and concerns in the classroom). Other postwar education programs may need to incorporate land-mine awareness, living with and responding to HIV/AIDS, and peace education.[59] This last aspect is intended to decrease the likelihood that children will seek violent solutions to the problems they later confront. In Somalia, for example, such peace-building programs have included teacher training and the distribution of workbooks and games that promote "the rights and responsibilities of children, awareness of others as equals, communication, conflict awareness/resolution, peace, justice and tolerance."[60]

Restoring lost educational opportunities is critical for both communal recovery and children's reintegration. Child soldiers will have missed out on months or years of basic instruction. For instance, one survey of ex–child soldiers in the DRC found that 45 percent had not even completed primary school.[61] Particular problems, then, are the frequent low levels of literacy and mathematical skills among ex-combatants, both of which can pose serious risks for their future well-being. One successful program in Sierra Leone is a "catch-up" program aimed at former child soldiers in interim care centers. The program is designed to move the children through core skills requirements over six months, so that they can rejoin their age cohort rather than return to school with children years younger.[62] Other potential programs include special scholarships for former child soldier students to attend local or foreign schools and universities, particularly for those who have lost their families.

As described in Chapter 6, the broader education system in war zones may have been severely damaged by the fighting. Consequently, post-conflict recovery programs must be sure to have proper support for the restoration of general schooling.

An additional aspect may be the need to set up vocational training programs.[63] Unfortunately, most post-conflict reintegration programs follow the trend in demobilization and provide such job skills and support programs only to adult ex-combatants. This, though, ignores both the wide presence of child soldiers in many conflicts and their own economic needs. An added problem is that many child soldiers may be too old to enroll in basic education programs or are now the primary wage earners of their families. If they lack the skills to compete in the economy, an entire generation may be left adrift and seek refuge in other warring groups or criminal activity.[64]

> *After I have finished my university I want to be a doctor or a teacher. Father God, I have a future plan for this country that will make this country develop. I thank God that I have survived, they did not kill me in the bush. They used to punish me, do all kinds of bad things to me, but they did not kill me. . . . Please support us. Right now we don't have books, we don't have pens, we don't even have uniforms. Let them send some things for us.*
>
> —A., age fifteen[65]

Vocational training is intended to give demobilized child soldiers—and the adults that they become—a chance to succeed at some valuable trade. It also steers them away from the economic pressures that often drew them into the conflict, and may do so once again. These skill sets may include civil service, agricultural, or industrial training. One positive example, the Don Bosco Rehabilitation & Skills Training Program in Liberia, offers vocational training to war-affected youths, including programs specifically designed to assist young teenage mothers.[66] In Sierra Leone, one innovative entrepreneur, Francis Steven George, even set up a vocational training center for former RUF rebels that teaches them computer and programming skills. As George described, "This would represent one of the best avenues for them because in the next economy, information literacy is going to be the key."[67]

As with broader development programs, the best of such vocational training programs are often linked to micro-credit initiatives, which extend the backing over the longer term.[68] These may include support in the formation of cooperatives or other associations in which a small group of young people can jointly undertake projects. The Don Bosco Center, for example, provides its graduates with the needed tools for their new trade, a small cash grant, and the advice of a small business advisor. In Sierra Leone, the Christian Children's Fund set up a micro-credit loan and payback program which helps groups of ex-combatants share a small loan to help purchase needed business start-up items, such as tools for farming or fabrics and dyes for textiles.[69]

> *After escaping the Lord's Resistance Army, I was trained as a carpenter. I hoped to earn enough money from digging to rent a place in town, but the digging makes barely enough money to feed and clothe my family, and often I trade onions for other goods instead of money. Now I don't believe I'll ever get to live in town and sell my chairs.* —M., age seventeen[70]

In a sense, the worst legacy of the child soldier experience is that it never ends, shaping the child's development and later adulthood. As such, the final element in any reintegration program must be sustained follow-up activities. These should aim at providing social and psychological support to ex–child soldiers and their families and communities. The activities should also seek to determine the whereabouts and activities of former child soldiers. This can help ensure that they do not fall through the cracks, or end up becoming involved in criminal or violent groups again. For example, in East Timor, one positive program created incentives (links to assistance programs) for demobilized soldiers to check back in with support groups. This helped ensure that they were adjusting well and steering clear of any negative activities, such as street crime or violence. In Sierra Leone, follow-up activities have included the organization of local committees at the district level, which provide community-based support for vulnerable children.

If possible, these activities should be coordinated between the relevant local government agencies and supporting civil society, humanitarian, and development organizations.[71] Linked with this should be a program to collect systematic data about the circumstances and conditions of the ex–child soldiers, which will be useful to both future policy and research.

Conclusions

The recovery of lost childhood is one of the most difficult challenges that the use of the child soldier doctrine has raised. A final important note is that much of what we know in this realm has been learned through hard experience. It remains as much of a developing art as it is a known process. What we do know for certain is that a child soldier's physical, psychological, social, and economic needs must be factored into post-conflict arrangements. To do otherwise risks the recovery of society writ large. Such programs must also seek to incorporate the best of modern expertise and techniques with local culture and perceptions.

The state of the field is still young, though. The lessons discussed here are not fully spread and certainly not universally accepted across the various child soldier conflict zones and postwar operations. We simply do not yet have a bedrock of established learning on which to rest. A priority for the international community, therefore, must be a comprehensive program to vet what does and does not work in child soldier demobilization, rehabilitation, and reintegration. It should then develop and disseminate the best practices in this realm, to assist program development and effectiveness.

CHAPTER 11

Looking Ahead

*I am praying for forgiveness so that more fruitful things can come
our way, praying that God will help us to become good people.*
—Z., age fourteen[1]

There used to be no need to formally prohibit the use of children as
soldiers. To send children into battle was once not only unconscionable
but also unthinkable. However, this practice is now one of the dreadful
realities of modern warfare. It is a new doctrine adhered to by a wide-
ranging set of conflict groups spread out across the globe. Indeed, the
conflicts that have not seen children serving as fighters are now the rar-
ity. A number of these wars fought by children are, in fact, even sustained by their very presence.

An Even Darker Future?

As we look to the future, perhaps most worrisome is that the underlying forces that led to the rise of this practice appear likely to stay in
place if no action is taken to amend them. World order remains in a
state of constant flux, with little end in sight to the panoply of wars and
smoldering conflicts that cover the international system. Diseases,
famine, mass poverty, and so on continue to darken the once hopeful
seeds of globalization. The result is that a generation of estranged and

isolated children is growing up without educational and economic opportunities, and without any hope of prospering. They make up the core of the child soldier recruiting pool in the present and future.

In turn, the predominant weapons of war remain cheap, widespread, and easily available to any would-be warring party with even an iota of initiative. Their accessibility allows the conversion of mass numbers of vulnerable, disconnected children into low-cost and expendable soldiers. They are abducted or recruited, quickly indoctrinated and trained, and then set loose on the battlefield.

Such is the new doctrine of child soldiers that has emerged over the last decades. It is taken advantage of by an increasing cast of unscrupulous warlords and power mongers. All they require is an opportunity and incentive; the mass breakdown in good governance and the potential for profits and power from war provide both. These leaders only need the willingness to transgress moral norms, which is made easier by the lack of any consequences.

Sadly, none of these factors will go away of their own accord and the consequences are quite dangerous. Children's recruitment and use in battle not only violates acceptable practices of war, but also makes conflicts both more likely and more bloody. It results in higher levels of human rights violations and atrocities committed against civilians and the child soldiers themselves. It also can lead to a virtual proliferation of conflict groups and warring parties. Almost any group is able to fight better and longer, for a wider variety of causes, many of them personalized, unpopular, or downright incoherent. Finally, the use of children as soldiers steals their very childhood, laying the groundwork for further strife.

So far, the response by the international community to this phenomenon has been limited in its effectiveness. While certainly directed by the right motives, the movement against child soldiering has made little headway if the standard for success is to end the present and future use of children on the battlefield. Activists have raised awareness and made great efforts to re-establish certain prohibitory regimes. But these regimes have remained fairly toothless. In turn, governments and the United Nations have been unhurried in implementing changes that might prevent, deter, or even mitigate the consequences. Political and military analysts share equal blame, as they have been slow to recognize the changes in warfare that child soldiers portend.

While the task of changing this path is daunting, it is not without hope. Making an effort to end the practice of child soldiers is a necessary one. It will not only alleviate some of the worst aspects of modern violence, but is also a means to reclaiming part of our lost humanity.

If there is any hope of halting the trend, the exploitation of children as weapons of war must be faced down in each of its stages: before, during, and after. Such global challenges as the spread of disease, mass poverty, the lack of human opportunity, and the global trade in cheap weaponry to various warring parties are important not only on their own merits, but because they carry a greater cost for us all. They lead to wider risks of war, enable terrorism, and sustain child soldier groups; each provides an even further imperative for serious action.

More direct preventative measures must also be taken to end child soldiering. Rather than relying on an unlikely or ephemeral change of heart among leaders who abuse children to do their bidding, we must set up realistic systems of punishment and deterrence. Such measures include the use of sanctions against child soldier leaders, supporters, and enablers, and the wider application of war crimes tribunals and labor laws.

These steps may not fully deter the use of the child soldier doctrine, and certainly will not end the practice at the very start. They will, however, at least take away some of its advantages and, most importantly, connect the practice of recruiting and using child soldiers with some form of realistic penalty. Thus, the decision calculus of those weighing whether or not to use children as soldiers will be altered. Moral norms will be finally backed with action.

Unfortunately, we cannot always choose our opponents or their behavior. If children are a new feature of contemporary war, then our professional militaries must be prepared for them. Grounding preparation and training in this reality is the only way to minimize the child soldier doctrine's harms and remove some of the benefits that opponents may gain in using it. Possible actions to take in response include developing intelligence profiles of child soldier opponents; building an effective counter-doctrine that incorporates new rules of engagement, use of psychological operations, employment of non-lethal weapons, and educated targeting; welcoming child soldier escapees and POWs; and managing the new stresses of public affairs.

Finally, post-conflict efforts can provide far better attention and support to the growing pool of children who have served as soldiers. If we do so successfully, they will be less likely to serve as soldiers again, and thus end a terrible cycle. Peace treaties and post-conflict planning must recognize who is now actually at war and the unique challenges that the widening use of the child soldier doctrine presents. Greater support must also be given to the difficult but important tasks of child soldier demobilization, rehabilitation, and reintegration. Former child soldiers must be treated as the victims they are. They require sustained and systematic support to allow them to regain the childhood and opportunities that were stolen from them.

Countless doctrines and modes of warfare have come and gone over the long march of history. War has been viewed as everything from a noble affair of feudal ideals, in which armored knights would test their honor and manliness, to an imperial burden, in which nations sought to prove their worth by seizing colonies in distant lands. In turn, allowable practices in battle have included everything from the right to keep captured soldiers as personal slaves to the release of poison gases designed to kill thousands at a time.

The child soldier doctrine will hopefully someday soon join these many other practices of war that have vanished. Perhaps, history will look back upon this period of child soldiers as an aberration, a short phase when the moral norms broke down but were quickly restored. It has been a long-held conviction that children have no place in war. To make it a reality once more, we need only to match the will of those who do evil with our own will to do good.

Optional Protocol to the Convention on the Rights of the Child on the Involvement of Children in Armed Conflict

The States Parties to the present Protocol,

Encouraged by the overwhelming support for the Convention on the Rights of the Child, demonstrating the widespread commitment that exists to strive for the promotion and protection of the rights of the child,

Reaffirming that the rights of children require special protection, and calling for continuous improvement of the situation of children without distinction, as well as for their development and education in conditions of peace and security,

Disturbed by the harmful and widespread impact of armed conflict on children and the long-term consequences it has for durable peace, security and development,

Condemning the targeting of children in situations of armed conflict and direct attacks on objects protected under international law, including places that generally have a significant presence of children, such as schools and hospitals,

Noting the adoption of the Rome Statute of the International Criminal Court, in particular, the inclusion therein as a war crime, of conscripting or enlisting children under the age of 15 years or using them to participate actively in hostilities in both international and non-international armed conflicts,

Considering therefore that to strengthen further the implementation of rights recognized in the Convention on the Rights of the Child there is a need to increase the protection of children from involvement in armed conflict,

Noting that article 1 of the Convention on the Rights of the Child specifies that, for the purposes of that Convention, a child means every human being below the age of 18 years unless, under the law applicable to the child, majority is attained earlier,

Convinced that an optional protocol to the Convention that raises the age of possible recruitment of persons into armed forces and their participation in hostilities will contribute effectively to the implementation of the principle that the best interests of the child are to be a primary consideration in all actions concerning children,

Noting that the twenty-sixth International Conference of the Red Cross and Red Crescent in December 1995 recommended, inter alia, that parties to conflict take every feasible step to ensure that children below the age of 18 years do not take part in hostilities,

Welcoming the unanimous adoption, in June 1999, of International Labour Organization Convention No. 182 on the Prohibition and Immediate Action for the Elimination of the Worst Forms of Child Labour, which prohibits, inter alia, forced or compulsory recruitment of children for use in armed conflict,

Condemning with the gravest concern the recruitment, training and use within and across national borders of children in hostilities by armed groups distinct from the armed forces of a State, and recognizing the responsibility of those who recruit, train and use children in this regard,

Recalling the obligation of each party to an armed conflict to abide by the provisions of international humanitarian law,

Stressing that the present Protocol is without prejudice to the purposes and principles contained in the Charter of the United Nations, including Article 51, and relevant norms of humanitarian law,

Bearing in mind that conditions of peace and security based on full respect of the purposes and principles contained in the Charter and observance of applicable human rights instruments are indispensable for the full protection of children, in particular during armed conflicts and foreign occupation,

Recognizing the special needs of those children who are particularly vulnerable to recruitment or use in hostilities contrary to the present Protocol owing to their economic or social status or gender,

Mindful of the necessity of taking into consideration the economic, social and political root causes of the involvement of children in armed conflicts,

Convinced of the need to strengthen international cooperation in the implementation of the present Protocol, as well as the physical and psychosocial rehabilitation and social reintegration of children who are victims of armed conflict,

Encouraging the participation of the community and, in particular, children and child victims in the dissemination of informational and educational programmes concerning the implementation of the Protocol,

Have agreed as follows:

Article 1

States Parties shall take all feasible measures to ensure that members of their armed forces who have not attained the age of 18 years do not take a direct part in hostilities.

Appendix

Article 2

States Parties shall ensure that persons who have not attained the age of 18 years are not compulsorily recruited into their armed forces.

Article 3

1. States Parties shall raise in years the minimum age for the voluntary recruitment of persons into their national armed forces from that set out in article 38, paragraph 3, of the Convention on the Rights of the Child, taking account of the principles contained in that article and recognizing that under the Convention persons under the age of 18 years are entitled to special protection.

2. Each State Party shall deposit a binding declaration upon ratification of or accession to the present Protocol that sets forth the minimum age at which it will permit voluntary recruitment into its national armed forces and a description of the safeguards it has adopted to ensure that such recruitment is not forced or coerced.

3. States Parties that permit voluntary recruitment into their national armed forces under the age of 18 years shall maintain safeguards to ensure, as a minimum, that:

(a) Such recruitment is genuinely voluntary;

(b) Such recruitment is carried out with the informed consent of the person's parents or legal guardians;

(c) Such persons are fully informed of the duties involved in such military service;

(d) Such persons provide reliable proof of age prior to acceptance into national military service.

4. Each State Party may strengthen its declaration at any time by notification to that effect addressed to the Secretary-General of the United Nations, who shall inform all States Parties. Such notification shall take effect on the date on which it is received by the Secretary-General.

5. The requirement to raise the age in paragraph 1 of the present article does not apply to schools operated by or under the control of the armed forces of the States Parties, in keeping with articles 28 and 29 of the Convention on the Rights of the Child.

Appendix

Article 4

1. Armed groups that are distinct from the armed forces of a State should not, under any circumstances, recruit or use in hostilities persons under the age of 18 years.

2. States Parties shall take all feasible measures to prevent such recruitment and use, including the adoption of legal measures necessary to prohibit and criminalize such practices.

3. The application of the present article shall not affect the legal status of any party to an armed conflict.

Article 5

Nothing in the present Protocol shall be construed as precluding provisions in the law of a State Party or in international instruments and international humanitarian law that are more conducive to the realization of the rights of the child.

Article 6

1. Each State Party shall take all necessary legal, administrative and other measures to ensure the effective implementation and enforcement of the provisions of the present Protocol within its jurisdiction.

2. States Parties undertake to make the principles and provisions of the present Protocol widely known and promoted by appropriate means, to adults and children alike.

3. States Parties shall take all feasible measures to ensure that persons within their jurisdiction recruited or used in hostilities contrary to the present Protocol are demobilized or otherwise released from service. States Parties shall, when necessary, accord to such persons all appropriate assistance for their physical and psychological recovery and their social reintegration.

Article 7

1. States Parties shall cooperate in the implementation of the present Protocol, including in the prevention of any activity contrary thereto and in the rehabilitation and social reintegration of persons

who are victims of acts contrary thereto, including through technical cooperation and financial assistance. Such assistance and cooperation will be undertaken in consultation with the States Parties concerned and the relevant international organizations.

2. States Parties in a position to do so shall provide such assistance through existing multilateral, bilateral or other programmes or, inter alia, through a voluntary fund established in accordance with the rules of the General Assembly.

Article 8

1. Each State Party shall, within two years following the entry into force of the present Protocol for that State Party, submit a report to the Committee on the Rights of the Child providing comprehensive information on the measures it has taken to implement the provisions of the Protocol, including the measures taken to implement the provisions on participation and recruitment.

2. Following the submission of the comprehensive report, each State Party shall include in the reports it submits to the Committee on the Rights of the Child, in accordance with article 44 of the Convention, any further information with respect to the implementation of the Protocol. Other States Parties to the Protocol shall submit a report every five years.

3. The Committee on the Rights of the Child may request from States Parties further information relevant to the implementation of the present Protocol.

Article 9

1. The present Protocol is open for signature by any State that is a party to the Convention or has signed it.

2. The present Protocol is subject to ratification and is open to accession by any State. Instruments of ratification or accession shall be deposited with the Secretary-General of the United Nations.

3. The Secretary-General, in his capacity as depositary of the Convention and the Protocol, shall inform all States Parties to the Conven-

tion and all States that have signed the Convention of each instrument of declaration pursuant to article 3.

Article 10

1. The present Protocol shall enter into force three months after the deposit of the tenth instrument of ratification or accession.

2. For each State ratifying the present Protocol or acceding to it after its entry into force, the Protocol shall enter into force one month after the date of the deposit of its own instrument of ratification or accession.

Article 11

1. Any State Party may denounce the present Protocol at any time by written notification to the Secretary-General of the United Nations, who shall thereafter inform the other States Parties to the Convention and all States that have signed the Convention. The denunciation shall take effect one year after the date of receipt of the notification by the Secretary-General. If, however, on the expiry of that year the denouncing State Party is engaged in armed conflict, the denunciation shall not take effect before the end of the armed conflict.

2. Such a denunciation shall not have the effect of releasing the State Party from its obligations under the present Protocol in regard to any act that occurs prior to the date on which the denunciation becomes effective. Nor shall such a denunciation prejudice in any way the continued consideration of any matter that is already under consideration by the Committee on the Rights of the Child prior to the date on which the denunciation becomes effective.

Article 12

1. Any State Party may propose an amendment and file it with the Secretary-General of the United Nations. The Secretary-General shall thereupon communicate the proposed amendment to States Parties with a request that they indicate whether they favour a conference of States Parties for the purpose of considering and voting upon the pro-

posals. In the event that, within four months from the date of such communication, at least one third of the States Parties favour such a conference, the Secretary-General shall convene the conference under the auspices of the United Nations. Any amendment adopted by a majority of States Parties present and voting at the conference shall be submitted to the General Assembly of the United Nations for approval.

2. An amendment adopted in accordance with paragraph 1 of the present article shall enter into force when it has been approved by the General Assembly and accepted by a two-thirds majority of States Parties.

3. When an amendment enters into force, it shall be binding on those States Parties that have accepted it, other States Parties still being bound by the provisions of the present Protocol and any earlier amendments they have accepted.

Article 13

1. The present Protocol, of which the Arabic, Chinese, English, French, Russian and Spanish texts are equally authentic, shall be deposited in the archives of the United Nations.

2. The Secretary-General of the United Nations shall transmit certified copies of the present Protocol to all States Parties to the Convention and all States that have signed the Convention.

Chapter 1: Children and War

1. Quoted in "Child Soldiers," Radio Netherlands, January 21, 2000, http://www.rnw.nl/humanrights/index.html.

2. John Keegan, *A History of Warfare* (New York: Knopf, 1993).

3. Michael Walzer, *Just and Unjust Wars: A Moral Argument with Historical Illustrations* (New York: Basic Books, 1992).

4. Michael Ignatieff, *The Warrior's Honor: Ethnic War and the Modern Conscience* (New York: Holt, 1998).

5. Human Rights Watch, *"You'll Learn Not to Cry": Child Combatants in Columbia* (New York, September 2003), p. 95.

6. Jane Green Schaller, "Children, Child Health, and War," paper presented at the IPA/WHO/UNICEF Pre-Congress Workshop on Assessment of the Mid-Decade Goals: Evaluation and Recommendations, Cairo, September 9–10, 1995.

7. Michael Klare, "The Kalashnikov Age," *Bulletin of the Atomic Scientists* 55, no. 1 (January/February 1999), http://www.bullatomsci.org/issues/1999/jf99/jf99klare.html.

8. United Nations, Report of the Expert of the Secretary General Graça Machel, "Impact of Armed Conflict on Children," Document A/51/306 & Add. 1., August 26, 1996; BBC, *Children of Conflict,* 1999, http://www.bbc.co.uk/worldservice/people/features/childrensrights/childrenofconflict/soldtxt.shtml.

9. "Doctrine is defined as the body of theory within which the armed forces must operate prescribing the methods and circumstances of their employment. Doctrinal provisions are generalizations gleaned from past experience about what functions well." David Keithley and Paul Melshein, "Past as Prologue: USMC Small Wars Doctrine," *Small Wars and Insurgencies* 8, no. 2 (autumn 1997): 88. For other extrapolations on "doctrine," please see U.S. Department of Defense, Joint Publication 1-02, *DOD Dictionary of Military and Associated Terms,* http://www.dtic.mil/doctrineljel/doddict/data/d/02018.html; Gunther E. Rothenberg, "Maurice of Nassau, Gustavus Adolphus, Raimondo Montecuccoli, and the 'Military Revolution' of the Seventeenth Century," in Peter Paret, ed., *Makers of Modern Strategy* (Princeton, NJ: Princeton University Press, 1986), esp. pp. 40–42.

10. Quoted in Rory Carroll, "Sham Demobilization Hides Rise in Congo's Child Armies," *The Guardian* (London), September 9, 2003.

11. The eighteen-year-old definition is drawn from the UNICEF international standard of age of maturity and is encoded in the international laws of war described later.

12. T. W. Bennet, *Using Children in Armed Conflict: A Legitimate African Tradition?* (Essex, UK: Institute for Security Studies, 2002), at http://www.essex.ac.uk/armedcon/Issues/Texts/Soldiers002.htm.

13. Many hold that the eighteen-year definition has its basis in cultural relativism. In addition to the aforementioned points that refute it, such an argument is undermined by the fact that during negotiations over the Additional Protocol, it was primarily the Western countries, including the United States, United Kingdom, and the Netherlands, that argued that they should be able to recruit under-eighteen-year-olds. Interestingly, eighteen is also the most common age that former child soldiers cite as being the proper minimum age for recruitment. UNICEF, *Adult Wars, Child Soldiers* (Geneva, 2003), p. 58.

Chapter 2: It's a Small World After All

1. "Stopping the Use of Child Soldiers," *New York Times,* April 22, 2002.

2. John Keegan, with Richard Holmes and John Gau, *Soldiers: A History of Men in Battle* (London: Sphere Books, 1987).

3. T. W. Bennet, *Using Children in Armed Conflict: A Legitimate African Tradition?* (Essex, UK: Institute for Security Studies, 2000), http://www.essex.ac.uk/armedcon/Issues/Texts/Soldiers002.htm.

4. John Paden, "Muslim Civic Culture and Conflict Resolution," Brookings manuscript, 2003, p. 127.

5. Women's Commission for Refugee Women and Children, *Against All Odds: Surviving the War on Adolescents,* July 2001.

6. Speech available at http://www.208.184.41.83/English/NormsandValues.html (accessed May 5, 2001).

7. William Shakespeare, *The Life of King Henry the Fifth,* Act IV, Scene 7, in *The Oxford Shakespeare,* http://www.bartleby.com.

8. James Brundage, *The Crusades: A Documentary History* (Milwaukee, WI: Marquette University Press, 1962), p. 213.

9. Esther Forbes, *Johnny Tremain* (New York: Yearly, 1944; reissued 1987).

10. Eleanor Bishop, *Ponies, Patriots, and Powder Monkeys: A History of Children in America's Armed Forces, 1776–1916* (Del Mar, CA: Bishop, 1982), p. 4.

11. Ibid., pp. 50–51.

12. John Cook, quoted in "Battery B, 4th Light Artillery's Medal of Honor Winners," http://www.Batteryb.com.

13. "Report on the Battle of New Market Virginia and aftermath, part 1, May 15, 1864," *VMI Annual Report,* July 1864, http://www.vmi.edu/~archtml/cwnmrpt.html.

14. Guido Knopp, *Hitler's Kinder* (Munich: Bertelsmann, 2000); Philip Baker, *Youth Led by Youth* (London: Vilmor, 1989).

15. Harendra de Silva, "Conscription of Children in Armed Conflict: Is It Martyrdom or Child Abuse?," paper presented at the British Association for the Study and Prevention of Child Abuse and Neglect Congress, Edinburgh, July 1997.

16. Save the Children, "Children of the Gun," Children in Crisis project report, September 2000, http://www.savethechildren.org/crisis.

17. Human Rights Watch, *"You'll Learn Not to Cry"*: *Child Combatants in Colombia* (New York, September 2003), pp. 4–5; Karl Penhaul, "Colombia's Force of Child Soldiers," *Boston Globe,* March 4, 2001.

18. Jan Mckirk, "Brutality of Child Army Shocks Colombia," *The Independent* (London), May 2, 2001.

19. Coalition to Stop the Use of Child Soldiers (CSC), "The Use of Child Soldiers in the Americas: An Overview," 2001, http://www.child-soldiers.org; Human Rights Watch, "Child Soldiers Used by All Sides in Colombia's Armed Conflict," press release, New York, October 8, 1998, http://www.hrw.org/hrw/press98/oct/childsold1008.htm.

20. CSC, "Action Appeal: Colombia," September 2002; *UNHCR News,* May 21, 2002.

21. Human Rights Watch, *"You'll Learn Not to Cry,"* p. 64.

22. Quoted in Jason Chrudy, "From Bosnian Child Soldier to U.S. Army Leader," *Stars and Stripes,* August 17, 2004.

23. Colonel Boris Okhtinsky, quoted in "Sausage, Shahid's Dream," *Moskovskie Novosti,* July 2, 2002.

24. CSC, "The Use of Children by OSCE Member States," Human Dimension Seminar on Children and Armed Conflict, Warsaw, May 23–26, 2000, http://www.child-soldiers.org.

25. "PKK Child Recruitment in Sweden," Children of War, September 1998.

26. Richard Reid, "The Impact of Armed Conflict on Children's Rights," *International Pediatric Association Journal* 6, no. 4 (October 1995), http://www.ipa-france.net/pubs/inches/inch6_4/reid.htm.

27. "Liberia: Child Soldiers Are Back on the Frontline," Integrated Regional Information Networks (IRIN), June 9, 2003; Somini Sengupta, "Soldiers of Misfortune," *The Hindu* (Madras), December 2, 2003.

28. The RUF in Sierra Leone is next with a six-year-old, closely followed by a number of armed groups with seven- and eight-year-olds. Rädda Barnen, *Childwar Database,* principal investigator: Henric Häggström, at http://www.rb.se (accessed November 2000).

29. Quoted in "Up to 15,000 Child Soldiers in Liberia, UN Says," IRIN, September 24, 2003.

30. Even after the overthrow of the regime behind the genocide, the fighting by children still continues. The Army for the Liberation of Rwanda (ALIR) rebel group recruits and sometimes abducts children for military service, some as young as ten years old. Rädda Barnen, *Children of War Newsletter,* no. 1/01 (March 2001), at http://www.rb.se.

31. "Up to 14,000 Children Used in War," IRIN, June 12, 2001.

32. Barnen, *Children of War Newsletter.*

33. International Labor Office, *Wounded Childhood: The Use of Children in Armed Conflict in Central Africa* (Geneva, 2003), p. 5.

34. Evelyn Leopold, "Congolese Kids Face Horrific Conditions," Reuters, June 17, 2003; "UN Finds Congo Child Soldiers," BBC News, February 21, 2001; "Amman Conference to Seek Ban on Use of Child Soldiers in Region, World," AFP, April 7, 2001; "DRC Child Soldiers," *Child Soldiers Newsletter* 3 (March 2002).

35. Emily Wax, "Boy Soldiers Toting AK-47s Put at Front of Congo's War," *Washington Post,* June 13, 2003; Anne Edgerton, "Rapid Deployment of Emergency Multinational Force Critical," Refugees International press release, June 2, 2003; AFP report, June 6, 2003.

36. Interviews with DRC experts, spring 2003.

37. "Articles Tell Palestinians' Side of Fight," *Los Angeles Times,* March 31, 2002. For one of the more reliable statistics on the intifada, please see the Information Center for Human Rights in the Occupied Territories, http://www.btselem.org.

38. Ian Brown, *Khomeini's Forgotten Sons: The Story of Iran's Boy Soldiers* (London: Grey Seal, 1990), p. 2.

39. Quoted in Karen Armstrong, *The Battle for God* (New York: Knopf, 2000), pp. 327–28.

40. Brown, *Khomeini's Forgotten Sons,* p. 39.

41. P. W. Singer, "Facing Saddam's Child Soldiers," Brookings Iraq Memo 8, January 2003.

42. Matthew Cox, "War Even Uglier When a Child Is the Enemy," *USA Today,* April 8, 2003; "Report: Marines Wounded in Fighting Late Wednesday in Iraq," AP, March 27, 2003; Alex Perry, "When Kids Are in the Cross Hairs," *Time,* April 21, 2003.

43. Martin Bentham, "Fedeyeen Use Children as Shields," *The Telegraph* (London), April 4, 2003.

44. Barbara Slavin, "U.S. Troops Clash with Exile Leader's Militia," *USA Today,* May 2, 2003.

45. Mary Beth Sheridan, "For Help in Rebuilding Mosul, U.S. Turns to Its Former Foes," *Washington Post,* April 25, 2003.

46. "Enemy Tactics, Techniques, and Procedures (TTP) and Recommendations," Third Corps Support Command briefing document, LSA Anaconda, Iraq, September 2003; Joseph Galloway, "Hurt Still Arriving at Army Hospital," *Charlotte Observer,* November 3, 2003; interviews with U.S. Army officers, November–December 2003.

47. Quoted in "Child Soldiers Square Up to U.S. Tanks," *Daily Telegraph* (London), August 23, 2004.

48. Ibid.

49. Neil Mackay, "Iraq's Child Prisoners," *Sunday Herald,* August 1, 2004; Richard Sisk, "Teen Held, U.S. Admits Juveniles in Abu Ghraib," New York *Daily News,* July 15, 2004.

50. U.S. Army Lt. Col. Barry Johnson, quoted in Sisk, "Teen Held."

51. Human Rights Watch, *Children in Sudan: Slaves, Street Children and Child Soldiers* (New York, September 1995).

52. CSC, *Child Soldier Use 2003: A Briefing for the 4th UN Security Council Open Debate on Children and Armed Conflict,* January 2004.

53. Rachel Stohl, "Child Soldiers Released in Sudan, Still No U.S. Action," *Weekly Defense Monitor* 5, no. 9 (March 1, 2001).

54. Carol Ann Berger, "From Cattle Camp to Slaughterhouse: The Politics of Identity Among Cuban-Educated Dinka Refugees in Canada" (master's thesis, University of Alberta, 2001); Human Rights Watch/Africa, *Civilian Devastation: Abuses by All Parties in the War in Southern Sudan* (New York, 1994).

55. Ellen Barry, "The Lost Boys," *Boston Globe,* January 7, 2001; Women's Commission, *Against All Odds.*

56. Colin Nickerson, "A Boy's Journey from Canada to Al Qaeda," *Boston Globe,* March 9, 2003; Joseph Farah, "Family of Canadian Teen Has Extensive al Qaida Ties," *World Net Daily,* September 6, 2002.

57. CSC, "Action Appeal: Afghanistan," *Child Soldiers Newsletter* 2 (December 2001).

58. P. W. Singer, "Pakistan's Madrassahs: Ensuring a System of Education, Not Jihad," Brookings Analysis Paper, no. 14, January 2002.

59. Hannah Beech Farkhar, "The Child Soldiers," *Time,* November 7, 2001.

60. Quoted in "Rescuing Former Child Soldiers," *Afghan Recovery Report,* Institute for War and Peace Reporting, May 19, 2004.

61. Adnan Laeeq, "Flowers on the Frontline," *Child Soldiers Newsletter* 5 (September 2002).

62. "Too Small to Be Fighting in Anyone's War," IRIN, December 12, 2003.

63. Interviews with U.S. Army officer, March 2004; Keith Richburg, "Taliban Maintans Grip Rooted in Fear," *Washington Post,* August 9, 2004.

64. CSC, *1379 Country Report,* 2002.

65. Quoted in Jessica Stern, *Terror in the Name of God* (New York: HarperCollins, 2003), p. 210.

66. Recent reports indicate that children between the ages of seven and twelve are fighting on both sides in Ambon. CSC, "Child Soldiers: A Human Security Challenge for ASEAN (Association of South East Asia Nations)," July 24, 2000, at http://www.child-soldiers.org.

67. Quoted in John McBeth, "Children of War," *Far Eastern Economic Review,* May 2, 2002.

68. Human Rights Watch, *My Gun Was as Tall as Me* (New York, 2002), p. 46; Coalition to Stop the Use of Child Soldiers, *Child Soldier Use 2003.*

69. "Philippines: Children Captured by Philippines Army," *Child Soldiers* 3 (March 2002). Amnesty International, "Child Soldiers Are the Real Victims," appeal, February 22, 2002.

70. Philip Pan, "Some Filipinos Say US Presence May Fuel Rebel Support," *Washington Post,* February 7, 2002, p. 13.

71. Rädda Barnen, *Children of War Newsletter.*

72. Robert Kaplan, "The Coming Anarchy," *Atlantic Monthly,* February 1994; Kaplan, *The Ends of the Earth: A Journey at the Dawn of the 21st Century* (New York: Ran-

dom House, 1996); Barry Buzan, Ole Wæver, and Jaap de Wilde, *Security: A New Framework for Analysis* (Boulder, CO: Rienner, 1998); Chester A. Crocker and Fen Osler Hampson, *Managing Global Chaos* (Washington, DC: United States Institute of Peace Press, 1996); Robert Cooper, *The Post Modern State and the World Order,* demos paper no. 19, 2d ed., 2000; Max Singer and Aaron Wildavsky, *Real World Order: Zones of Peace/Zones of Turmoil* (Chatham, UK: Chatham House, 1993); Yahya Sadowski, *The Myth of Global Chaos* (Washington, DC: Brookings, 1998).

73. Data on Rädda Barnen, *Childwar Database;* Taylor Seyboldt, ed., *SIPRI Yearbook 2002: Armaments, Disarmament and International Security* (Oxford, UK: Oxford University Press, 2002), Appendix IA, Uppsala Conflict Data Project.

74. Data from Rädda Barnen, *Childwar Database.* These figures also blunt the spurious arguments that the standards against use of child soldiers are Western derived. No culture considers its members mature at these young ages, nor do their prior histories of warfare indicate such use of pre-teen warriors.

75. UNICEF, *Adult Wars, Child Soldiers* (Geneva, 2003), p. 19.

76. International Labor Office, *Wounded Childhood,* p. 36.

77. Ilse Derluyn et al., "Post Traumatic Stress in Former Child Soldiers," *The Lancet,* March 13, 2004.

78. "Child Soldiers," Radio Netherlands, January 21, 2000, http://www.rnw.nl/humanrights/index.html.

79. Human Rights Watch, *"You'll Learn Not to Cry,"* p. 64.

80. Save the Children, "Children of the Gun"; United Nations, Report of the Expert of the Secretary General, Graça Machel, "Impact of Armed Conflict on Children," Document A/51/306 & Add. 1, August 26, 1996.

81. Data on overall combatant figures from Taylor Seyboldt, ed., *SIPRI Yearbook 2000: Armaments, Disarmament and International Security* (Oxford, UK: Oxford University Press, 2000), Appendix IA, Uppsala Conflict Data Project.

82. United Nations, Report of the Expert of the Secretary General, 1996.

83. Stohl, "Child Soldiers Released."

84. BBC, *Children of Conflict,* 1999, http://www.bbc.co.uk/worldservice/people/features/childrensrights/childrenofconflict/soldtxt.shtml.

85. CSC, "The Use of Child Soldiers in the Americas: An Overview," 2001; Human Rights Watch, "Child Soldiers Used by All Sides in Colombia's Armed Conflict."

86. Amnesty International news release, AMR 45/003/200159/01, April 5, 2001.

87. Center for Defense Information (CDI), "The Invisible Soldiers: Child Combatants," *Defense Monitor* 26, no. 4 (1997), http://www.cdi.org/oldsite/dm/1997/issue4 (accessed September 2000).

88. Robyn Dixon, "In Russia, Military Helps Orphaned Boys Soldier On," *Los Angeles Times,* February 24, 2001.

89. Data from Barnen, *Childwar Database.* See also Dyan Mazurana and Susan Mckay, "Child Soldiers: What About the Girls?," *Bulletin of the Atomic Scientists* 57, no. 5 (September/October 2001) 31–35. Mazurana and Mckay, "Girls in Militaries, Paramili-

taries, and Armed Opposition Groups," paper presented at International Conference on War-affected Children, Winnipeg, Canada, September 2000.

90. Mike Wessells, "Child Soldiers," *Bulletin of the Atomic Scientists* 53, no. 6 (November/December 1997); CSC, *Child Soldier Use 2003: A Briefing for the 4th UN Security Council Open Debate.*

91. Rory Carroll, "Everyone's Afraid of Her," *The Guardian* (London), August 25, 2003.

92. Quoted in Human Rights Watch, *"You'll Learn Not to Cry,"* p. 19.

93. Quoted in "Girls Without Guns: An Agenda on Child Soldiers for Beijing Plus Five," CSC, June 4, 2000, http://www.child-soldiers.org; see also "Sri Lanka, Stop Inciting Children to Kill," http://www.opsick.com, April 2002.

94. P. G. Rajamohan, "Arming the Children," *South Asia Intelligence Review* 2, no. 35 (March 15, 2004).

95. Alex Spillius, "Red Army Brings Terror to Land of the Gurkhas," *Electronic Telegraph* 1961 (October 7, 2000), http://www.telegraph.co.uk/et?ac=003586312928943&pg=/ et/00/10/7/wgurk07.html; quote from "Girls Without Guns"; *Asia Child Rights Newsletter,* January 22, 2003.

96. Interviews with military analyst, June 2001; "Nepal Accuses Sri Lanka's Tamil Tigers of Supporting Maoists Rebels," AFP, June 14, 2002.

97. Yvonne Kearins, "The Voices of Girl Child Soldiers," Quaker UN Office (New York, October 2002), p. 7.

98. Women's Commission, *Against All Odds,* p. 20.

99. CSC, "The Use of Child Soldiers in the Americas: An Overview," 2000, http://www.us-childsoldiers.org/child_soldiers/child-sold.html.

100. Greg Taylor, "Innocence Stolen," *Christianity Today,* July 10, 2000; Danna Harman, "Hard Return for Uganda's Lost Children," *Christian Science Monitor,* August 27, 2002.

Chapter 3: The Underlying Causes

1. The book won the French equivalent of the Pulitzer Prize. The title means that Allah is not obliged to be just in everything below, or, in other words, "Life ain't fair." Ahmadou Kourouma, *Allah n'est pas obligé* (Paris: Seuil, 2000).

2. Population Institute, briefing notes, March 2003.

3. Figures from UN Human Settlements Program, "The Challenge of Slums," October 2003; Paul Collier, "How to Stem Civil Wars, It's the Economy, Stupid," *International Herald Tribune,* May 21, 2003; Michael Renner, "The Global Divide: Socioeconomic Disparities and International Security," in Michael Klare and Yogesh Chandrani, *World Security: Challenges for a New Century* (New York: St. Martin's Press, 1998), p. 275.

4. Figures from the U.S. Department of Labor, Bureau of International Labor Affairs (Washington, DC, 2003) and UN Population Fund, *State of World Population: Making 1 Billion Count* (New York: UNFPA, 2003).

5. Karl Vick, "Big Rise in Hunger Projected for Africa," *Washington Post,* September 4, 2001.

6. Renner, "Global Divide," p. 273.

7. Population Institute, briefing notes.

8. Thomas Homer-Dixon, "Synchronous Failure: The Real Danger of the 21st Century," paper presented to Security for a New Century Group, December 1, 2003.

9. Brian A. Nichipork, *The Security Dynamics of Demographic Factors* (Santa Monica, CA: RAND, 2001); Thomas Homer-Dixon, "Environmental Scarcities and Violent Conflict: Evidence from Cases," *International Security* 19, no. 1 (summer 1994): 5–40; J. P. Platteau and C. André, "Land Relations Under Unbearable Stress: Rwanda Caught in the Malthusian Trap" (CRED paper, University of Namur, Belgium, February 1996), pp. 1–39. See also the Project on Environment, Population, and Security, http://www.library.utoronto.ca/pcs/eps.htm.

10. Richard Cincotta, Robert Engelman, and Daniele Anastasion, *The Security Demographic: Population Issues in Post–Cold War Armed Conflict* (Washington, DC: Population Action International Report, 2003).

11. P. W. Singer, "AIDS and International Security," *Survival* 44, no. 1 (spring 2002): 145–58.

12. Additionally, this is heightened for adult woman, killing at even higher rates, such that the death rate for women in Africa in their twenties is twice that of women in their sixties. Rachel Swarns, "Study Says AIDS Is Now Chief Cause of Death in South Africa," CNN.com, October 16, 2001.

13. Christian Mesquida and Neil I. Warner, "Male Age Composition and Severity of Conflicts," *Politics and Life Sciences* 18, no. 2 (September 1999): 181–89; Richard Morin, "Boy Trouble," *Washington Post,* June 24, 2001; "Natural-Born Killers," *Profiles,* May 1999.

14. Jack Goldstone, *Revolution and Rebellion in the Early Modern World* (Berkeley: University of California Press, 1991); Richard P. Cincotta, "Are Proportions of Young Males and Measures of Institutional Capacity Meaningful Predictors of Vulnerability to IntraState Conflict?," paper presented at Population Association of America meeting, Atlanta, May 9, 2002; H. Moller, "Youth as a Force in the Modern World," *Comparative Studies in Society and History* 10 (1967): 237–60; Valkerie Hudson and Andrea den Boer, *Bare Branches: The Security Implications of Asia's Surplus Male Population* (Cambridge, MA: MIT Press, 2004).

15. Cincotta, Engelman, and Anastasion, *Security Demographic,* p. 48.

16. Raymond Copson, "AIDS in Africa," Congressional Research Service Issue Brief IB10050, May 14, 2001; International Crisis Group (ICG), "HIV/AIDS as a Security Threat," ICG Report, June 19, 2001, www.intl-crisis-group.org; National Intelligence Council, "The Global Infectious Disease Threat and Its Implications for the United States," NIE 99-17D, January 2000, http://www.cia.gov/cia/publications/nie/report/nie99-17d.html; P. W. Singer, "AIDS and International Security," *Survival* 44, no. 1 (spring 2002): 145–58.

17. Sharon LaFraniere, "Millions of AIDS Orphans Strain Southern Africa," *New York Times,* December 24, 2003.

18. "South Africa AIDS Orphans Struggle to Survive," CNN.com, June 21, 2001; "HIV/AIDS: The Impact on Social and Economic Development," 2001; National Intelligence Council, 2001; UN Population Fund, *State of World Population*.

19. Claire Bisseker, "Africa's Military Time Bomb," *Johannesburg Financial Mail,* December 11, 1998.

20. Mark Duffield, "Internal Conflict: Adoption and Reaction to Globalisation," The Cornerhouse, Briefing 12, 1999.

21. There were 59 wars in 2001, 53 in 2002. The determination of what is a "war" or conflict zone is one of those odd political science disputes over something that should be quite simple. Many studies use raw statistical measures, such as whether a thousand people have been killed or not, but this appears to be driven by arbitrary, and often inaccurate, figures and not connected to the context of the violence and its impact. For example, the respected Stockholm International Peace Research Institute, uses whether there were 1,000 battle deaths in the year. Project Ploughshares, a well-regarded Canadian organization, defines a war on 1,000 deaths cumulative. For a deeper discussion of the problems in such measures, please see Nicholas Sambanis, "Defining and Measuring Civil War: Conceptual and Empirical Complexities," manuscript, Yale University, 2002. For the purposes of this book, the more policy-relevant National Defense Council Foundation count, which combined political, social, economic, and military measures, both qualitative and quantitative, to determine whether a state is at conflict or not, is used. It has also been among the best predictors of future violence. National Defense Council Foundation, *World Conflict List 2002* (December 2002). It also closely matches the Control Risks Group firm's International Political and Security "Risk Map," the general standard used by businesses and the insurance industry in evaluating risk. The CRG report, though, also contains a forward-looking element. Unfortunately, it finds that the security situation will worsen in the next few years, with risk ratings jumping by 23 percent from 2003 to 2004. Control Risks Group, RiskMap, http://www.crg.com/html, 2003. The International Crisis Group, one of the most widely respected policy research units, concurred with these findings of global distress, finding some seventy situations of current or potential conflict. International Crisis Group, *CrisisWatch,* November 2003.

22. Jon Lee Anderson, *Guerillas* (New York: Times Books, 1992), p. 161.

23. Deborah Smith, "Children in the Heat of War," *Monitor on Psychology* 32, no. 8 (September 2001).

24. UN Population Fund, *State of World Population,* p. 8.

25. Save the Children-UK, *War Brought Us Here,* (London, 2000). Some refugee experts think that this figure may be a high estimate, potentially exaggerated for political reasons.

26. "Children of War," International Regional Information Networks (IRIN), June 14, 2001.

27. Renuka Senanayake, "Sri Lanka: Peace Garden for Children in War Zone," *Inter Press Service,* April 19, 2001.

28. Save the Children, "Children of the Gun," Children in Crisis project report, September 2000, http://www.savethechildren.org/crisis.

29. Dan Jacobs, "Protecting Children from the Scourge of War," Consultative Group on Early Childhood Care and Development, *Coordinator's Notebook,* no. 10 (October 1991): 6.

30. Women's Commission for Refugee Women and Children, *Against All Odds: Surviving the War on Adolescents,* July 2001, p. 8.

31. Daniel Bergner, *In the Land of Magic Soldiers: A Story of Black and White in West Africa* (New York: Farrar, Straus and Giroux, 2003), p. 45.

32. Quoted in Hamilton Wende, "From Schoolboy to Soldier," BBC, September 20, 2003.

33. R. L. Punamaki, "Can Ideological Commitment Protect Children's Psychological Well-being in Situations of Political Violence?" *Child Development* 67 (1996): 55–69.

34. Theresa Stichick and Claude Bruderlein, "Children Facing Insecurity: New Strategies for Survival in a Global Era," Harvard Program in Humanitarian Policy and Conflict Research Policy Paper, March 2001.

35. Paul Salopek, "The Guns of Africa: Violence-Wracked Nations Are Dumping Grounds for World's Arsenals," *Seattle Times,* February 27, 2002; Daniel Smith and Rachel Stohl, "Small Arms in Failed States: A Deadly Combination," paper written for Failed States and International Security Conference, Purdue University, April 8–11, 1999.

36. Michael Klare, "The Kalashnikov Age," *Bulletin of the Atomic Scientists* 55, no. 1 (January/February 1999).

37. Robert Neild, "Expose the Unsavory Business Behind Cruel Wars," *International Herald Tribune.* February 17, 2000.

38. Center for Defense Information (CDI), "The Invisible Soldiers: Child Combatants," *Defense Monitor* 26, no. 4 (1997).

39. Quoted in "Child Soldiers," Radio Netherlands, January 21, 2000, http://www.rnw.nl/humanrights/index.html.

40. Charles Cobb, "Arms and Africa on UN Agenda This Week," AllAfrica.com, July 9, 2001.

41. Bonn International Center for Conversion (BICC), *An Army Surplus—The NVA's Heritage,* BICC Brief No. 3 (1997).

42. Cobb, "Arms and Africa on UN Agenda This Week."

43. Klare, "Kalashnikov Age."

44. Sarah Aird et al., "Mozambique: The Battle Continues for Former Child Soldiers," Youth Advocate Program International Resource Paper, 2001.

45. Stavros Stavou and Robert Stewart, "The Reintegration of Child Soldiers and Abducted Children: A Case Study of Palaro and Pabbo Gulu District," in *Act Against Child Soldiers in Africa: A Reader* (South Africa: ISS, 2002).

46. United Nations, Report of the Expert of the Secretary General, Graça Machel, "Impact of Armed Conflict on Children," Document A/51/306 & Add. 1, August 26, 1996.

47. Quoted in Rachel Stohl, "Targeting Children: Small Arms and Children in Conflict," *Brown Journal of International Affairs* 9, no. 1 (Spring 2002): 281.

48. Sam Kona, quoted in Karl Vick, "Small Arms' Global Reach Uproots Tribal Traditions," *Washington Post,* July 8, 2001.

49. Peter Lock, "Illicit Small Arms Availability," paper presented at Third International Berlin Workshop—Consolidating Peace through Practical Disarmament, Berlin, July 2–5, 1998.

50. David Kaiser, *Politics and War* (Cambridge, MA: Harvard University Press, 1990).

51. Brian Wood and Johan Peleman, "The Arms Fixers," *PRIO Report,* (Oslo, March 1999).

52. Michael Ignatieff, *The Warrior's Honor: Ethnic War and the Modern Conscience* (New York: Holt, 1998).

53. Mats Berdal and David Malone, *Greed and Grievance: Economic Agendas in Civil Wars* (Boulder, CO: Rienner, 2001); Tamara Makarenko, "A Model of Terrorist-Criminal Relations," *Jane's Intelligence Review,* August 2003, pp. 6–10.

54. Metz, *Armed Conflict,* p. 24.

55. Collier, "How to Stem Civil Wars."

56. Paul Collier and Anke Hoeffler, "Greed and Grievance in Civil War," World Bank Policy Research Paper, no. 2355, May 2000.

57. Paul Collier, *Economic Causes of Civil Conflict and Their Implications for Policy,* World Bank Report, June 15, 2000.

58. Blaine Harden, "Africa's Gems: Warfare's Best Friend," *New York Times,* April 6, 2000.

59. Carl von Clausewitz, *On War,* trans. Peter Paret and Michael Howard (Princeton, NJ: Princeton University Press, 1976), p. 75.

60. Scott Wilson, "Colombian Fighters Drug Trade Is Detailed," *Washington Post,* June 25, 2003; Mary Kaldor, *New and Old Wars* (Stanford, CA: Stanford University Press, 1999), p. 102.

61. James Dao, "The War on Terrorism Takes an Aim at Crime," *New York Times,* April 7, 2002.

62. A typical example is the FARC in Colombia, which started out as a Marxist revolutionary group and is now a prime player in the international cocaine trade. Klare, "Kalashnikov Age."

63. Duffield, "Internal Conflict."

64. UNICEF, *Children Affected by Armed Conflict: UNICEF Actions* (New York, 2002), p. 3.

65. Kaldor, *New and Old Wars,* p. 1.

66. Crawford Young, *Ethnic Diversity and Public Policy* (New York: St. Martin's Press in association with UNRISD, 1998), p. 114.

67. Stephen Metz, *Refining American Strategy in Africa* (Carlisle, PA: U.S. Army War College, Strategic Studies Institute, April 2000), p. 11, http://carlisle-www.army.mil/usassi/ssipubs/pubs2000.htm.

68. Christopher Clapham, *Africa and the International System: The Politics of State Survival* (New York: Cambridge University Press, 1996), p. 156.

69. "They'd Make You Kill Your Parents," *Toronto Star News,* July 23, 2000.

70. Human Rights Watch, *Children in Sudan: Slaves, Street Children and Child Soldiers* (New York, 1995), http://www.hrw.org/reports/1995/Sudan.htm.

71. "Children in the North East War: 1985–1995," University Teachers for Human Rights briefing, no. 2 (June 20, 1995); Ilene Cohen and Guy Goodwin-Gill, *Child Soldiers* (Oxford, UK: Clarendon, 1994).

72. International Labor Office, *Wounded Childhood: The Use of Children in Armed Conflict in Central Africa* (Geneva, 2003), p. 26.

73. John Otis, "Rebel Held: Child Soldiers," *Houston Chronicle,* August 3, 2001.

74. "To Child Soldier, 14, War Was 'Shoot or Be Killed,' " Reuters, June 12, 2001.

75. Alcinda Honwana, "Children of War: Understanding War and War Cleansing in Mozambique and Angola," in Simon Chesterman, ed., *Civilians in War* (Boulder, CO: Rienner, 2001), p. 128.

76. Remy Ourdan, "Africa's Small Soldiers," *Foreign Policy,* (May/June 2001): 74–75.

Chapter 4: How Children Are Recruited into War

1. UN panel, "Reclaiming Our Children," UN headquarters, transcript, May 7, 2002.

2. "MONUC Denounces Recruitment of Child Soldiers by Lubanga's UPC/RP," International Regional Information Networks (IRIN), February 7, 2003.

3. Amnesty International, "Breaking God's Commands"; "The Destruction of Childhood by the Lord's Resistance Army Report," AFR 59/01/97, September 18, 1997.

4. Rohan Gunaratna, "LTTE Child Combatants," *Jane's Intelligence Review,* July 1998.

5. Rachel Stohl, "Targeting Children: Small Arms and Children in Conflict," *Brown Journal of International Affairs* 9, no. 1 (spring 2002): 281.

6. Ilene Cohen and Guy Goodwin-Gill, *Child Soldiers* (Oxford, UK: Clarendon, 1994).

7. One child interviewed in May 1997 claimed, "Rebels who had captured girls who were not beautiful or smart were beaten by the others for shaming them." Amnesty International, "Breaking God's Commands."

8. Gunaratna, "LTTE Child Combatants."

9. Human Rights Watch, *Children in Sudan: Slaves, Street Children and Child Soldiers* (New York, September 1995).

10. Ibid.

11. Tom Masland, "Leaders Gather at the U.N. This Week to Discuss the World's Kids, Including Child Soldiers," *Newsweek,* May 6, 2002.

12. Mike Wessells, "Child Soldiers," *Bulletin of the Atomic Scientists* 53, no. 6 (November/December 1997).

13. Ibid.

14. International Children's Institute, "Children Forced to Fight," http://www.icichildren.org.

15. Amnesty International, "Breaking God's Commands."

16. John Otis, "Rebel Held: Child Soldiers," *Houston Chronicle,* August 3, 2001.

17. UNICEF, *Adult Wars, Child Soldiers* (Geneva, 2003), p. 19.

18. International Labor Office, *Wounded Childhood: The Use of Children in Armed Conflict in Central Africa* (Geneva, 2003).

19. Center for Defense Information (CDI), "The Invisible Soldiers: Child Combatants," *Defense Monitor* 26, no. 4 (1997), http://www.cdi.org/dm/1997/issue4.

20. *American Morning,* CNN, transcript, May 10, 2002.

21. Save the Children, "Children of the Gun," Children in Crisis project report, September 2000, http://www.savethechildren.org/crisis.

22. Refugees International, "Children in the Eastern Congo: Adrift in a Sea of War and Poverty," February 6, 2002; "DRC: Minimal Net Reductions in Child Soldiers," *Child Soldiers Newsletter* 3 (March 2002).

23. UNICEF, *Adult Wars, Child Soldiers* (Geneva: 2003), p. 19.

24. Document provided to author by I., a former child soldier, June 2002.

25. Ed Cairns, *Children and Political Violence* (Cambridge, MA: Blackwell, 1996), p. 114–15.

26. Hannah Beech Farkhar, "The Child Soldiers," *Time,* November 7, 2001.

27. Quoted in Paul Salopek, "The Guns of Africa," *Seattle Times,* February 27, 2002.

28. CDI, "Invisible Soldiers."

29. Gunaratna, "LTTE Child Combatants."

30. "Girl Soldiers: Challenging the Assumptions," *Geneva Reporter* 21, no. 3 (July 2002); Yvonne Kearins, "The Voices of Girl Child Soldiers," Quaker UN Office newsletter (New York, October 2002).

31. International Labor Office, *Wounded Childhood,* p. 25.

32. ICI Oregon Foundation, "War: A Child's Perspective," 2001. Note: His best friend was later captured by his unit. Despite his speaking up for him, the friend was knifed to death.

33. CDI, "Invisible Soldiers."

34. Ibid.

35. Cairns, *Children and Political Violence,* p. 130.

36. UNICEF, "Child Soldiers: Demobilization in Southern Sudan," February 2001.

37. Erik Erikson, *Childhood and Society* (Harmondsworth, UK: Penguin, 1965); Kim Triandis, *Individualism and Collectivism* (London: Sage, 1994); Ruth Benedict, *The Chrysanthemum and the Sword* (London: Routledge and Kegan Paul, 1967); David Pryce-Jones, "Priests of Killing," *National Review,* April 22, 2002, pp. 19–20. These differ from "guilt" cultures, which are more individualistic. Both clearly have their issues.

38. Interviews with former child soldiers, Arlington, Virginia, 1998.

39. ICI Oregon Foundation, "War: A Child's Perspective."

40. Roger Rosenblatt, *Children of War* (New York: Doubleday, 1983), p. 101.

41. International Labor Office, *Wounded Childhood,* p. 31.

42. "Child Soldiers," Radio Netherlands, January 21, 2000, at http://www.rnw.nl/humanrights/index.html.

43. Tom Kamara, "Children Remain 'Useful,'" *The Perspective,* January 24, 2001. Note: Taylor won the war and obviously did not keep his promise.

44. John Hughes, "Children at War," *Christian Science Monitor,* October 28, 1987.

45. Cohen and Goodwin-Gill, *Child Soldiers.*

46. Quoted in Human Rights Watch, *"You'll Learn Not to Cry": Child Combatants in Colombia* (New York, September 2003), p. 5.

47. Craig Davis, "A Is for Allah, J Is for Jihad," *World Policy Journal* 19, no. 1 (spring 2002): 90–94.

48. Shah Muhammad, *Riyazi Barayi inf-I chaharum* (Peshawar, Pakistan: Taj Mahal Company, 1987), p. 50. Information kindly supplied by Craig Davis.

49. Wessells, "Child Soldiers."

50. Jon Lee Anderson, *Guerrillas* (New York: Times Books, 1992), p. 68.

51. BBC, *Children of Conflict,* 2002, at http://www.bbc.co.uk/worldservice/people/features/childrensrights/childrenofconflict/soldtxt.shtml.

52. Gunaratna, "LTTE Child Combatants."

53. Harendra de Silva, "Conscription of Children in Armed Conflict: Is It Martyrdom or Child Abuse?," paper presented at the British Association for the Study and Prevention of Child Abuse and Neglect Congress, Edinburgh, July 1997.

54. "Children in the North East War: 1985–1995," University Teachers for Human Rights briefing, no. 2 (June 20, 1995).

55. Gunaratna, "LTTE Child Combatants."

Chapter 5: Turning a Child into a Soldier

1. Quoted in "Child Soldiers," Radio Netherlands, January 21, 2000, http://www.rnw.nl/humanrights/index.html.

2. John Lynn, *The Bayonets of the Republic: Motivation and Tactics in the Army of Revolutionary France, 1791–94* (Urbana: University of Illinois Press, 1984).

3. Ibid., pp. 23–24.

4. Elbridge Colby, *Masters of Mobile Warfare* (Princeton, NJ: Princeton University Press, 1943), p. 83.

5. Anthony Kellett, *Combat Motivation: The Behavior of Soldiers in Battle* (Boston: Kluwer-Nijhoff, 1982), p. 134.

6. Steven T. Ross, *From Flintlock to Rifle: Infantry Tactics, 1740–1866* (London: Cass, 1979), p. 24.

7. Mike Wessells, "Child Soldiers," *Bulletin of the Atomic Scientists* 53, no. 6 (November/December 1997).

8. U.S. Department of State, *Human Rights Report, 2002* (Washington, DC, 2003).

9. M. Deutch, "Psychological Roots of Moral Exclusion," *Journal of Social Issues* 46, no. 1 (1990): 21–25; Albert Bandura, "Mechanisms of Moral Disengagement," in Walter Reich, ed., *Origins of Terrorism* (New York: Cambridge University Press, 1998), pp. 161–191.

10. For instance, one eleven-year-old veteran of the group is able to talk about how in

one village raid he took a baby by the legs and bashed its head against the walls till its brain matter came out. When inactive, the child soldier felt bored and restless. The sight of blood obsesses him; Harendra de Silva, "Conscription of Children in Armed Conflict: Is It Martyrdom or Child Abuse?," paper presented at the British Association for the Study and Prevention of Child Abuse and Neglect Congress, Edinburgh, July 1997.

11. Deutch, "Psychological Roots of Moral Exclusion," pp. 21–25; Bandura, "Mechanisms of Moral Disengagement."

12. Robert Jay Lifton, *The Nazi Doctors: Medical Killing and the Psychology of Genocide* (New York: Basic Books, 1986), pp. 126, 427.

13. They came up with this from watching videos of Hollywood action movies.

14. Emily Wax, "Toting AK-47s Instead of Bookbags," *Washington Post*, August 25, 2003.

15. "Children in the North East War: 1985–1995," University Teachers for Human Rights Briefing, no. 2 (June 20, 1995).

16. Danna Harman, "Aid Agencies Help to Rid Child Soldiers of War's Scars," *Christian Science Monitor*, October 30, 2001.

17. Tom Masland, "Leaders Gather at the U.N. This Week to Discuss the World's Kids, Including Child Soldiers," *Newsweek*, May 6, 2002.

18. Cole Dodge, *Reaching Children in War* (Oslo, Norway: Sigma Forlut, 1991), p. 57.

19. Basildon Peta, "Mass Murder and Cannibalism Claims Emerge in Congo," *The Independent* (London), May 24, 2003.

20. "Child Soldiers," Radio Netherlands.

21. Ibid.

22. Human Rights Watch, *"You'll Learn Not to Cry": Child Combatants in Colombia* (New York, September 2003), p. 96.

23. Mike Wessells, "Child Soldiers."

24. Ilene Cohen and Guy Goodwin-Gill, *Child Soldiers* (Oxford, UK: Clarendon, 1994).

25. "Child Soldiers," Radio Netherlands.

26. UNICEF, *Adult Wars, Child Soldiers* (Geneva, 2003), p. 19.

27. Human Rights Watch, *"You'll Learn Not to Cry,"* p. 80.

28. International Labor Office, *Wounded Childhood: The Use of Children in Armed Conflict in Central Africa* (Geneva, 2003), p. 43.

29. "Release Child Soldiers, UNICEF Tells Fighting Groups," IRIN, October 9, 2003.

30. Rohan Gunaratna, "LTTE Child Combatants," *Jane's Intelligence Review*, July 1998; Yvonne Kearins, "The Voices of Girl Child Soldiers," Quaker UN Office, October 2002, p. 7.

31. Human Rights Watch, *"You'll Learn Not to Cry,"* p. 47.

32. Women's Commission for Refugee Women and Children, *Against All Odds: Surviving the War on Adolescents*, July 2001.

33. As one eight-year-old put it, "At a camp we were trained to use guns. Those who

disobeyed had their ears and fingers cut off. I didn't want to participate in the killing but they threatened to shoot me if I refused to do it." "Over 100,000 Children Bear Arms in Africa," *Ofeibea Quist-Arcton* (Johannesburg), June 13, 2001.

34. Cohen and Goodwin-Gill, *Child Soldiers.*

35. Human Rights Watch, *"You'll Learn Not to Cry,"* p. 76.

36. Ellen Nakashima, "Burma's Child Soldiers Tell of Army Atrocities," *Washington Post,* February 10, 2003.

37. Coalition to Stop the Use of Child Soldiers, Yearly Report 2001.

38. M. Fraser, *Children in Conflict* (Harmondsworth, UK: Penguin, 1974).

39. Jessica Reaves, "Should the Law Treat Kids and Adults Differently?," *Time,* May 17, 2001.

40. "Child Soldiers," Radio Netherlands.

41. Ismene Zarifis, "Sierra Leone's Search for Justice and Accountability of Child Soldiers," *Human Rights Brief* 9, no. 3 (Spring 2002): 18–21.

42. Masland, "Leaders Gather at the U.N."

43. "Sierra Leone: IRIN Focus on Children with an Uncertain Future," International Regional Information Networks (IRIN), July 9, 2001; Sue Loughlin, "A Preliminary Assessment of Past and Current Drug Use Among Former Child Ex-Combatants in Sierra Leone," *UNICEF Report,* August 2000.

44. Wessells, "Child Soldiers."

45. "Child Soldiers," Radio Netherlands.

46. Quoted in Ivan Watson, "Sierra Leone: Redeeming Child Soldiers," *Chronicle of Foreign Service,* July 23, 2001.

47. Jean H. Lee, "Ex-U.N. Leader: Children Define War," AP, March 21, 2001.

48. Masland, "Leaders Gather at the U.N."

49. Wessells, "Child Soldiers."

50. Quoting a Defense Intelligence Agency interview; Cohen and Goodwin-Gill, *Child Soldiers.*

51. Quoted in "Children in Armed Conflict," World Vision position paper, Policy and Research Department, June 1999.

52. "Child Soldiers," Radio Netherlands.

53. Ibid.

54. Document provided to author by I., a former child soldier, June 2002.

55. Interview with British military officer, Quantico, Virginia, May 2002.

56. United Nations, Report of the Expert of the Secretary General, Graça Machel, "Impact of Armed Conflict on Children," Document A/51/306 & Add. 1., August 26, 1996.

57. Gunaratna, "LTTE Child Combatants."

58. A tactic later copied by al Qaeda for use against the USS *Cole.* From its use of suicide bombings to child soldiers, the LTTE has been one of the more innovative terrorist groups.

59. F. B. Abagye, "Perspective on the Problems and Challenges of ECOWAS Regional Security Paradigm: The Role of the Military in the Protection of War-affected

Children in West Africa," paper presented at the International Conference on War-affected Children, Winnipeg, Canada, September 11, 2000.

60. Interview with private military soldier, September 2004. Report corroborated by CENTCOM briefing slides, April 2004.

61. Interview with military expert, Washington, DC, August 2001.

62. Interview with military expert, Washington, DC, August 2001.

63. Hannah Beech Farkhar, "The Child Soldiers," *Time,* November 7, 2001.

64. Gunaratna, "LTTE Child Combatants."

65. Interview with British military expert, August 2001.

66. E. Gargan, "In Uganda, a Children's Army," *International Herald Tribune,* August 5, 1986.

67. Neil Boothby, "Working in the War Zone: A Look at Psychological Theory and Practice from the Field," *Mind and Human Interaction* 2, no. 2 (1990): 33.

68. Adnan Laeeq, "Flowers on the Frontline," *Child Soldiers Newsletter* 5 (September 2002).

69. Christopher Hamner, "An Army of One? Combat Motivation, Unit Cohesion, and Technological Change in Infantry Combat," John M. Olin Institute for Strategic Studies, Harvard University, presentation, October 2001.

70. Jon Lee Anderson, *Guerrillas* (New York: Times Books, 1992), p. 217.

71. "Child Soldiers," Radio Netherlands.

72. Ibid.

73. Women's Commission for Refugee Women and Children, *Against All Odds.*

74. Ibid.

75. Quoted in Human Rights Watch, *The Scars of Death* (New York, 2001).

76. "Army: Mourners Forced to Eat Corpse," Reuters, April 29, 2002; "Uganda: Horrors of LRA Child Captivity," IRIN, April 24, 2003.

77. de Silva, "Conscription of Children in Armed Conflict"; Human Rights Watch, *"You'll Learn Not to Cry."*

78. Human Rights Watch, *"You'll Learn Not to Cry,"* p. 111.

79. Women's Commission, *Against All Odds,* p. 19.

80. "Child Soldiers," Radio Netherlands.

Chapter 6: The Implications of Children on the Battlefield

1. Quoted in CSC, *Child Soldiers Newsletter* 4 (June 2002).

2. F. B. Abagye, "Perspective on the Problems and Challenges of ECOWAS Regional Security Paradigm: The Role of the Military in the Protection of War-affected Children in West Africa," paper presented at the International Conference on War-affected Children, Winnipeg, Canada, September 11, 2000.

3. Robert Rotberg, "Failed States in a World of Terror," *Foreign Affairs* 81, no. 4 (July/August 2002): 127–40.

4. "Africa: Clinton Legacy Alive Under Bush," IRIN, February 8, 2001.

5. "UN Envoy Considering Taliban Meeting," CNN.com, October 30, 2001.

6. "Al-Qaida Bomb Suspects Hid in Liberia," AP, June 1, 2004.

7. The rebel RUF and agents of al Qaeda traded in millions of dollars of "blood diamonds," with a reported rise in purchasing before the 9/11 attacks in New York City as the groups tried to gain hard assets. Douglas Farah, "Al Qaeda Cash Tied to Diamond Trade," *Washington Post,* November 2, 2001.

8. UNICEF, *Children Affected by Armed Conflict: UNICEF Actions* (New York, 2002), p. 35.

9. For more on this, please see P. W. Singer, *Corporate Warriors* (Ithaca, NY: Cornell University Press, 2003).

10. "Uganda: Increased Abduction and Recruitment of Child Soldiers," International Regional Information Networks (IRIN), August 16, 2003.

11. Unfortunately, the current literature on civil war termination fails to take this new doctrine into account. For example, Barbara Walter's work is the touchstone of the field, but looks only at civil wars prior to 1990, thus not accounting for the advent of child soldier doctrine. Walter, "Designing Transitions from Civil War," *International Security* 24, no. 1 (summer 1999); Walter and Jack Snyder, *Civil Wars, Insecurity, and Intervention* (New York: Columbia University Press, 1999); Walter, "The Critical Barrier to Civil War Settlements," *International Organization* 51, no. 3 (summer 1997).

12. International Crisis Group, *Sierra Leone: Time for a New Military and Political Strategy,* ICG Africa Report, no. 28 (April 11, 2001).

13. Human Rights Watch, *The Scars of Death* (New York, 2001).

14. "Child Soldiers," Radio Netherlands, January 21, 2000, http://www.rnw.nl/humanrights/index.html.

15. Robert Bates, "Prosperity and Violence: The Political Economy of Development," unpublished paper, 2000.

16. Tom Kamara, "Sierra Leone: A Search for Peace Against the Odds," *WriteNet Country Papers,* paper no. 21 (1999).

17. Amnesty International, "Breaking God's Commands."

18. Samson Mulugeta, "Rebels of Terror in Uganda," *Newsday,* March 28, 2004.

19. Stavros Stavou and Robert Stewart, "The Reintegration of Child Soldiers and Abducted Children: A Case Study of Palaro and Pabbo Gulu District," in *Act Against Child Soldiers in Africa: A Reader* (South Africa: ISS, 2002), available at www.iss.co.za.

20. Peter Strandberg, "End of a Long Nightmare," *Mail & Guardian,* July 26, 2002.

21. T. R. Gurr, ed., *A Global Survey of Armed Conflicts, Self-Determination Movements and Democracy* (College Park: Center for International Development and Conflict Management, University of Maryland, 2000); Chaim Kaufmann, "Possible and Impossible Solutions to Ethnic Civil Wars," *International Security* 20, no. 4 (spring 1996): 136–75, esp. p. 142; Jacob Bercovitch, "The Nature of the Dispute and the Effectiveness of International Mediation," *Journal of Conflict Resolution* 37, no. 4 (1993): 3–25. For an opposite view, see David Mason and Patrick Fett, "How Civil Wars End: A Rational Choice Approach," *Journal of Conflict Resolution* 40, no. 4 (December 1996): 545–568, Mason and Fett did not find the number of deaths statistically significant, but like the other literature on civil wars, their data was backward looking, not accounting for the introduction of the

new doctrine. Moreover, they measured only battle deaths, missing the true shift of civil wars towards primarily civilian-directed violence.

22. Tom Masland, "Leaders Gather at the U.N. This Week to Discuss the World's Kids, Including Child Soldiers," *Newsweek,* May 6, 2002.

23. Human Rights Watch, *"You'll Learn Not to Cry": Child Combatants in Colombia* (New York, September 2003), p. 88.

24. Ibid., p. 67.

25. *Today,* NBC, transcript May 10, 2002.

26. In cases in Latin America, government forces reportedly have deliberately killed even the youngest children in peasant communities on the grounds that they, too, could be "dangerous." Center for Defense Information (CDI), "The Invisible Soldiers: Child Combatants," *Defense Monitor* 26, no. 4 (1997), http://www.cdi.org/dm/1997/issue4.

27. Coalition to Stop the Use of Child Soldiers (CSC), *1379 Country Reports,* 2002, p. 25.

28. Stavou and Stewart, "Reintegration of Child Soldiers."

29. Physicians for Human Rights, "War-related Sexual Violence in Sierra Leone," Population Assessment Report, 2002.

30. P. W. Singer, "AIDS and International Security," *Survival* 44, no. 1 (spring 2002): 145–58.

31. In fact Oxygen network did a documentary on it. Operation Fine Girl at http://www.witness.org.

32. "Child Soldiers," Radio Netherlands.

33. Reported being abducted, beaten, raped, and forced to become a rebel's "wife." She was released during the latter stages of her pregnancy and now has a baby girl. Physicians for Human Rights, "War-related Sexual Violence in Sierra Leone."

34. Khadija Alia Bah, "Rural Women and Girls in the War in Sierra Leone," Conciliation Resources Occasional Paper, 1999.

35. Strandberg, "End of a Long Nightmare."

36. Human Rights Watch, *"You'll Learn Not to Cry,"* p. 58.

37. Mark Frankel, "Boy Soldiers," *Newsweek,* August 14, 1995, p. 45.

38. Interview with former child soldier, June 2002.

39. "Child Soldiers," Radio Netherlands.

40. Ian Brown, *Khomeini's Forgotten Sons: The Story of Iran's Boy Soldiers* (London: Grey Seal, 1990).

41. United Nations, Report of the Expert of the Secretary General, Graça Machel, "Impact of Armed Conflict on Children," Document A/51/306 & Add 1., August 26, 1996.

42. Ibid.

43. Human Rights Watch, *Scars of Death.*

44. Amnesty International, "Breaking God's Commands."

45. Interview with DRC expert and NGO representative, June 2001.

46. Figures from http://www.reality.lanka.com, accessed November 2000.

47. Quoted in *The Use of Children by OSCE Member States,* CSC, Human Dimen-

sion Seminar on Children and Armed Conflict, Warsaw, May 23–26, 2000, http://www
.child-soldiers.org.

48. CSC, "Girls Without Guns: An Agenda on Child Soldiers for Beijing Plus Five,"
June 4, 2000, http://www.child-soldiers.org.

49. Sarah Aird et al., "Mozambique: The Battle Continues for Former Child Soldiers," Youth Advocate Program International Resource paper, 2001.

50. United Nations, "Impact of Armed Conflict on Children."

51. Jane Green Schaller, "Children, Child Health, and War," paper presented at the
IPA/WHO/UNICEF Pre-Congress Workshop on Assessment of the Mid-Decade Goals:
Evaluation and Recommendations, Cairo, September 9–10, 1995.

52. Mike Wessells, "Child Soldiers," *Bulletin of the Atomic Scientists* 53, no. 6
(November/December 1997).

53. Interview with expert on Sudan, July 2002.

54. Tom Kamara, "Children Remain 'Useful,' " *The Perspective,* January 24, 2001.

55. Douglas Farah, "Sierra Leone Rebels Contemplate Life Without Guns," *Washington Post,* April 14, 2001; Ivan Watson, "Sierra Leone: Redeeming Child Soldiers," *San
Francisco Chronicle,* July 23, 2001.

56. Bory Seyni, "After Liberia, Sierra Leone, Is Guinea Next?" Panafrican News
Agency, October 20, 2000; Human Rights Watch, "Back to the Brink: War Crimes by
Liberian Government and Rebels, a Call for Greater International Attention to Liberia
and the Sub Region," Action Appeal, 2002.

57. Human Rights Watch, "Trapped Between Two Wars," August 2003; International Regional Information Networks (IRIN), January 29, 2003.

58. "Peace Here Means War Somewhere Else," *The Economist,* June 23, 2001.

59. Interview with former child soldier, June 2002.

60. Human Rights Watch, *Scars of Death.*

61. Physicians for Human Rights, "March 2000 Delegation to Sierra Leone Preliminary Findings and Recommendations," March 2000.

62. Aird et al., "Mozambique."

63. Dan Jacobs, "Protecting Children from the Scourge of War," Consultative Group
on Early Childhood Care and Development, no. 10 (October 1991): 8.

64. BBC, "*Children of Conflict,*" 1997, http://www.bbc.co.uk/worldservice/people/
features/childrensrights/childrenofconflict/soldtxt.shtml.

65. Human Rights Watch, *Scars of Death.*

66. UNICEF, *Children Affected by Armed Conflict: UNICEF Actions* (New York, 2002).

67. Information from United Nations Office for the Coordination of Humanitarian
Affairs, 2004. Emily Wax, "In Uganda, Terror Forces Children's Nightly Flight," *Washington Post,* February 13, 2004.

68. Martin Teicher, "Scars That Won't Heal: The Neurobiology of Child Abuse,"
Scientific American, March 2002.

69. Ilse Derluyn et al., "Post Traumatic Stress in Former Child Soldiers," *Lancet,*
March 13, 2004.

70. CDI, "Invisible Soldiers."

71. International Children's Institute, "Children Forced to Fight," http://www.childrensinstitute.org.

72. A. Dawes, "The Effects of Political Violence on Children," *International Journal of Psychology* 25, no. 2 (1990): 13–31.

73. Aird et al., "Mozambique."

74. Phil Ashby, "Child Combatants: A Soldier's Perspective," *The Lancet* 360 (December 2002): s11–12.

75. "Child Soldiers," Radio Netherlands.

Chapter 7: The New Children of Terror

1. Jack Kelley, "The Sickening World of Suicide Terrorists," *USA Today,* June 26, 2001.

2. "National Roundup," *Miami Herald,* April 23, 2003; Human Rights Watch, "U.S. Guantánamo Kids at Risk," April 24, 2003; Bruce Auster and Kevin Whitelaw, "Terror's Cellblock," *U.S. News & World Report,* May 12, 2003; Michelle Faul, "U.S. Defends Detaining Teens," AP, June 28, 2003. There is an unknown added number between sixteen and eighteen that the United States has held in the general adult population, contrary to both U.S. and international law on how children should be treated during detention.

3. Nancy Gibbs, "Inside 'The Wire,' " *Time,* December 8, 2003.

4. "Palestinian Teen Stopped with Bomb Vest," CNN.com, March 25, 2004.

5. Gal Luft, "The Palestinian H-Bomb," *Foreign Affairs* 81, no. 4 (July/August 2002): 5; CSC, *1379 Report,* 2002, p. 54; Suzanne Goldenberg, "A Mission to Murder," *The Guardian,* June 11, 2003; Johanna Mcgeary, "Inside Hamas," *Time,* March 29, 2004.

6. Interview with U.S. security agency official, Washington, DC, December 2003.

7. "Enemy Tactics, Techniques, and Procedures (TTP) and Recommendations," Third Corps Support Command briefing document, LSA Anaconda, Iraq, September 2003.

8. "Teenage Boys Trained by Paramilitary Group," *Guardian Weekly* (London), November 29, 2000.

9. U.S. State Department, *Report on Human Rights,* 1997, Colombia section. UNICEF-Colombia, Situation Report, April 22, 2003.

10. Rohan Gunaratna, "LTTE Child Combatants," *Jane's Intelligence Review,* July 1998.

11. "Teenage Boys Trained by Paramilitary Group."

12. Jack Kelley, "Street Clashes Now Deliberate Warfare," *USA Today,* October 23, 2000; Herb Keinon, "Israel to the UN: Keep Palestinians from Using Kids as Shields," *Jerusalem Post,* November 8, 2000; D. Kuttab, "A Profile of the Stone Throwers," *Journal of Palestine Studies* 17 (1988): 14–23.

13. Nasra Hassan, "An Arsenal of Believers," *The New Yorker,* November 19, 2001.

14. Gehud Auda, *Palestinian Suicide Bombing: Description and Evaluation,* Ahram Strategic Papers, no. 114 (2002); Hassan, "Arsenal of Believers."

15. Daniel Williams, "Bomber Unleashed Secret Rage," *Washington Post,* April 14, 2002.

16. Samir Kouta, quoted in *Al Alam al Yom,* January 24, 1995.

17. "The Appeal of Suicide Bombers Grows," AP, April 28, 2002.

18. Alan Krueger and Jitka Maleckova have argued the opposite in a highly cited study. Krueger and Maleckova, "Education, Poverty, Political Violence and Terrorism: Is There a Causal Connection?" NBER Working Paper no. w9074, July 2002, http://papers.nber.org/papers/W9074. However, many analysts believe that the study was highly limited in its purview, looking only at one case that was suboptimal in selection, and thus flawed in its methodology. Omer Taspinar, "Promoting Educational and Economic Opportunity in the Islamic World," Brookings Monograph, 2003.

19. Jessica Stern, "Islamic Extremists: How Do They Mobilize Support?" USIP Presentation, April 17, 2002.

20. Ibid.

21. Jessica Stern, *Terror in the Name of God* (New York: HarperCollins, 2003), p. 51; "The Appeal of Suicide Bombers Grows," Associated Press, April 28, 2002.

22. Stern, *Terror in the Name of God,* p. 219.

23. Amy Waldman, "Sri Lanka's Young Are Forced to Fill Ranks of Endless Rebellion," *New York Times,* January 6, 2003.

24. *South Asia Intelligence Review,* August 2, 2002.

25. Kelley, "Sickening World of Suicide Terrorists."

26. David Pryce-Jones, "Priests of Killing," *National Review,* April 22, 2002, pp. 19–20.

27. Roni Shaked, a terrorism expert and former officer in Shin Bet, quoted in Kelley, "Sickening World of Suicide Terrorists."

28. "PA Mufti of Jerusalem and Palestine Discusses the Intifada," *Al-Ahram Al-Arabi,* October 28, 2000, via MEMRI, November 8, 2000.

29. John F. Burns, "Palestinian Summer Camp Offers the Games of War," *New York Times,* August 3, 2000.

30. Franz Fanon, *The Wretched of the Earth* (New York: Grove, 1963), p. 93.

31. Colin Nickerson, "A Boy's Journey from Canada to Al Qaeda," *Boston Globe,* March 9, 2003.

32. Quoted in "Child Soldiers Square Up to U.S. Tanks," *Daily Telegraph* (London), August 23, 2004.

33. Mcgeary, "Inside Hamas."

34. James Garabino, "A Note on Children and Youth in Dangerous Environments: The Palestinian Situation as a Case Study," Erickson Institute, Chicago, undated.

35. Hassan, "Arsenal of Believers."

36. For example, one in *Al-Istiqlal,* the Palestinian Authority's newspaper, read:

"With great pride, The Palestinian Islamic Jihad marries the member of its military wing . . . the martyr and hero Yasser-Adhami, to the black-eyed [virgins]." From Yotam Feldner, " '72 Black-eyed Virgins': A Muslim Debate on the Rewards of Martyrs," MEMRI paper, 2002, http://www.memri.org.

37. Hassan, "Arsenal of Believers."

38. Chris Hedges, "The Glamour of Martyrdom," *New York Times,* October 29, 2000; *Al Hayat-Al Jadida,* October 27, 2000, from Palestinian Media Watch, Jerusalem.

39. Quoted in Stern, *Terror in the Name of God,* p. 221.

40. David Kupelian, "Trouble in the Holy Land: Jerusalem Cleric Praises Child 'Sacrifices,' " WorldNetDaily.com, November 10, 2000.

41. From the May 19, 1999; February 6, 1998; August 10, 1998; and July 2, 1998, broadcasts. Translation of Palestinian television shows, available at www.cnsnews.com/specialreports/jihadtranslation.htmnl (accessed October 15, 2002). Video of "Children's Club" clips can be downloaded at http://www.israelnationalnews.com/english/radio/ram/eng-video/jihad-80.ram. The first to raise the issue was the 1998 film *Jihad for Kids* produced by the organization Peace for Generations.

42. Emily Wax, "Outrage Spreads in Arab World," *Washington Post,* March 30, 2003.

43. Walter Laquer, *No End to War* (New York: Continuum, 2003), p. 91.

44. "Profile of a Suicide Bomber," CNN.com, December 15, 2001.

45. Haim Malka, "Must Innocents Die? The Islamic Debate on Suicide Attacks," *Middle East Quarterly* (spring 2003).

46. David Van Biema, "Why the Bombers Keep Coming," *Time,* December 17, 2001; Pryce-Jones, "Priests of Killing," pp. 19–20; Hamza Hendawi, "Gaza's Children Worship Martyrdom," AP, May 14, 2002.

47. Huda Al-Husseini, an Arab journalist with the London-based daily *Al-Sharq Al-Awsat,* quoted in Kupelian, "Trouble in the Holy Land."

48. Its first human bomber, Ala'a al-Kahlout, even wore shorts, a T-shirt, a cap, and dark glasses before climbing aboard a bus in 1993 and blowing it up. Hassan, "Arsenal of Believers."

49. Auda, *Palestinian Suicide Bombing; Al-Sharq Al-Awsat,* August 8, 2001.

50. Martin Cohn, "The Teen Soldiers Who Refused to Die," *Toronto Star,* January 18, 2002.

51. Hassan, "Arsenal of Believers."

52. Stern, *Terror in the Name of God,* p. 51.

53. Laquer, *No End to War,* p. 83.

54. Amos Harel, "Portrait of the Terrorist as a Young Man," *Ha'aretz Daily,* April 23, 2002.

55. Dewayne Wickham, "Root Out the Seeds of Terrorism in Sub-Saharan Countries," AP, April 14, 2003.

56. Stern, *Terror in the Name of God.*

57. "The Appeal of Suicide Bombers Grows," AP, April 28, 2002.

Chapter 8: Preventing Child Soldiers

1. Remarks made to UN Special Session on Children, May 8, 2002.

2. Julian Borger and Charlotte Denny, "Monterrey: U.S. Will Seek Advice on Spending Aid," *The Guardian* (London), March 21, 2002; for more on this, see The Reality of Aid project located at http://www.devinit.org/realityofaid.

3. UNICEF, *Children Affected by Armed Conflict: UNICEF Actions* (New York, 2002), p. 3.

4. Lael Brainard, "The Administration's Budget for Global Poverty and HIV/AIDS: How Do the Numbers Stack Up?," Brookings Institution Analysis Paper, February 24, 2003.

5. "Great Lakes: U.S. Labor Department Lends Support to Combat Use of Child Soldiers," International Regional Information Networks (IRIN), December 19, 2003.

6. UN Population Fund, *State of the World Population,* 2003, p. 51.

7. "Missing the Target on Small Arms," *Japan Policy & Politics,* July 30, 2001.

8. Mei-Ling Hopgood, "Let World Bear Arms: Bush Won't OK Measures to Ban Guns," *Atlanta Journal-Constitution,* July 10, 2001.

9. William Godnick and Helena Vazquez, "Small Arms Control in Latin America," *International Alert Latin America MISAC Report,* March 2003.

10. For example, Jeffrey Legro, *Cooperation Under Fire: Anglo-German Restraint During World War II* (Ithaca, NY: Cornell University Press, 1995); Richard Price, *The Chemical Weapons Taboo* (Ithaca, NY: Cornell University Press, 1997); Ward Thomas, *The Ethics of Destruction: Norms and Force in International Relations* (Ithaca, NY: Cornell University Press, 2001); Nina Tannenwald, "The Nuclear Taboo: The United States and the Normative Basis of Nuclear Non-Use," *International Organization* 53, no. 3 (summer 1999).

11. Paul Bohannan, *Law and Warfare: Studies in the Anthropology of Conflict* (New York: Natural History Press, 1967), p. 23.

12. Richard Price, "Reversing the Gun Sights: Transnational Civil Society Targets Land Mines," *International Organization* 52, no. 3 (summer 1998): 613–44.

13. For example, in the IT world, a norm "(from *norma,* Latin for carpenter's level) is a model of what should exist or be followed, or an average of what currently does exist in some context, such as an average salary among members of a large group." See http//:www.whatis.techtarget.com.

14. Price, "Reversing the Gun Sights"; Martha Finnemore, *National Interests in International Society* (Ithaca, NY: Cornell University Press, 1996).

15. Michael Desch, "Culture Clash: Assessing the Importance of Ideas in Security Studies," *International Security* 23, no. 1 (summer 1998): 141–70.

16. Rachel Stohl, "Children in Conflict: Assessing the Optional Protocol," *Journal of Conflict, Security and Development* 2, no. 2 (2002).

17. Amy Waldman, "Sri Lanka's Young Are Forced to Fill Ranks of Endless Rebellion," *New York Times,* January 6, 2003; "Amnesty Slams Sri Lanka Rebels on Child Soldiers," Reuters, May 2, 2002; "S. Lankan Tamil Tigers Abduct More Children to Be Soldiers: Truce Monitors," Xinhua, October 12, 2003; "Sri Lanka: Child Recruitment

Continues Despite Ceasefire," *Child Soldiers Newsletter* 3 (March 2002); Human Rights Watch, "Sri Lanka: Former Tamil Tiger Child Soldiers Remain at Risk" (New York, April 27, 2004); Coalition to Stop the Use of Child Soldiers (CSC), *Child Soldier Use 2003: A Briefing for the 4th UN Security Council Open Debate on Children and Armed Conflict,* January 2004.

18. Interview with human rights expert, Washinton, DC, June 2002.

19. Rory Carroll, "Sham Demobilization Hides Rise in Congo's Child Armies," *The Observer* (London), September 9, 2003.

20. Both issued public communiqués in 2002. Human Rights Watch, "Erased in a Moment," October 2002.

21. Watchlist on *Children and Armed Conflict Newsletter,* November 2001, http://www.theirc.org.

22. Jacky Mamou, "Soldier Boys and Girls," *Le Monde diplomatique,* September 2001, http://www.monde-diplomatique.fr/2001/09/13soldiers.

23. Refugees International, "Child Soldiers in the Congo," April 4 and 30, 2001.

24. Interview with human rights expert, Washington, DC, June 10, 2003.

25. Interview with human rights expert, Washington, DC, June 17, 2002.

26. Located at http://www.spacegroove.com/josephkony. It has a message of greeting from Kony and also a page on "why democracy will tramp under Maj. Gen. Joseph Kony's powerfull leadership of LRA and it's powerfull Political System [*sic*]."

27. Jon Lee Anderson, *Guerrillas* (New York: Times Books, 1992), p. 5.

28. CSC, *Child Soldier Use 2003,* p. 3.

29. Waldman, "Sri Lanka's Young Are Forced to Fill Ranks of Endless Rebellion."

30. The coalition's annual report also makes a pointed parallel between sexual crimes that are not equivalent. It likened the FARC's "sexual freedom" policy, which includes forcing young girl soldiers to wear interuterine devices and even killing a fifteen-year-old who got pregnant regardless, with a single incident in 1997 where a British army recruit was raped by her drunken drill instructor (who was later put in jail for the crime). While both actions are inexcusable, there is a distinct difference between the overall policy of an entire organization and the deviant behavior of an individual within an organization, who is then properly punished. CSC, *Child Soldiers: An Overview* (New York, 2001).

31. Vince Crawley, "17-Year-Old Soldiers Can't Be Trigger Pullers," *Army Times,* March 18, 2002.

32. This philosophy is known as the Boyd, or OODA (Observation-Orientation-Decision-Action) loop, first established by Colonel John Boyd. Grant Hammond, *The Mind of War: John Boyd and American Security* (Washington, DC: Smithsonian Press, 2001).

33. Andrew Phillip of Amnesty International, quoted in Carroll, "Sham Demobilization Hides Rise in Congo's Child Armies."

34. "War Crimes Tribunal in Sierra Leone," *Child Soldiers Newsletter* 3 (March 2002).

35. "World Criminal Court Launched," CNN.com, March 11, 2003.

36. Jessica Reaves, "Should the Law Treat Kids and Adults Differently?," *Time,* May 17, 2001.

37. Faul, "U.S. Defends Detaining Teens."

38. Nancy Gibbs, "Inside 'The Wire,' " *Time,* December 8, 2003.

39. Ismene Zarifis, "Sierra Leone's Search for Justice and Accountability of Child Soldiers," *Human Rights Brief* 9, no. 3 (May 2002); Christina Clark, "Juvenile Justice and Child Soldiering: Trends, Dilemmas, Challenges," *Child Soldiers Newsletter* 3 (March 2003); Amnesty International, "Child Soldiers, Criminals or Victims?," December 2000.

40. Tom Masland, "Voices of the Children: We Beat and Killed People," *Newsweek,* May 13, 2002.

41. "Chaos and Cannibalism Under Congo's Bloody Skies," *The Observer,* August 17, 2003.

42. Brian Wood and Johan Peleman, *The Arms Fixers,* PRIO Report, March 1999; Jakkie Cilliers and Christian Dietrich, *Angola's War Economy* (Pretoria: Institute for Security Studies, 2000).

43. Rachel Stohl, "The Smallest Warriors: Child Soldiers, " Center for Defense Information Report, October 1999, http://www.cdi.org/atp/ChildSoldiers/resoures .html.

44. Emmanuel Kwesi Aning, "Regulating the Illicit Trade in Natural Resources," *Ghanaian Chronicle,* November 24, 2003; "How UN Rewarded President of Liberia," *Financial Times,* July 1, 2003; William Kistner, "Timber, Taylor . . . Guns and Money," *Washington Post,* July 23, 2003. Just as an illustration, French companies imported $13 million worth of illicit Liberian timber from Taylor in the period of January to June 2000. In turn, it is thought that 15 percent of two species of wood used in U.S. flooring products ended up in stores here.

45. Declan Walsh, "UN Cuts Details of Western Profiteers from Congo Report," *The Independent* (London), October 27, 2003.

46. Nicol Innocenti, "About 800,000 Children Used as Soldiers," *Financial Times,* June 13, 2001.

47. Meghan O'Sullivan, *Shrewd Sanctions* (Washington, DC: Brookings Institution, 2003).

48. Interview with expert on DRC, June 2003.

49. On Unocal, see Daniel Fisher, "Kabuled Togeher," *Forbes,* February 4, 2002, http: //www.forbes.com/global/2002/0204/020.html; Brooke Shelby Biggs, "Pipe Dreams," *Mother Jones,* September–October 2001, http://www.motherjones.com/news/feature/2001/ 10/pipedreams.html. On Robertson, see Colbert I. King, "Pat Robertson's Gold," *Washington Post,* September 22, 2001; Abraham M. Williams, "Pat Robertson Engages in Illegal Mining Operation in Liberia," *The Perspective,* December 4, 2001.

See generally Phillip van Niekerk, "The Business of War: Making a Killing," International Consortium of Investigative Journalists, October 28, 2002, http://www .publicintegrity.org/bow/report.aspx?aid=147.

50. Paul Collier and Anke Hoeffler, "Greed and Grievance in Civil War," World Bank Policy Research Paper, no. 2355 (May 2000); William Reno, *Warlord Politics and African States* (Boulder, CO: Rienner, 1998).

51. Anthony Davis, "Tiger International," *Asia Week,* July 28, 2000.

Chapter 9: Fighting Children

1. Aaron Zitner, "Wars Take Some Nasty Turns on City Streets," *Los Angeles Times,* March 30, 2003.

2. Coalition to Stop the Use of Child Soldiers (CSC), *The Use of Children by OSCE Member States,* Human Dimension Seminar on Children and Armed Conflict, Warsaw, May 23–26, 2000, http://www.child-soldiers.org.

3. Major Alan Marshall, in his debriefing, quoted in Al Venter, "Sierra Leone: A Disreputable Debacle," *Soldier of Fortune,* January 2001. In the end, more children died because of this decision, illustrating the dilemmas tactical commanders face.

4. Marie Colvin and James Clark, "How the Hi-Tech Army Fell Back on Law of the Jungle and Won," *Sunday Times* (London), September 17, 2000, http://www.sunday-times.co.uk/news/pages/sti/2000/09/17/stifgnafro3003.html.

5. "Operation Certain Death," *Sunday Times* (London), March 7, 2004. The shifting ratio of dead to wounded in professional forces can be credited to modern body armor and improvements in medicine.

6. E-mail exchanges with U. S. Marine officer, stationed off Liberia, July 2003.

7. Nicholas Fiorenza, "Rumble in the Jungle," *Armed Forces Journal,* August 2003, p. 16.

8. David Keithley and Paul Melshein, "Past as Prologue: USMC Small Wars Doctrine," *Small Wars and Insurgencies* 8, no. 2 (autumn 1997): 91.

9. E-mail exchanges with U. S. Marine officer, stationed off Liberia, July 2003.

10. Zitner, "Wars Take Some Nasty Turns on City Streets."

11. Interview with CIA expert, Washington, DC, June 5, 2001.

12. Major Alandian Sosa, Uruguayan army, quoted in Emily Wax, "Boy Soldiers Toting AK-47s Put at Front of Congo's War," *Washington Post,* June 13, 2003.

13. U.S. Department of State, *Country Reports on Human Rights,* 2002. Child soldier sections available at http://www.cdi.org/issues/childsoldiers/child-soldiers-global.cfm.

14. F. B. Abagye, "Perspective on the Problems and Challenges of ECOWAS Regional Security Paradigm: The Role of the Military in the Protection of War-affected Children in West Africa," paper presented at the International Conference on War-affected Children, Winnipeg, Canada, September 11, 2000.

15. Colin Nickerson, "A Boy's Journey from Canada to Al Qaeda," *Boston Globe,* March 9, 2003.

16. Interview with former U. S. Army officer, Boston, June, 2001.

17. Ibid.

18. Adnan Laeeq, "Flowers on the Frontline," *Child Soldiers Newsletter,* September 2002.

19. Chris Tomlinson, "Child Soldier Tells Tales of War," AP, May 7, 2001.

20. Human Rights Watch, *"You'll Learn Not to Cry"*: *Child Combatants in Colombia* (New York, September 2003), p. 62.

21. Bob Woodward, *The Commanders* (New York: Simon & Schuster, 1991).

22. Martin Cohn, "The Teen Soldiers who Refused to Die," *Toronto Star,* January 18, 2002.

23. Quoted in Tara McKelvey, "Where Girls Are Trained to Kill," *Marie Claire,* November 2002, p. 66.

24. Christopher Hamner, "An Army of One? Combat Motivation, Unit Cohesion, and Technological Change in Infantry Combat," John M. Olin Institute for Strategic Studies, Harvard University, presentation, October 2001.

25. For the soldiers' reaction see Stephen Ambrose, *Citizen Soldiers* (New York: Simon & Schuster, 1997), ch. 19.

26. Matthew Cox, "War Even Uglier When a Child Is the Enemy," *USA Today,* April 8, 2003.

27. Interviews with British military officers, Washington, DC and London, 2002.

28. Interview with former U.S. military officer, Washington, DC, June 2001.

29. Human Rights Watch, *The Scars of Death* (New York, 2001).

30. As one military expert argues, "The use of NATO tactics as taught by the U.S. Army and Brits is totally useless. Forget NATO movement styles and action drills." Interview with former U.S. military officer, Boston, July 2001.

31. Hamner, "An Army of One?"

32. "Effects-Based Operations," Department of Defense briefing, March 19, 2003, http://www.defenselink.mil/news/Mar2003/g030318-D-9085.html.

33. Indeed, during the war in Sierra Leone, the town of Bumbuna was kept free by the presence of a single forward air controller who could direct air attacks on rebel forces. Eventually, they just steered clear of the town.

34. Interview with former U.S. military officer, Washington, DC, June 2001.

35. Ibid.; see also P. W. Singer, "Facing Saddam's Child Soldiers," *Brookings Iraq Memo* 8, January 2003.

36. M. Dando, ed., *Non-Lethal Weapons: Technological and Operational Prospects* (London: Jane's Publishing, 2000); J. Alexander, "An Overview of the Future of Non-Lethal Weapons," *Medicine, Conflict & Survival* 17, no. 3 (2001); see also the Department of Defense Joint Non-Lethal Weapons Program, http://www.jnlwd.usmc.mil/default.asp.

37. Quoted in Mike Barber, "Non-Lethal Weapons Give Military More Options," *Seattle Post,* April 8, 2002.

38. Sasha Kishinchand, "Child Soldiers: The Case for Non-Lethal Weapons," Role of American Military Power (RAMP) paper, winter 2002.

39. Council on Foreign Relations, "Nonlethal Weapons and Capabilities," Task Force Report, 2004, p. 13.

40. Colvin and Clark, "How the Hi-Tech Army Fell Back."

41. In Sierra Leone, RUF fighters were unintimidated by the light armored personnel carriers (APCs) of the UN peacekeeping forces and even seized them and repainted them for their own use.

42. Somini Sengupta, "Congo War Toll Soars as U.N. Pleads for Aid," *New York Times,* May 27, 2003.

43. Interview with former U.S. military officer, Washington, DC, June 2001.

44. Rohan Gunaratna, "LTTE Child Combatants," *Jane's Intelligence Review,* July 1998.

45. UNHCR, *Guidelines on the Protection and Care of Refugee Children,* 1994, Section 7, Article III.

46. Laeeq, "Flowers on the Frontline."

47. Major General George Fay, *Investigation of Abu Ghraib Detention Facility and 205th Military Intelligence Brigade,* AR 15-6, August 2004. Josh White and Thomas Ricks, "Iraqi Teens Abused at Abu Ghraib," *Washington Post,* August 24, 2004.

48. Quoted in White and Ricks, "Iraqi Teens Abused at Abu Ghraib."

49. Disturbingly, at the time of writing, because of jurisdictional problems and a lack of political will to investigate the firms, not one of these private contractors identified by the U.S. military as committing cirmes at Abu Ghraib had been charged with a crime, let alone legally punished. For more on this aspect, see P. W. Singer, "The Contract the Military Needs to Break," *Washington Post,* September 13, 2004. The quote on contractors is from Major General George Fay, *Investigation of Abu Ghraib Detention Facility and 205th Military Intelligence Brigade,* AR 15-6, August 2004. For more information on the role of CACI employees in the abuses at Abu Ghraib prison, see Osha Gray Davidson, "Contract to Torture," *Salon,* August 9, 2004.

50. Abagye, "Perspectives on the Problems and Challenges of ECQWAS." Similar programs were run by SFOR in Bosnia and KFOR in Kosovo, with positive results.

51. Rädda Barnen, *Children of War Newsletter* 1/01 (March 2001).

52. Interview with British military officers, Washington, DC and London, June 2002.

Chapter 10: Turning a Soldier Back into a Child

1. UNICEF, *Adult Wars, Child Soldiers* (Geneva, 2003).

2. Center for Defense Information (CDI), "Child Combatants: The Road to Recovery," September 10, 1998, http://www.cdi.org/atp/childsoldiers/weekly2.html.

3. Coalition to Stop the Use of Child Soldiers (CSC), "Child Soldiers Report," 2001, http://www.child-soldiers.org/report2001/countries/liberia.html.

4. Sarah Aird et al., "Mozambique: The Battle Continues for Former Child Soldiers," Youth Advocate Program International Resource Paper, 2001.

5. "Angola: Former Child Soldiers Forgotten," Integrated Regional Information Networks (IRIN), April 29, 2003; Human Rights Watch, *Forgotten Fighters, Child Soldiers in Angola* (New York, 2003).

6. "Sierra Leone: IRIN Focus on Children with an Uncertain Future," IRIN, July 9, 2001.

7. Aird et al., "Mozambique."

8. John McBeth, "Children of War," *Far Eastern Economic Review,* May 2, 2002.

9. Ismene Zarifis, "Sierra Leone's Search for Justice and Accountability of Child Sol-

diers," *Human Rights Brief* 9, no. 3 (May 2002); McBeth, "Children of War." In Sierra Leone's second largest city, Bo, the rehabilitation period is much shorter because of the sheer number of former combatants. "The children stay here a maximum of one week," says Alois Babab of Christian Brothers, a local group. "They receive counseling, and during that week, our social workers try to find the children's parents. We speak with the parents and the community to see if they are willing to accept the child. If they aren't, we try to find a foster parent until the situation has stabilised and the child can return home."

10. U.S. House of Representatives, testimony by Anne Edgerton of Refugees International, House Committee on International Relations, May 5, 2001.

11. CDI, "Child Combatants."

12. F. B. Abagye, "Perspective on the Problems and Challenges of ECOWAS Regional Security Paradigm: The Role of the Military in the Protection of War-affected Children in West Africa," paper presented at the International Conference on War-affected Children, Winnipeg, Canada, September 11, 2000.

13. See "Policy Options Paper: Improving United States Support to Demobilization, Demilitarization, and Reintegration in Sub-Saharan Africa," OSD, International Security Affairs, Office of African Affairs, May 2002.

14. UNICEF, "Lessons Learned—DRC," 2002, http://www.ginie.org/ginie-crises -links/childsoldiers/congo2.html.

15. R. Muggah, "Globalisation and Insecurity: The Direct and Indirect Effects of Small Arms Availability," *IDS Bulletin* 32, no. 2 (April 2001); *Small Arms Survey 2001: Profiling the Problem* (Oxford, UK: Oxford University Press, 2001); R. Muggah and P. Batchelor, *Development Held Hostage: Assessing the Effects of Small Arms on Human Development,* UN Development Program Report, August 2001.

16. Quoted in "Liberians Riot over Weapons Cash," BBC, December 12, 2003.

17. "Child Soldiers in the Congo, Business as Usual," Refugees International report, April 1, 2003.

18. Ibid.

19. USAID, *Guide to Program Options in Conflict-Prone Settings,* Office of Transition Assistance, September 2001.

20. Victoria Graham, "Rwanda's Former Child Soldiers Find Help," *UNICEF Feature,* 1995, http://www.unicef.org/features/feat145.htm.

21. "Men, Women, and Children Disarm in MODEL Stronghold," IRIN, April 20, 2004.

22. J. D. Kiznie et al., "The Psychiatric Effects of Massive Trauma on Cambodian Children," *Journal of the American Academy of Child Psychiatry* 25 (1986): 370.

23. David McGuire, "Technology to the Rescue," *Washington Post,* April 21, 2003; for more on Child Connect, see also http://www.aidworks.com/cconnect.asp.

24. Jo Boyden and Sara Gibbs, *Children of War: Responses to Psycho-Social Distress in Cambodia* (Geneva: UNSRID, 1997).

25. Women's Commission for Refugee Women and Children, *Against All Odds: Surviving the War on Adolescents,* July 2001.

26. International Labor Office, *Wounded Childhood: The Use of Children in Armed Conflict in Central Africa* (Geneva, 2003), p. 51.

27. Dan Jacobs, "Protecting Children from the Scourge of War," Consultative Group on Early Childhood Care and Development, no. 10 (October 1991): 11.

28. Ilse Derluyn et al., "Post Traumatic Stress in Former Child Soldiers," *Lancet,* March 13, 2004.

29. National Center for Post-Traumatic Stress Disorder, created within the Department of Veterans Affairs in 1989, http://www.ncptsd.org.

30. Tom Masland, "Leaders Gather at the U.N. This Week to Discuss the World's Kids, Including Child Soldiers," *Newsweek,* May 6, 2002.

31. Pat Mendoza, a Global Outreach missionary who works with children in Gulu, quoted in Greg Taylor, "Innocence Stolen," *Christianity Today,* July 10, 2000.

32. International Children's Institute, *Literature Review of: Psychosocial Programming for Children in Refugee Camps,* January 2000, http://www.icichildren.org; Ivan Watson, "Sierra Leone: Redeeming Child Soldiers," *San Francisco Chronicle,* July 23, 2001.

33. Stavros Stavou and Robert Stewart, "The Reintegration of Child Soldiers and Abducted Children: A Case Study of Palaro and Pabbo Gulu District," in *Act Against Child Soldiers in Africa: A Reader* (South Africa: ISS, 2002).

34. Ibid.

35. S. Breznitz, *The Denial of Stress* (New York: International Universities Press, 1983).

36. Mike Wessells, "Child Soldiers," *Bulletin of the Atomic Scientists* 53, no. 6 (November/December 1997).

37. "Sierra Leone," IRIN.

38. "Child Soldiers," Radio Netherlands, January 21, 2000, http://www.rnw.nl/humanrights/html/general.html.

39. Jacobs, "Protecting Children from the Scourge of War," p. 8.

40. Danna Harman, "Aid Agencies Help to Rid Child Soldiers of War's Scars," *Christian Science Monitor,* October 30, 2001. See also International Medical Corps, at http://www.imc-la.com.

41. International Children's Institute, *Literature Review.*

42. K. Miller et al., *Playing to Grow: Creative Education Workshops for Children* (Ann Arbor, MI: OCSL, 1993); International Children's Institute, *Literature Review.*

43. National Center for Post-Traumatic Stress Disorder. There is some controversy regarding exposing children to the events that scare them. However, the majority of studies have found that it is safe and effective to use CBT for children with PTSD.

44. Document provided to author by I., a former child soldier, June 2002.

45. CDI, "Child Combatants."

46. UNICEF, *Adult Wars, Child Soldiers,* p. 65.

47. Interviews, 2001–2003; OIM Mission Colombia, "Support Program for Ex–Combatant Children," 2003; Neil Boothby, "Working in the War Zone: A Look at Psychological Theory and Practice from the Field," *Mind and Human Interaction* 2, no. 2 (1990): 33.

48. International Labor Office, *Wounded Childhood,* p. 53.

49. Taylor, "Innocence Stolen."

50. International Labor Office, *Wounded Childhood,* p. 54.

51. Stavou and Stewart, "Reintegration of Child Soldiers."

52. UNICEF, "Lessons Learned, Sierra Leone," 2001, http://www.ginie.org/ginie-crises-links/childsoldiers/child-sierra.html.

53. Stavrou and Stewart, "Reintegration of Child Soldiers."

54. "Child Soldiers," Radio Netherlands.

55. Rädda Barnen, *Children of War Newsletter* 1/01 (March 2001).

56. For other examples see Alcinda Honwana, "Children of War: Understanding War and War Cleansing in Mozambique and Angola," in Simon Chesterman, ed., *Civilians in War* (Boulder, CO: Rienner, 2001) pp. 123–42.

57. International Children's Institute, *Literature Review of Psychosocial Programming for Children in Refugee Camps* (Toronto: ICI, 2001)

58. Ilene Cohen and Guy Goodwin-Gill, *Child Soldiers* (Oxford, UK: Clarendon, 1994).

59. Global Information Networks in Education, "About Ginie-Programs," August 1999, http://www.ginie.org/about/ginie1-report/final-report3.html.

60. Global Information Networks in Education, "Educating a War-Torn Society: Peace Education," September 2000, http://www.ginie.org/ginie-crises-links/pr/somalia.html.

61. International Labor Office, *Wounded Childhood,* p. 56.

62. UNICEF, *Children Affected by Armed Conflict: UNICEF Actions* (New York, 2002), p. 41.

63. UNICEF, "Assistance to Child Soldiers in Sierra Leone," 2002, at http://www.ginie.org/ginie-crises-links/childsoldiers/sierraleone2.html.

64. Theresa Stichick and Claude Bruderlein, "Children Facing Insecurity: New Strategies for Survival in a Global Era," Harvard Program in Humanitarian Policy and Conflict Research Policy Paper, March 2001.

65. Tom Masland, "Voices of the Children: We Beat and Killed People," *Newsweek,* May 13, 2002.

66. "Empowering Liberia's Youth," *Salesian Bulletin,* 2001, http://www.salesians.org.uk/html/empowering_liberia_s_youth.html: Catherine Langevin-Falcon, "Vocational Education Gives War-Affected Children a New Start," UNICEF child soldier report, 2000.

67. "Child Soldiers to Swap Guns for PCs," BBC, March 25, 2002.

68. The best example of this is the Grameen Bank in Bangladesh; for more information, please go to http://www.grameen-info.org.

69. Michael Wessells and Davidson Jonha, "Creating Life Options in Sierra Leone Through Skills Training and Employment Generation," *Child Soldiers Newsletter* 9 (September/October 2003).

70. Women's Commission for Refugee Women and Children, *Against All Odds.*

71. UNICEF, "Rwanda: Lessons Learned and Actions Taken Thus Far," UNICEF document (Kigali, Rwanda, 2001).

Chapter 11: Looking Ahead

1. Tom Masland, "Voices of the Children: We Beat and Killed People," *Newsweek,* May 13, 2002.

A NOTE ON THE TYPE

This book was set in Adobe Garamond. Designed for the Adobe Corporation by Robert Slimbach, the fonts are based on types first cut by Claude Garamond (c. 1480–1561). Garamond was a pupil of Geoffroy Tory and is believed to have followed the Venetian models, although he introduced a number of important differences, and it is to him that we owe the letter we now know as "old style." He gave to his letters a certain elegance and feeling of movement that won their creator an immediate reputation and the patronage of Francis I of France.

Composed by North Market Street Graphics
Lancaster, Pennsylvania
Printed and bound by Berryville Graphics
Berryville, Virginia
Designed by Virginia Tan

355